Celestial Pantomime

Celestial Pantomime

POETIC STRUCTURES OF TRANSCENDENCE

JUSTUS GEORGE LAWLER

New Haven and London   Yale University Press   1979

Designed by Sally Harris
and set in VIP Janson type.
Printed in the United States of America by
Halliday Lithograph, West Hanover, Mass.

Published in Great Britain, Europe, Africa, and
Asia (except Japan) by Yale University Press,
Ltd., London. Distributed in Australia and
New Zealand by Book & Film Services, Artarmon,
N.S.W., Australia; and in Japan by Harper & Row,
Publishers, Tokyo Office.

Library of Congress Cataloging in Publication Data

Lawler, Justus George.
  Celestial pantomime.

  Includes index.
  1. Poetics.   2. English poetry–History and criticism.
3. American poetry–History and criticism.   I. Title.
PN1042.L35   808.1   78-21964
ISBN 0-300-02323-5

For Harold Bloom
and to the memory of
W. K. Wimsatt

The thing I hum appears to be
The rhythm of this celestial pantomime.

"The Man with the Blue Guitar"

CONTENTS

PREFACE

The title of this book is taken from a poem by Wallace Stevens, and the chapter titles are intended to pay homage to him by way of "The Comedian as the Letter C"—that letter being the glyph of one of the recurrent structures examined herein. I had given some thought to calling the book "Wild Criticism," after the example of John O'Neil's *Wild Sociology*, since I have sought to make my readings of various poems exploratory and provocative.

One of the structural patterns I will discuss in some detail is the parenthetic insertion; and this pattern may be regarded as having shaped the format of this book. The first two and the last two chapters are more speculative and generalizing than are the six central chapters of more "practical" criticism which might thus be read first. Those chapters treat of, in order: chiasm and parenthesis; enjambment; coda of reversal; coda of irony; prepositionalizing, refrains, journey motifs; mono-polysyllabic collisions and oscillatory imagery. I have included line numbers only for citations from long poems. Wherever I have italicized words in quoted passages as an aid to discussion I have assumed the device will be sufficiently apparent to readers without any "italics added" notation.

This book is dedicated to two quite different critics from whom I have learned much; my debt to others is acknowledged throughout these pages. Lastly, I must express my gratitude for support in various ways and in various undertakings to Thomas Altizer, Ray L. Hart, Christopher Kauffman, and Werner Mark Linz.

J. G. L.

May 26, 1978

xi

PART ONE: ONTOLOGY

1: *Caduceus*

Almost all music critics and many literary critics share in common with the explicators and program annotators of *Harper's Bazaar*, *Vogue*, and *Women's Wear Daily* a penchant for eloquence about the arrangement and organization of this or that material, and a long silence as to why this or that particular arrangement or organization is to be regarded as pleasing. Why are these pleatings, tuckings, foldings, and drapings especially attractive? Is the "golden section" beautiful because it appears everywhere in nature and art, and we have grown accustomed to its space; or is it beautiful because of some quality intrinsic to it, beyond mere ubiquity; and is there some counterpart to this quality in a "beautiful" line of poetry? To ask such questions is to broach the crucial issue in criticism, the most vexing, the most controversial, and the most seemingly unresolvable.

Primarily in reaction to certain dicta of the New Critics, but also in response to a generalizing or "interdisciplinary" trend within the humanities, the practice of literary criticism for the past two decades or so has concentrated on the artwork not as a self-contained monad but as a relational entity possessing a history and emerging out of a social context. As a consequence of this generalizing drift, at present much criticism consists in the transmission of the poem through the grid of one or another of the social and behavioral sciences; and the poem is viewed, say, as the distillation of sincerity, the manifestation of psychic tensions, the vehicle of primitive myth or archetypal symbol, the product of economic repression, the interface of individual and community, or more likely, as a combination of all of these. The fruitfulness of this hybrid enterprise, which may as well be called "communal criticism," has become evident in a flood of critical works that are almost universally acknowledged as exemplifying the renewal of the humanities, their return from academic isolation in the intense inane of the New Criticism, and their entrance into the common market of ideas.

But however admirable all contributions to the common good by definition are, the federalist principle tends to worry one that these may be sacrificial contributions which ultimately impoverish the contributor, and thus in the long run work against that same common good. In the well-adjusted polity, what used to be called the "commonwealth of letters," it was by each segment of the whole pursuing its own *finis operis*, and pursuing it to the fullest, that the overall equilibrium of the society was maintained. This was the principle of self-reliance that Emerson proclaimed as a way of life, the principle of self-interest that Tocqueville discerned in emerging democracies, and the principle of sectarianism and sectionalism that Madison made cardinal in *The Federalist* papers. It is a principle as ancient as the concept of the cycle of learning, each radius of which focuses its light back on the common humane center; but, to paraphrase Hopkins, its *own* light—not the beams of the other disciplines.

The issue is whether one can in fact talk of poetry as having its own "proper end," "its own light," or whether poetry may be, as communal criticism maintains, merely the ground on which all the other human sciences meet. It is well known that Northrop Frye sees the act of literary criticism, as opposed to the critical act in each of the auxiliary disciplines, entailing a combination of all related knowledge: "all these interests are seen as converging on literary criticism instead of receding from it into psychology and history and the rest." The literary critic may thus be regarded as a kind of polymath of the polymyth, and literature, instead of being one radius in the wheel of knowledge, is the hub of the wheel, or the wheel itself.

Now, possibly all this is so, but again the tradition raises a worry in that poetry has conventionally been defined as the *doctrina infima*, the knowledge that was some place beneath the *scientia rectrix* of metaphysics and the *doctrina sacra* of theology. But for communal criticism the gods that Boucher killed, in anticipation of Nietzsche and modern antitheologies, are utterly dead, along with all future metaphysics. Perhaps if only by default, poetry, as Arnold on the wrong grounds anticipated, is the new ruling science. Unfortunately, such a claim is suspect because it is in no way unique but common among practitioners of every "human science," from anthropology, psychology, sociology to history; we have heard it all before from Freud, Marx, Lévi-Strauss, and others.

In the face of all these equally strong claimants to the intellectual throne, it is obvious that poetry cannot define its unique rights in terms of an equally dubious centrality; some other differentia must be sought. Poets do not differ from, say, historians or metaphysicians in an interest in the totality of existence; nor is there any difference in a concern with the concrete; all are concerned with the universal as with the specific. Nor can it be that only poets and not, say, metaphysicians employ patterned images and patterned sounds; again, to a greater or lesser degree they both do. Nor, to take *in extremis* what some see as the ultimate defining element, can one maintain that poets differ from, say, historians by arranging their material flush left, random right. Any gibbon at a typewriter would do the same.

This seems to exhaust the possible differentiae. To employ traditional language, in terms of substance there is no adequate distinction with regard either to content or to organization of that content. In terms of accident there is no adequate distinction with regard to appearance. But since common sense tells us poetry is not sociology, history, metaphysics, there must be some differentia. Again, to use traditional language, if the differentia cannot be found in material causality (content) or formal causality (organization), it must be found in final causality (purpose). As to purpose, since all intellectual constructs organize content with a view to communication, there is only one possible alternative remaining: that is, that one type of construct communicates primarily something about the content and the other communicates primarily something about the organization itself.

This solution, which all that follows will try to explicate, avoids the traditional dichotomies that have to do not with final causality but with material and formal. This solution also avoids the cul-de-sac of arguing that, in poetry form and content, pattern and seman-

tic statement are inextricably welded, whereas in the verbal constructs of historians, sociologists, and such, the two can be sun-
dered. In fact, everyone knows the latter is not true. A passage of
Gibbon or Darwin or Veblen does not admit of that kind of split-
ting or abstracting: the two constituents are as fused as in any
poem. *Etiam in dicendo* (by which he meant "prose"), there is a kind
of hidden music, said Cicero. This solution also avoids the kind of
otiose distinction Eliot indulged in when he talked about "poems in
which we are moved by the music and take the sense for granted,"
or the equally vacuous distinction of Valéry, after Malherbe, of
defining prose as walking speech and poetry as dancing speech.

If the ultimate purpose of poetry is the employment of patterned
ideas, images, and sounds, to communicate something about the
patterns (and of course, by that fact, about the semantic content)
one must wonder what is the meaning of that communicated pattern. Because nothing has meaning save in relation to something
else, and if the patterns by definition do not find their essential
meaning in themselves or in the communication of what may rather
grossly be called lexical statement, and if we have exhausted the
constituents of the poem, then these patterns must find their meaning in something outside the poem. I am in pursuit, then, of something outside the poem, of which the patterns in the poem are the
representation or mime. That "something," I will seek to show, is
akin to Stevens's "central poem," in which all lesser poems find
their ultimate meaning.

Making use of the impoverished language of matter-form,
content-structure, or their analogues, I have said that in the other
(nonaesthetic) disciplines the structure exists to clarify or reinforce
the content, whereas in poetry the content exists, at least partially,
though distinctively and uniquely, to clarify or make manifest the
nature of the structure—which structure is in turn related to some
ultimate structure to be assayed shortly. Although it is the content
that usually makes the structure accessible, once one has gained
entrance, that structure may be seen not as merely illuminating the
content but as illuminating the mysterious "central poem" as well.

All this seems to sound like various doctrines of "significant
form" or "expressive form," and there is no quarrel here with those
terms, derived mainly from painting, sculpture, and music, except

when they are treated as though they were statements of a solution to the problem of artistic communication rather than as further definitions of the problem. We cannot say that we are moved by the expressive form of a given painting, unless we can show what makes that particular form expressive as opposed to another which is presumably either nonexpressive, or is a "nonform." To rely on "expressive form" to explain the effect of a given artwork is to explain one problem by another problem; it is like explaining the mystery of being in the world by invoking a Being "outside" the world whose very nature is posited as totally inexplicable. Thus, it is of little help to be told by exponents of the notion of "expressive form" like Susanne Langer, "The meanings which pure visual forms and musical patterns convey are nameless because they are logically uncongenial to the structure of language. They will presumably never have literal handles." Philosophically, this is merely a sophisticated obscurantism; theologically, it is an aesthetic Barthism; it is to take refuge in a facile understanding of religion's *Deus ineffabilis*, Langer's "nameless one," of whom nothing can be said that is true. A better ontology and a better aesthetic (compare Tennyson's "The Ancient Sage") would argue that although the mystery of Being and the mystery of beauty are situated in a translogical or, better, paralogical realm they must be spoken about in words, and these words do convey true "names," though never exhaustively, of the reality being considered.

Since I am talking about "structure," perhaps a historical illustration of the meaning to be attached to that term will be helpful. Every school child reading the *Aeneid* is filled with sympathy for Dido and contempt for what seems the caddish behavior of Aeneas—Robert Graves, even into his eighties polemicizing against Vergil, never recovered from that first response. Love *should* outweigh duty, and we should applaud Dido as she turns with gesture stern from her false friend's approach. Saint Augustine recalls in the *Confessions* (in what is for us, given his own emergent priggishness, a very telling passage) how he had wept over the Vergilian text. But all these are responses to the narrative rather than to what Tennyson called the stateliest *measure* every molded by the lips of man. One response to that kind of structure has been expressed by John Henry Newman in the *Grammar of Assent* when he talks of

Vergil's "pathetic half lines, giving utterance, as the voice of Nature herself, to that pain and weariness, yet hope of better things, which is the experience of her children in every time." And though G. E. Duckworth, one of the most interesting modern interpreters of the *Aeneid*, integrates these broken lines into the overall work, Newman's judgment remains unshaken. He was a structuralist *avant la parole*, and one may say in his terms that the *story* of Aeneas and Dido can be apprehended by Notional Assent, but the *structure*, which may apparently have little to do with plot and narrative, can be apprehended only by Real Assent.

The title to this chapter is "Caduceus," a term which on the first level defines the poem as serpentine, after Coleridge, Rossetti, and Hulme, among others. On the second level, "Caduceus" relates to Hermes, bearer of that lithe charm, and thus to this project of a hermeneutic of structures. On the third level, where I want to pause briefly, "Caduceus" is the name given to that insigne which was borne before a herald who was about to announce an edict or proclaim a royal arrival; as such, it is cognate to "kerygmatic," which is in turn a word that Rudolf Bultmann put into widespread currency as conveying the mode whereby the gospel message affected the believing Christian. That term, *kerygmatic*, can be adapted *mutatis mutandis*, to the context of poetry—and in fact, Bultmann first employed the word in a work dedicated to his former colleague Heidegger who had himself only gradually over the years come to realize the unique burthen of poetic speech.
Bultmann, relying on fairly conventional comparative studies, best summarized by Thorlief Boman, of Greek and Jewish *Denkformen*, contrasted the biblical "Word of God" with the Greek *logos* and noted of the former that

> The fundamental factor is that here "being spoken" does pertain to the word and that it is this spoken word which shows man his place in the world and his road to salvation. But in the Greek concept the decisive characteristic is lacking. The word is not a summons in the true sense and it is not a temporal event in a specific situation, an event in a specific history. In the Greek view everything still rests on content.

That Bultmann harnesses an elaborate philosophical dialectic to his notion of kerygma (and is of course writing as a Christian believer) need not detain us here. The significant conclusion is that, in the perennial conflict between Hebraism and Hellenism, literary critics have generally opted for the latter: "everything still rests on content." Whereas, as I shall try to show, regardless of what a poem is about in terms of "plot" or narrative, its structures are intrinsically ambivalent, pointing indeed, on the one hand, to that plot and narrative but, on the other, to man's "place in the world" and, one might even say, to his "road to salvation."

Perhaps to draw the distinction between the word as *content* and the word as *summons* is still to be needlessly vague. "Word" itself only rarely conveys (as in, "I give you my word") an existential event, and we need here a term which can stand over against "word" as merely conceptual pointer. That term is ready at hand and has been the almost instinctive choice of aesthetic "believers" down through the centuries. And no matter how much its use in this context is decried by more rigorously minded thinkers, the term recurs with unremitting persistency. It bespeaks the power of this subterranean current in all the arts and particularly in poetry that, however constantly frustrated and opposed, the use of this term nevertheless breaks through from the underground in age after age.

From Plato's "mousike," through Quintilian, through the translation of Pseudo-Pythagoras by Marsilio Ficino, up to the founding of Dadaism—which Hugo Ball testified took its name from Pseudo-Dionysius—"music" has been the term that constantly recurs in any attempt to express the undefinable and ineffable elements in all communication. "Music" may be thought of as the ineradicable heresy—standing as Gnosticism to Christianity—in orthodox literary criticism. To be sure, the use and abuse of the term in Poe and Lanier, Pater and Hopkins, Eliot and Valéry, and scores of lesser figures have been abundantly documented, indeed have been demonstrated by John Crowe Ransom, Northrop Frye, Donald Davie, and most recently, John Hollander. And they have been irrefutable in all that they have said. Yet, like another Gnostic heresy, the teaching of the Kabbalah, which has been shown by George Steiner to be a most fruitful source of understanding the nature of language and by Harold Bloom to be a most fruitful source of understanding interpoetic relationships, the metaphor of music, the rich freight it bears, quite literally from Plato to the present, must be introduced in any treatment of the power of the nonconceptual in poetry. The poet is the shepherd of being, poetry is the dwelling place of being, and as Rilke said long before Heidegger, *Gesang ist Dasein*. The presiding muse of any consideration of poetic structures is the "one" of Fictive Music. Thus, in what follows I shall be using the analogy of music for all those figural patterns in a poem which communicate through, over, and beyond the lexical statement as such.

Now, it is unquestionable that the very nature of a spoken art requires some kind of "ear," which the isolated critic silently puzzling a poem is not likely to develop. Moreover, if comprehending a poem requires some kind of aural tact and Johnson is the first great literary critic in the history, or at least the first great common reader, the critical tradition may be tainted at the wells; not only did he dislike music because as he himself said it interfered with the "contemplation" of his "ideas"—true Hellenist he—but his judgments on versification, on the "numbers," are so invariably flawed that they have long gone without defenders. So, too, with the second most influential common reader, Arnold, of whom Geoffrey Tillotson observes, "Aesthetically he experienced almost nothing when hearing music." Thus our most influential critics both suffered from that affliction known in Quintilian as "stumbling at the vestibule of the ear"—a failing which has also afflicted many of their followers.

Hic Rhodus. It is past time for illustration of the larger project. Geoffrey Hartman has pointed up some implications of the connection he sees between the flower listing in "Lycidas" and that in the "Ode to a Nightingale." The connection is suggestive, though it is not unlikely that if one tabulated all the flower lists from Chaucer on the catenations among poems so surveyed would be proportionately suggestive. Thus, one might as well link Milton's jessamine with the jasmine of Stevens's "Asides on the Oboe" and confirm the nexus by pointing out that the first stanza of the latter poem is concerned with the demise of the classical offices of prophet (read *divine poet*), priest, and king and that Milton is concerned equally with the death of a poet-priest, King.

In the examples that follow, I am aware of the brevity of each. But this is an essay in micropoetics by contrast with the macropoetics of those who are engaged in psychological, sociological, "tonal," or archetypal criticism. To be preoccupied with the building blocks is not to be indifferent to the architecture; indeed, the architecture is often the expanded expression of the constituent blocks; they determine the ultimate shape, which grows like a crystal, like a coral reef, like Emerson's "Limestone of the Continent." The procedure I am following is analogous to that which Jacques Monod argues for when he maintains that all of the life sciences are derived from a study of the molecules of which the cell is made up. Though probably a better exemplar of what I hope to do in the following chapters—and more accurately invoked than Monod—is Lévi-Strauss, who sees his work centered not on full-scale myths but on the aggregate of fragmentary myths which he calls "mythemes." And though Lévi-Strauss seems perversely deaf to the high claims of poetry—a perversity for which he has been ceremonially roasted by Harold Bloom and Octavio Paz—his method of slowly assembling homologous elements to construct a unified myth is very similar to what I shall be attempting here.

The passage Geoffrey Hartman made reference to is the following from Keats:

> I cannot see what flowers are at my feet,
>   Nor what soft incense hangs upon the boughs,
> But, in embalmed darkness, guess each sweet
>   Wherewith the seasonable month endows
> The grass, the thicket, and the fruit-tree wild;
>   White Hawthorn, and the pastoral eglantine;
>   Fast fading violets cover'd up in leaves;
>   And mid-May's eldest child,
>   The coming musk-rose, full of dewy wine,
>   The murmurous haunt of flies on summer eves.

The pattern of interest here is:

$$\overset{1}{\text{The grass,}} \overset{1\quad 2}{\text{ the thicket,}} \text{ and } \overset{1\quad 2\quad 3}{\text{the fruit-tree wild}}$$

Figurally, the movement is one of accretion, of syllabic expansion, similar to the classic instance which Kenneth Burke with his fine ear for this kind of patterned symbolization first pointed out:

$$
\begin{array}{cccccccccc}
1 & & 1 & 2 & & 1 & 2 & 3 & & 1 & 2 & 3 & 4
\end{array}
$$

Friends, Romans, countrymen, lend me your ears

One moves from the immediate and definite out toward the unlimited. It is a structure of enlargement and aspiration similar to that of Keats in "The Eve of St. Agnes":

She knelt, so pure a thing, so free from mortal taint

And of Hopkins:

I look, I lift up, I lift up heart

Less nobly, it is the aggrandizement in which "each man himself becomes a giant" in Stevens's "Gigantomachia":

A mask, a spirit, an accoutrement

In the "Ode to a Nightingale" one expects the enumeration to conclude with the first triad at "wild," but so compelling is the momentum of this expansive remembrance that Keats continues to enlarge his list to include more and more items over the next five lines. Now, what is equally fascinating about this figure is that it is the reverse of an earlier pattern which displayed the poet as shrinking more and more into his solitariness, that is, as moving from fullness to vacuity:

$$
\begin{array}{ccccccc}
1 & 2 & 3 & & 1 & 2 & & & 1
\end{array}
$$

The weariness, the fever, and the fret

Syllabically, this is a kind of diminuendo expressive of the poet's growing isolation.

This kind of pattern on a different scale may help in discovering that elusive element, whose pursuit has been the concern of much recent criticism, the "tone" of a work. Ants Oras has noted that consonant clusters in *The Faerie Queene* generally come at the beginning of a word. Such steady repetition of a kind of syllabic decrescendo in Spenser may account, at least partially, for the air of leisure, even of lassitude, that pervades that work—at least by contrast with the air of urgency, one might say of eschatological expectancy, that seems to prevail in *Paradise Lost*, where the opposite cluster pattern predominates.

To return briefly to that third stanza of Keats's "Ode to a Nightingale," in the line, "Here where men sit and hear each other groan," it is immediately apparent that the heavy monosyllables retard the forward movement and thus express the brokenness, the gaps in all human community, the unbridgeable chasm between man and neighbor. But we are bade not to read the words of the bard but to "hear the voice"; and if one heard the line spoken, this sense of the disjunction of man from man would be intensified even more as the listener tried to sort out his response to expectations of a parallel structure which—startlingly—are here unfulfilled. The listener, unlike the mere reader, would anticipate something like, "Here, where men sit and here—? . . . where they stand." The temporal lag induced from one's befuddlement at the ambiguity of "here"-"hear" would bring home all the more effectively the distance, the psychic and spatial lag, between persons.

Each of these patterns I have cited reinforces the poem's theme, and I will of necessity make use of that kind of more or less conventional interpretation of structure in many of the illustrations to come—but primarily as support for my larger hermetic argument which will try to validate the significance of certain patterns over and beyond semantic context. One may take a small step toward that goal by noting that one of the best American speculative students of music, Leonard B. Meyer, in *Music, the Arts, and Ideas* defines musical *meaning* as that which "arises when an antecedent situation, requiring an estimate of the probable modes of pattern continuation, produces uncertainty about the temporal-tonature of the unexpected consequent." This is precisely what has happened in the Keats line above; and though one might question Meyer's definition when he relates it to "information theory," there is no doubt that what I have called "befuddlement" (an aspect of *surprise*) and he calls "uncertainty" is ingredient in aesthetic meaning.

Since the pattern of accretion and diminution shall not be taken up later in this book, two more instances can be adduced—instances which, again, seem to open up as significant relationships within a poem and between poems as do similarity or identity of theme and imagery. In one of the "Marguerite" poems, Arnold

moves toward a condition of isolation akin to that of Keats in the
third stanza of the "Ode to a Nightingale":

> Yet she, chaste queen, had never proved
> How vain a thing is mortal love,
> Wandering in heaven, far removed.
> But thou hast long had place to prove
> This truth—to prove, and make thine own:
>
>   1   2   3   1   2   1
> "Thou hast been, shalt be, art, alone."

The word "alone" here functions as *summatio*, a type of coda I shall
examine more closely in chapter 5. This numerical decrescendo in
the verbs echoes an even more renowned poem of love, but of love
fulfilled rather than of love frustrated (where I take Helen Gardner's reading in the last line):

> And now good morrow to our waking soules,
> Which watch not one another out of feare;
> For love, all love of other sights controules,
> And makes one little roome, an every where.
> Let sea-discoverers to new worlds have gone,
> Let Maps to others, worlds on worlds have showne,
> Let us *possesse* our world, each *hath* one, and *is* one.

Here the evolution is more subtly expressed, but the pattern is the
same and may be described as tracing the movement from multiplicity to unity, from the plane of the pure "it" which is owned and
possessed (for example, I *possess* a car) through the intermediate
plane of the "it" touched by personhood (for example, I *have* a dog)
to the plane of "being" and oneness with the "thou" (for example, Je
est un autre). This present distinction between "having" and "being" is based on Gabriel Marcel, not on Merleau-Ponty who re-
verses Marcel's order; but as an interesting corollary, it should be
noted that Marcel equates *avoir* with *voir* and thus explicates Donne's
ceasing to "watch one another" once the plane of "having" has
been abandoned. Lastly, since the artwork is made up of patterns
that are congruent one with another, the final line of Donne's poem
may be recognized as a condensation—a true *summatio*—of all the

preceding lines of the poem, as one moves from the clumsy sexual grapplings of the first stanza through the harmonious bonding together of the lovers in the second to their perfect union in the third. The experience of that movement is one of the ways Bultmann's "spoken word" (or better, the experience of that movement is one of the ways a poem's "music") "shows man his place in the world."

Although I shall for pedagogical purposes generally correlate this "music" with the theme of a given poem, there is, I repeat, a danger in overemphasizing the role of context. Thus there are, as everyone has experienced, certain sequences of musical notes that seem to be intrinsically pleasing, that is, intrinsically significant. The latter stand out like "Three Blind Mice" at the end of "God Save the Queen," "Twinkle, Twinkle, Little Star" in the "Surprise Symphony," or "The Farmer in the Dell" in the "Academic Festival Overture." For someone to feel a sense of profanation at the presence of nursery tunes in these putatively lofty contexts is to let theme or genre (here expressed by the titles) deafen one to these self-communicating melodies. Moreover, I have intentionally confined these musical examples to unsophisticated airs that have grown out of folk art on the assumption, to be elucidated shortly, that they may best reflect or resonate that ultimate structure which I have earlier identified with Stevens's "central poem."

Northrop Frye has said that "The Adonis myth in 'Lycidas' is the structure of 'Lycidas.' It is in 'Lycidas' in much the same way that the sonata form is in the first movement of a Mozart symphony." But there may be in "Lycidas" an anterior structure similar to Schoenberg's musical *Grundgestalt*, a structure which, however momentary and epiphanic in our grasp of it, still communicates to the listener. That anterior structure may differ from the Adonis myth or any other myth, just as in Jung "the archetype per se" differs from the "archetypal image," or as in Lévi-Strauss the mytheme differs from the myth.

A parallel to Frye's utilization of the Adonis myth may be found in a passage from Cassirer which I cite because of the parallel itself, but even more because it provides a pointer to the direction I am about to take. In *Language and Myth* Cassirer discusses at length various anthropological studies which show "how primitive mystic conception originally grasps only the great, fundamental qualitative contrast of light and darkness, and how it treats them as one essence, one complex whole, out of which definite characters only gradually emerge"—or more baldly, how the primitive mind went from unity to multiplicity in denominating the heavenly powers and gods. At great length are cited anthropological surveys that show that among "the Cora Indians" "the conception of the nocturnal heaven and the diurnal heaven must have preceded that of the sun, the moon, and the separate constellations." And at even greater length illustrations from "the Avesta" and "ancient Mexicans" are marshaled. It is to wonder: no reference whatever to the one tradition, and a more ancient one at that, and one that would speak directly to each of his readers, Genesis, in which the creation of light precedes the creation of the heavenly bodies—"No back yard cheepers for that connoisseur," as Stevens wrote of Audubon. All this is merely to argue that the microstructures to be examined in what follows may be more primordial, more immediate, and more relevant than what many readers of poetry might characterize—if at Professor Frye's urgings they recognize them at all—as "Greek fairy tales." So much for the parallel; now, the direction.

At some point, presumably at the very point where this differentiation of the global totality and the multiple attributions or personifications occurred, human speech, or more accurately, human utterance emerged. It emerged when the first primate experienced himself as separated from that totality surrounding him and, in response to that separation, "outered" what was within himself. No one knows how that emotive outering became denotive sound, and it is a commonplace that there are almost as many theories about the genesis of language as there are theorists. Fortunately, there is no need here to hack one's way through the thicket of language's beginning. What does seem indubitable is that this outering, this utterance had about it some kind of "shape" or form that assuaged its "speaker's" fear, concern, and fascination at this mystery confronting him.

Now, it seems not unlikely that, given the continuity, however tenuous, of human speech over the ages, something of that aboriginal form is going to perdure, and that if it does, it will manifest itself in that speech which is by definition most disclosive of radical man, that is, in poetry. I suggest this, and what is supportive of it in the following pages, with complete diffidence since it is purely a hypothesis which may support my larger argument, while being in no way essential to it.

One speculates, admittedly with what is currently being called a logocentric bias, on the nature of language, guided, now, by the invaluable maxim: when in doubt, read Blake—in this case, the introduction to the *Songs of Innocence*. Here, man dwelling in primordial chaos (valleys wild), undifferentiated from that chaos (piping songs of happy glee), encounters something both fascinating and transcendent (child on a cloud) to which he is compelled to respond with an utterance which is at once somewhat adequate and somewhat inadequate (laughed, wept). But it is a *response*: man utters an *Antwort* to a *Wort*. It is not as Merleau-Ponty maintains in *Phenomenology of Perception* an utterance "whereby man *superimposes* on the given world the world according to man." This is postlapsarian, and a prefigurement of Lacan. With Whorf, one may say grammar shapes thinking; contra Lacan, one cannot say words create things. For if one looks at the Genesis story, man does not "superimpose" his world on the given world in the act of naming the animals; rather, with Milton (*PL* 8. 352), man brings them to their own true fulfillment by asserting his kinship, his unity, with them, a unity which to modern man, as Muir says in "The Horses," is a "long-lost archaic companionship." Merleau-Ponty goes back not to the "first" attempts at language but to that Urizenic moment when man is seeking to dominate, and ultimately exploit, the given world. This is indeed the *modern* eon, the beginning of technology rampant, as William Leiss and Jackson Cope from totally different perspectives have noted.

Speech born in Beulah is the "laughing song" of Blake's poem and the "smiling" godhead of Milton's "Nativity Ode," of *Paradise Lost* (5. 718), and *Paradise Regained* (1. 129); and this is the closest approximation to the laughter of the child on the cloud; that laughing song is subsequently articulated temporally by an ensemble of sounds in the narrative we would call primitive myth; the narrative will extrapolate itself in embellishments, variations, glosses, commentaries, and so on, until by that process of entropic mimesis (I stained the water clear) called "acculturation" it may be difficult to recognize the original narrative, much less its primordial generative ensemble of sounds. Lyric poets will instinctively, and more often than not unwittingly, resuscitate those sounds in their own more diffuse posterior creations, and literary critics pursuing Whitehead's "chain of symbolic references" (And I wrote; and I stained; and I made; and I plucked) will compare and combine these attenuated narratives and, perhaps, when as skilled as Professor Frye, divine at two removes the original narrative—though they may find it difficult to discover the primordial articulated ensemble of sounds, an ensemble which *one would like to believe* (I emphasize the tentativeness of all of this) is isomorphic with the patterns to be examined later in this book. Says Stevens in "Notes toward a Supreme Fiction" (4):

> There was a myth *before* the myth began,
> Venerable and articulate and complete,
>
> *From this* the poem springs. . . .

The whole is a development not too unlike that described in the well-known beginning of *The Raw and the Cooked,* that book being denominated by Lévi-Strauss as "the rough draft of a third-order code," "with the myths themselves being second-order codes, and language being the first-order code." This syncopates the Blakean schema somewhat, but in any case it is the "first-order" that is the focus of what follows.

Cassirer cites the following Uitoto text: "In the beginning the Word gave the Father his origin." Cassirer—like Merleau-Ponty and Lacan an almost compulsive Kantian—reads this literally, whereas a more traditional understanding would affirm that the Word gave the Father his origin in *this world* by "expressing" him. That is the meaning of the following from the prologue to John's Gospel where one reads: "No one has ever seen God; it is God the only Son, ever at the Father's side, who has *revealed* him." The verb "revealed" here is in French translated "expliqué"; the Greek is "exēgeisthai." The Son is thus the exegete of the Father; he is the first literary critic; he explicates God and is the model for all literary criticism in which ideally the Explicator is the Text and the Text is the Explicator, while the Commentary which joins the two is the Spirit. Thus the doctrine of the *filioque* is ratified. The Spirit

proceeds from the Father *and the Son*: the Commentary proceeds
from the Text and the Explicator. And thus is also ratified a brilliant interpretation of the *Verbum factum* passage by John Meagher
in which the received reading is amended to "And the Word was
made Spirit and dwelt among us." The translation of Text through
Explicator can only come by way of the Commentary which represents "among us" in a refracted and diffuse fashion the original
impulse of the Text.

Acting on a derivative maxim, "if in doubt after reading Blake,
read Stevens," one may sketch these strata—now with "The Idea of
Order at Key West" as guide.

> She sang beyond the genius of the sea.
> The water never formed to mind or voice,
> Like a body wholly body, fluttering
> Its empty sleeves; and yet its mimic motion
> Made constant cry, caused constantly a cry,
> That was not ours although we understood,
> Inhuman, of the veritable ocean.

One hears the "empty" noise of the water; let us say, in the context
of Frye's original example of "Lycidas," one hears the "theatrical"
and "tinsel" third-order narrative of the poem as it appears in its
printed form. One may be aware of the second-order "genius of the
sea," that is, of the Adonis myth in "Lycidas," but through this one
hears that which sings "beyond" the myth, that is, one hears the
primordial generative musical ensemble. But Stevens with Blake
tells us, "what *she* sang was what she *heard*," that is, her song is the
Antwort to the *Wort* of the child on the cloud.

Frye's own method has been compared to that of peeling an
onion (though one never quite reaches the core), and he himself has
compared it to the game, "Twenty Questions." The best illustration of what I have been describing is d'Indy's tone poem "Ishtar"
(Milton's "queen and mother both"), in which the original complicated orchestration is successively simplified through phrase after
phrase, as veil after veil is removed (Hopkins's "parings of
paradisiacal fruit"), until one is in the presence of the pure, naked
melody (Stevens's "sister and mother and diviner love"). Those
intervening veils, orders, strata need not be examined further here;

they have been studied fully by others, most notably and most ingeniously by Frye himself. It is the roots of the figural patterns that penetrate those strata and find their ground in the primordial utterance that I would like to imagine I am tracing.

Now, none of this means that the poetry we know develops through a kind of reverse-refractive process: the poet does not wend his way back through known poems and behind them through their narrative myths, and then behind the latter to their ultimate paleostructures, and then, after all this, having discerned such structures, reduplicate them in the context of his own poem. The process is not mimetic, imitation of a prior imitation, but ontomimetic, imitation of "being" itself. And to employ Rilke's metaphor, just as primitive man's *Antwort* was an unmediated response to the primordial *Wort,* so the poet's *Gesang* is an unmediated response to *Dasein.* "What *she* sang was what she *heard*": "being."

To deny this immediate and nondiscursive encounter with being would entail something akin to what in theology has been called the heresy of "traditionalism." In the late eighteenth and early nineteenth century when it became apparent to everyone, atheist and honest believer alike, that there was no way of logically coming to a knowledge of the existence of God, a "primitive revelation" from God attesting to his own existence was posited by several religious thinkers, notably de Maistre and de Lamennais. This revelation became the *traditum* being handed down through generations and so accounting for present-day man's knowledge of God. The heresy of traditionalism in poetry relies on the doctrine of "rules of art" and, in answer to the question of how one knows a specific poem here and now to be beautiful, affirms that it is so because it conforms to the rules of art. The question necessarily arises as to how right rules of art are determined; and the only answer is that they are deduced from existing works of avowedly great art, which are known to be great because of their conformity to, and so forth and so on. The regress into infinity can only be checked by a regress into absurdity, which must posit some primitive revelation of the first great work of art from which were deduced the first rules.

But the poet, possibly as distinct from the literary critic or the philosopher, does not track his way back to the primal *Wort*; like Adam or Tharmas, that *Wort* addresses him directly, and his poem constitutes the *Antwort.* As Quintilian noted, the *carmen* precedes the *observatio carminis*. That the heresy of traditionalism is not dead may be seen in periodic efforts to resurrect the Arnoldian doctrine of touchstones; the heresy is cautiously skirted by E. D. Hirsch writing on the concept of genre: "All philosophical texts are called philosophical texts"; it is wholeheartedly embraced by Stanley Fish in his outré gnome: "You can only read what you've already read"; and it is endorsed from the musical side by the conductor and composer Deryck Cooke in *The Process of Musical Composition*: "what we call 'inspiration' must be an unconscious creative re-shaping of already existing materials in the tradition." This is a hoary notion that dies hard and is very close to the Renaissance identification of translator as traducer and of poetic treason as deviation from tradition.

That the tradition is an influence, and a potent one, has been demonstrated overwhelmingly by Harold Bloom. But the other side of Bloom's coinage is that if there is an "ephebe" there *must* be a strong poet, and the latter is almost by definition the poet who responds to something more than the tradition, responds to something prior to the tradition. The poet, then—and I here employ an example that should speak to Bloom's Kabbalistic model—is like Rabbi Simeon ben Yohai who according to pious legend gave birth to the Zohar in the darkness of his own cave of quietude where he had no books to read and had to rely entirely upon his own inner vision of the book of splendor.

If it is true, as I am suggesting, that poetic patterns are not learned by the poet primarily through the study of other poets' works but are his own unthematized and spontaneous response to the same reality that mystified primitive man—if this is more or less true—one has to wonder about the universality of these patterns. The old Jones-Málinowski debate erupting in the Anti-Oedipus of Deleuze and Guattari must make anyone chary of grandiose claims; so, it is the better part of parsimony to regard these patterns and their significance as suggestive formats, deriving from the experience of one language area within the occidental *orbis terrarum*, which may perhaps be helpful in the discernment of similar such patterns in other poetries.

However, as shall be made clear shortly, I do embrace the universality of the fundamental mystery that gives rise to these patterns. "The thing I hum appears to be / The rhythm of this celestial pantomime." That mystery is threefold in its composition of man's relation to some transcendent "other," his relation with some contingent "other," and his relation with the "other" that is discovered in himself. Presumably, if language is the creation that grapples with this mystery, then each language will develop certain figural strategies analogous to those I shall be analyzing in the relatively narrow confines of English-language poetry. The common grammatical structures and the common sound symbolism that Noam Chomsky and Dell Hymes have descried would seem to support this presumption.

In the light of all this speculation (Stevens's "*appears* to be"), one could respond to Frye on "Lycidas," without blurring the genres or forgetting the *Laokoön*, that in that poem it is the "sonata form" *itself* that must be studied, and beyond that the phrases that constitute such form, because these phrases and form will be discovered as "the structure" of that poem. I do not mean this in the sense of Saintsbury or Hanford substituting talk about "the beautiful music" of "Lycidas" for close reading, or in the sense of Finney's fine musicological interpretation of the poem. I mean that there are certain figural patterns, certain architectural motifs, the recurrence of which constitutes the "deep structure" of the poem. Frye's Adonis myth is at best a secondary or tertiary shaping factor. Very briefly, that foundational structure is the undular rise and fall of the narrative voice, similar to the "up-down" pattern I discuss in more detail in chapter 8. In "Lycidas" the "strain of a higher mood" and "dread voice" descending to the "frail thoughts" of the poet himself create this pattern, which is summarized in line 172: "So Lycidas, sunk low, but mounted high." This ascending-descending motif pairs the following sections: 1–35; 36–84; 85–131; 132–151, with the final ascent 152–185 drifting off into the personal coda of 186 and what follows.

It should be clear from what I have said thus far that I will only indirectly be concerned with traditional metrics; and this is because, first, the meters generally function mainly as a mood-setting backdrop to the narrative element in the poem—Ransom's notion of homage to the Platonic ideas—and second, when metrical variations are conventionally introduced they function merely to reinforce meaning. Certainly, in what follows many structures will be related to meaning—or at least meaning provides access to them— but others, and perhaps the more significant, will function "musically"; that is, they are affective and effective as figural patterns over and beyond their patent context. Lastly, I am not concerned with traditional metrics because the subject has been so extensively treated, but often, as by classical rhetoricians, to the point of enervation by repetition of the same commonplace conclusions. Perhaps it has been this very concentration, combined with our "hobby-horsical" devotion to the old manuals, that has diverted attention from other, richer figural formats.

There is, however, one aspect of these standard structural devices which has a strong bearing on the preceding discussion and which has not been adequately treated in the handbooks, primarily because it is a fairly widespread modern practice that the manualists knew as a relatively rare deviation. I refer to the slant rhymes or pararhymes given currency by Wilfred Owen and his imitators. Grierson somewhat tautologically observed that the second rhyme constitutes a muting of the first. That seems obvious; but why a poet would find this muting attractive remains problematic. Empson whimsically, but as always very pointedly, thought its purpose was to set the listener's teeth on edge and thus link satanic speech in *Paradise Lost* with Owen's detestation of a satanic war. But the practice in Owen is much too ubiquitous— entailing several different variations—in even the nonwar poems for that explanation to be widely applicable.

Dramatically, such a shift gives the verse a note of suspiration; like the dactyl and the trochee, the half-rhyme introduces a tone of passivity, acquiescence, even defeat, not unlike Spenser's consonant clusters. The following is a good illustration from "Futility":

> Think how it wakes the seed—
> Woke, once, the clay of a cold star.
> Are limbs so dear-achieved, are sides
> Full-nerved—still warm—too hard to stir?

But in a deeper sense, just as resonant of the tragic, these successive mutings point up the nature of that unveiling process examined above, and which Milton refers to in *Paradise Lost*: "Immediate are the Acts of God, . . . but to human ears / Cannot without *process of speech* be told" (7. 176–79). The initial inspiration—one thinks again of Blake's supratemporal laughing song—is complicated as it is refracted into the temporal and the sequential, just as the primordial utterance suffers luxation as it passes through its successive manifestations in primitive myth, in the narratives that derive from that myth, and in the glosses and diminished images of those narratives.

Here is another and clearer illustration of this Wort-Antwort "process":

> Leaves
>> Murmuring by myriads in the shimmering trees.
> Lives
>> Wakening with wonder in the Pyrenees.
> Birds
>> Cheerily chirping in the early day.
> Bards
>> Singing of summer scything thro' the hay.

Here the slanting entropic process from unity to multiplicity is counterpointed with the direct half-rhymes of Leaves-Lives, and so on. Similarly, in Owen's "Apologia pro poemate meo," the triplets represent the activating and temporalizing-by-diffusion of the initially unified inspiring Wort:

> Merry it was to laugh there—
>> Where death becomes absurd and life absurder
>> For power was on us as we slashed bones bare
>> Not to feel sickness or remorse of murder.

> I, too, have dropped off fear—
>> Behind the barrage, dead as my platoon,
>> And sailed my spirit surging, light and clear
>> Past the entanglement where hopes lay strewn.

And one may note that in the last stanza we have another counterpointing between the structure which is entropic and the lexical meaning which is incremental.

That Owen, often described as an innovator, is writing out of an old tradition suggests once again the possibly universal, "deepstructure" character of these patterns. Owen, almost certainly unknowingly, was merely introducing a variation on a form which had flourished in several languages during the Renaissance, which is extant in several kinds of permutations, and which was known as *carmen correlativum*. The following from Sidney's *Astrophil and Stella* (no. 77) is very similar to the passages above by Owens:

> Those lookes, whose beames be joy, whose motion is delight,
> That face, whose lecture shewes what perfect beautie is:
> That presence, which doth give darke hearts a living light:
> That grace, which Venus weepes that she her selfe doth misse:
> That hand, which without touch holds more than Atlas might:
> Those lips, which make death's pay a meane price for a kisse.

The pattern admits of the same interpretation as above: first comes the aboriginal insight (Stevens's "ultimate Plato") then the analogue (Frye's "myth"), an analogue which never exhausts or even perfectly approximates the initial inspiring impulse; then the "plot" of a particular poem, and lastly its commentaries.

Finally, it should be emphasized that the illustrations of structures that follow can hardly claim to be exhaustive; as I have said, the entire project is provisory. This is not, then, an attempt at any kind of *epitome troparum ac schematum*. It is at best a roughly drawn map of a few significant patterns.

II: *Catechesis*

This exercise in cartography begins with an axiom and an assumption. The axiom is that the beautiful object is congruent with what is commonly called "human nature"; otherwise, man would not find such an object beautiful at all. The assumption entails a myth proferring an explanation of that nature. The entire map—which like most provisional maps is a kind of collage—will be constructed by moving back and forth between the putatively beautiful object and the myth, in the hope that this dialectic crisscross will illuminate both elements as well as the nature of the relationship itself. The myth is rudimentary, and though it is endorsed directly neither by philosophical school nor by religious doctrine, it is implicated in both and in fact should be as congenial to a Stevensian fictionist as to a Freudian reductionist, and as congenial to someone who believes man's "soul" participates a personal God as to someone who believes man is nothing more than a portable and compendious sack of acids and enzymes. Put most conventionally, the myth affirms that man has a sense of having come forth from unity, of dwelling halfway between unity and disunity, and of therefore wanting to return to unity, but to a unity which, precisely because it is attained by journeying through disunity, must somehow be a higher state than that originally remembered. The development of this myth is the major theme of M. H. Abrams's remarkable study, *Natural Supernaturalism*; but whether or not one regards the myth as "true," there is no doubt that either in its religious form or in its secularized version it has been a major influence on almost all Western poetry.

26

I continue on this rudimentary note. Because the ultimate criterion of credibility is the satisfaction and "pleasure" experienced by the knowing subject, I shall first look at certain framings of language that by common consent "make one happy," that is, are "beautiful"; and then seek to discern how and why they are such. My emphasis is, as I have said, on the framing of language, not on its statements; on the nondiscursive patterns in language, not on its lexical content—recognizing, again, that as with all verbal sequences it may not always be possible to separate what they state from the way they are organized. But it is the pattern, not the paraphrasable meaning as such, that is my primary concern.

I am therefore in search of standards but, even more, of the reason why certain lines of poetry are accepted as standards. Every undergraduate has been told that, whereas Shakespeare's Touchstone is the declared enemy of the didactic and moralizing, Arnold's touchstones relate almost invariably to a literal meaning with which Arnold was sympathetic because it conveyed something of his own moral outlook: "E'n la sua volontade è nostra pace" (approved by Eliot also, and one suspects on Arnoldian grounds); "And courage never to submit or yield / And what is else not to be overcome"; and "which cost Ceres all that pain / To seek her through the world" (the latter an important fragment but sanctioned, one suspects, only for its evocation of chin-up conduct). So, too, with the negative touchstones Arnold supplied for prose in "The Literary Influence of Academies." The prose he lauds as "prose of the centre," "prose without the note of provinciality," is contrasted with four passages redolent of oral-anal imagery, all highly offensive to mid-Victorian moral sensibilities. But in the "touchstones" I have to do with, the patent moral content, the statement, is relatively negligible, and for that reason among others the texts are all the more profoundly "human" in their bearing and concomitantly all the more profoundly "beautiful."

The issue would be burked if one began with a conception of man—the provisional myth above—and sought to have this conception somehow ratified by the statements in certain poems. Since somehow man and poetry are correlative—otherwise poetry wouldn't be pleasing at all—one should not be surprised if "human nature" defined by philosophers as *Geist in Welt*, *esprit incarné*, existence-essence, *en-soi/pour-soi*, universal-concrete were congruent with poetry defined by Carlyle as the "infinite with the finite," or by Browning as "the infinite in the finite." The terms are all analogous one with the other as each is only the periphrasis of some common undefinable paradox—again, embodied in Stevens's "giant on the horizon." Whether among German Romantic philosophers and their heirs, including Kierkegaard, or among English Romantic poets and their heirs, the definitions merge so that man and poetry are isomorphic. As Milton declared in *An Apology for Smectymnus*, "I was confirmed in this opinion that he who would not be frustrate of his hope to write well hereafter in laudable things, ought himself to be a true poem, that is, a composition and *pattern* of the best and honorable things."

A defective approach, as I say, would be to take up unknown lines of verse and determine whether they state something about this isomorphism: those that do, good; those that don't, bad. But this would be like constructing an ethical theory without ever having performed an ethical act; and since ontologically "feeling is first" (or as moralists say, the experience of conscience takes primacy), like all apriorisms, this approach would lead only back to Arnold and the influence of academies or, among critics, to the intermediate strata that much "communal" criticism is devoted to. The preferable mode of beginning is to take avowedly admirable texts—on the likely premise that they are such precisely because of their connaturality with "human nature"—and see how their structure may convey something of that nature and its relation to its world.

A start can be made with that passage from Milton which Arnold had applauded:

> Not that fair field
> Of Enna, where Proserpin gath'ring flow'rs
> Herself a fairer Flow'r by gloomy Dis
> Was gather'd, which cost Ceres all that pain
> To seek her through the world. . . .
>
> [*PL* 4.268–72]

One does not experience here merely another overtone of the eternal note of sadness, though that is what the statement is all about. What one has here is not only the juxtaposition of flowers and pain, a common enough theme, not only the chiastic structure I shall examine more closely in the next chapter, not only a collision of mellifluous polysyllables with stark monosyllables—though of course one does have all this. But I am seeking the basic pattern, am in search of the shape of Stevens's "central poem" of which all these paradoxic structures are only the multiple reflections. That central poem disclosed by its lesser mimes is the relation of limned foreground to unlimited background, the relation of individual, concrete, particular, single, temporal, to universal, absolute, eternal, and so on (synonyms can be supplied *ad libitum* depending on one's intellectual tastes and terminological armory). When one experiences that relation, not serially as in the above description but synoptically and nondiscursively, one is placed in his or her proper stance or, more cautiously, we have communicated to us the meaning of our heuristic myth—hence, delight. We seem to know what we are: we are, in the sense of the Milton prose passage, being "poetic."

It would obviously take one much too far afield to try to "prove" these definitions of "what we are" in relation to the mysterious cosmos. I repeat, one must suspend judgment on the validity of the definitions as such and view them also as hypotheses employed in an effort to make sense out of a particular poetic pattern. All knowledge is predicated on adoption of some hypothesis (for example, Heraclitus's fifty-ninth fragment: "You must join together things whole and things not whole"), which is then tested against the empiric data—in the present instance, tested against certain recurrent literary themes and structures. One certainly doesn't have to affirm apodictically belief in this myth as such—though the fact that this basic myth and its ramifications were unquestionably the matrix of the English poetic tradition might certainly incline one toward a tentative credence.

From a poem much admired by Yeats, I take another simple illustration with a view to a more complicated exegesis later, the induction to Lionel Johnson's "By the Statue of King Charles at

Charing Cross"—the title itself suggests its own affinities with the Milton text: the splendid, the wounded, the chiastic.

> Somber and rich, the skies
> Great glooms, and starry plains;
> Gently the night wind sighs;
> Else a vast silence reigns.
>
> The splendid silence clings
> Around me: and around
> The saddest of all Kings,
> Crown'd, and again discrown'd.

Thus is the tragedy of human existence defined. Against the immense screen of the seemingly indifferent absolute is projected the figure not merely of a fallen man but of a man, in Aristotle's terms, fallen from the highest estate, and now remembered only in effigy. This is Caesar dead and turned to clay, precisely not to keep the wind away but to signify the encompassment of all contingencies by what our forebears' myth specified as the "sky god." It is this encompassment that these lines evoke: Wordsworth's and Robinson's man against the sky, the man who is defined as the nexus of the absolute and the contingent or, as I said earlier, as the nexus of unity-disunity.

A corollary of the original simple myth would be that it is only when contingent, disunified man experiences the passion for absolute unity that his tragic nature is exposed; only when man experiences this dislocation which is constituted by his own duality can there be tragedy. There is thus but one step from tragedy to comedy; it is the step from duality to triviality. Comedy, as a consequence, takes place only where multiplicity, totally though temporarily, smothers man's aspiration to unity, and where nothing has any real importance because nothing has any real meaning. Comedy is beyond good and evil, beyond morality. In a monadic world there is no meaning and no morality, because meaning and morality always demand a comparison, a duality, a relationship with something totally "other." Hence, the grossly comic is described as "a panic"—a totality of disconnected multiplicities. And—returning to our poem—this is why the relationship that Johnson's lines convey is tragic: the threatening, overarching horizon and the limned individual.

Even what we suspect on many other grounds is probably bad verse tends to move us by imposing this "human," and therefore essentially tragic, posture, as when almost unwillingly one responds to the pattern of Browning's "Love among the Ruins":

> Where the quiet-colored end of evening smiles
>   Miles and miles
> On the solitary pastures where our sheep
>   Half asleep

And this is also why, for all their mournful rhetoric, there is little tragic accent, because little "human" structure, in the following from *In Memoriam*—anodynes Lionel Johnson in the passage above might almost seem to have been hurling back across the decades at Tennyson:

> I will not shut me from my kind,
>   And lest I stiffen into stone,
>   I will not eat my heart alone,
> Nor feed with sigh a passing wind;
>
> What profit lies in barren faith,
>   And vacant yearning, though with might
>   To scale the heaven's highest height,
> Or dive below the wells of death.
>
> [No. 108]

For Pascal, man as such suffers the *misères d'un roi dépossédé*, the "sublime misery" of the discrowned Charles Stuart. But the prototype of the dispossessed king in English letters, whose perfect circular creation was shattered at his fall, is Arthur whose pasch is described by an earlier Tennyson than the author of *In Memoriam*:

> So all day long the noise of battle rolled
> Among the mountains by the winter sea,
> Until King Arthur's table, man by man,
> Had fallen in Lyonnesse about their lord
> King Arthur; then, because his wound was deep,
> The bold Sir Bedivere uplifted him.

"Because his wound was deep": one is startled at how casually this phrase is interjected, and how ineffectually it collides with the vast panorama that forms the backdrop of the great king's maiming. The structural similarities to the other texts above are clear enough even to the concluding staccato monosyllables, "his wound was deep," as in "to seek her through the world." Equally clear is the movement of the passage from Pascal's *éspaces infinis* to the human creature *blessé par le mystère*. But we have a new change rung on that "et ego in Arcadia" theme that Panofsky so brilliantly explicated and that is so understandably recurrent in our literature—as in these most memorable lines of *Manfred*:

> upon such a night
> I stood within the Coliseum's wall,
> 'Midst the chief relics of almighty Rome;
> The trees which grew along the broken arches
> Waved dark in the blue midnight, and the stars
> Shone through the rents of ruin; from afar
> The watch-dog bayed beyond the Tiber; and
> More near from out the Caesar's palace came
> The owl's long cry.

[3.4]

We have more than this, however fine it is, in Tennyson's life-death, present-past, near-far cluster. The very casualness of the tragedy of this dispossessed Caesar is shocking. "Then, because his wound was deep," is almost a parenthetic insertion, almost only a slight interruption breaking momentarily the movement of the whole period. "The creature," says Cusanus, "stands between God and nothing." It would seem that man, even the greatest man, so seemingly Promethean, may be simply a mere afterthought in the forward-flowing tide of things. Man may be only a sob or sigh of "the great breath," only, as Donne implies, a demisemiquaver in the musique of the absolute.

Hence, perhaps, the gasp, the poignancy, of such parenthetic utterances as those that follow, and those that I shall examine more closely in the next chapter:

> Or bid the soul of Orpheus sing
> Such notes as, *warbled to the string*,

Drew iron tears down Pluto's cheek
And made Hell grant what Love did seek.
["Il Penseroso," 105–08]

or again,

Perhaps the self-same song that found a path
Through the sad heart of Ruth, when, *sick for home,*
She stood in tears amid the alien corn.
["Ode to a Nightingale"]

or inversely,

Old Eben Flood, *climbing alone one night*
Over the hill between the town below
And the forsaken upland hermitage
That held as much as he should ever know
On earth again of home, paused warily.
["Mr. Flood's Party"]

In the last instance I return to my earlier figure of that wounded chief of whom both Ruth and the "sad virgin" are only pale counterparts, for Eben is also Roland at Roncevaux ("like Roland's ghost"), Arthur in Lyonnesse, even as all likenesses of broken kings tragically destroyed in quest of the absolute may be only analogues of the central poem of the absolute unity engulfing and giving meaning to the contingent fragment.

As I have noted, the movement in the texts from Johnson and Tennyson is from the great glooms of the universal reaches down to the slight, bent figure of the isolate individual. Within this infinite frame, the damaged image of finitude is trapped. This is tragedy of the kind Bossuet essayed in prose in a memorable "oraison funèbre" ("the noblest of all his compositions," said the rhetorician Hugh Blair), which moved through long, stately periods, then through shorter clauses to the pithy fulcrum (my "parenthesis") proclaiming: "the queen is dead." The format is that of the ever-widening gyre, at the foot of which stands the helpless falconer.[1]

---

1. It may be remembered that Yeats's "mere *an*archy" would be traditionally defined as the condition of a kingdom dispossessed of its monarch. But this "mere" is also the paradoxic murderous-innocent sea, which is an aspect of Eben *Flood,* a manifestation of Stevens's paradoxic "giant on the horizon," and the backdrop (the "winter sea") of Arthur's passing.

But if, as Donne affirmed with much of the tradition of poetic and religious myth, "death doth touch the Resurrection," then the glyph that Bossuet should have been homiletically drawing is not merely that of the triangle on its tip, Yeats's gyre, the terrifying whirlpool of Phlebas the Phoenician:

————————————————————

————————————————

————————————

————

——

The glyph should have been something more: something similar to the structure of Herbert's "Easter Wings," a structure which would complement the tragic structures I have cited above by moving circularly from infinite to finite and then by a *reditus* from that finite back to the infinite:[2]

> Lord, who creadst man in wealth and store,
> Though foolishly he lost the same
> Decaying more and more
> Till he became
> Most poore:
> With thee
> O let me rise
> As larks, harmoniously
> And sing this day thy victories:
> Then shall the fall further the flight in me.

And in fact that is exactly what Herbert's contemporary did do in the structure of his sermon on the dispossessed queen:

> Après tant de maux et tant de traverses, elle ne connut plus d'autres ennemis que ses péchés. Aucun ne lui sembla léger: elle en faisait un rigoureux examen; et, soigneuse de les expier

2. Herbert's poem was originally printed vertically, that is, as the convergence of two pointed structures with hyperbolically flared sides. The figure thus represents the flight upward into the infinite.

par le pénitence et par les aumônes, elle était si bien préparée, que la mort n'a pu la surprendre, encore qu'elle soit venue sous l'apparence du sommeil. *Elle est morte, cette grande reine.* Et par sa mort elle a laissé un regret éternel, non seulement à Monsieur et à Madame, qui, fidèles à tous leurs devoirs, ont eu pour elle respects si soumis, si sincères, si persévérants, mais encore à toux ceux qui ont eu l'honneur de la servir ou de la connaître. Ne plaignons plus ses disgrâces, qui font maintenant sa félicité.

"Disgrâces qui font la félicité": this may be translated as contingencies and finitudes which make absolutes and infinities: the caged skylark of Hopkins is free; the swan of Mallarmé escapes "l'horreur de col où le plumage est pris"; multiplicity is swallowed up in unity (to paraphrase the text used by virtually all the Royalist poets in their tributes to Charles I).

"Death, thou art swallowed up in victory": we are here at the heart of that paradox where, again, the poetic myth converges with that of religion and philosophy. "The way up is the way down"—a text universal from the Upanishads to the Kabbalah to Pascal. "Unless a corn of wheat fall into the ground and die, it abideth alone." For the priest-poet Herbert, like the priest-poet Donne, like the priest-poet Bossuet, like the priest-poet Hopkins, indeed, like the priest-poet Mallarmé—since at this point all myths converge and all poets are priests[3]—the tragic cycle of trapped lark and swan is broken precisely by "imping" the broken creaturely wing to the wing of that phoenix of the absolute which some call Yahweh, others the "not-yet," others "being's ground," and so on.

Similarly, there is a real agreement, a real convergence of the poet's "luxe, calme, et volupté" (which Gide in his *Journals* characterized as the perfect definition of the work of art) and the mystical philosopher's "lux, pax, et voluptas" (which Pico della Mirandola in *De Ente et Uno* saw as the goal of all human striving). And both

---

3. In the tradition that culminates in Romanticism every humane achievement should be both priestly and poetic—another aspect of M. H. Abrams's "natural supernaturalism": thus, Ranke and Burckhardt on the historian; Carlyle and Emerson on Shakespeare, Carew on Donne, and Milton on himself; Heidegger on the philosopher; Rahner on the theologian; and Bloom on the strong critic.

Baudelaire and Gide, along with Herbert and the whole soaring company I have cited above, would have agreed with Pico's answer to the inevitable question: "Sed quid dabit pennas ut illuc volemus?" All would agree that these "easter wings" are supplied only by "Amor eorum quae sursum sunt"—of that "sursum," more shortly. Witnesses to the myth unanimously affirm that only the eros from above can draw the eros from below; only the absolute made concrete can give the concrete the gift of the absolute. Hence, the fascination of all religions with a paradoxic deity, Krishna-Kali, Brahman-Atman, Siva-Sakti, Word-flesh; and the fascination of poets like Hölderlin, Rilke, and Stevens with an ultimate hyphenating principle, an absolute-contingent, a god-man. Though with different symbolizations, all respond alike to Amy Lowell's self-answering question: "Christ! what are patterns for?"

The complete glyph of the infinite-finite-infinite pattern would approximate, then, the pyramidic figure Cusanus had his disciples contemplate, which is homologous with a twentieth-century Cusanian's (Kenneth Burke's) "dialectical pyramid," as well as with Lévi-Strauss's "culinary triangle." And just as the golden section engenders the Pythagorean five-pointed star, so the triangular convergence of Herbert's poem and Bossuet's peroration engenders the Kabbalistic six-pointed star, a symbol Yeats detected in his own vision of the intersecting spirals, at the midpoint of which alone—at the very core of the paradox—were fulfillment and union attained.

It is clear, then, the distortion that was wrought above for catechetical reasons in not proferring the whole introduction to the "Morte d'Arthur." For Arthur, so the legend had it, with all his wounds was to live again: "I pass but shall not die." He too was to embrace and be embraced by the absolute. The female figures on his death barge, like Goethe's "mothers," stand as mediators of that absolute. Hence, the complete text, "Kabbalistically" we may now see, moves in circular fashion from the infinite to the finite and then out into the infinite again; and the whole is identical with the patterns of Herbert and Bossuet.

> So all day long the noise of battle rolled
> Among the mountains by the winter sea,
> Until King Arthur's table, man by man,

> Had fallen in Lyonnesse about their lord
> King Arthur; then, because his wound was deep,
> The bold Sir Bedivere uplifted him,
> Sir Bedivere, the last of all his knights,
> And bore him to a chapel nigh the field,
> A broken chancel with a broken cross,
> That stood on a dark strait of barren land.
> On one side lay the ocean, and on one
> Lay a great water, and the moon was full.

The basic pattern is figured forth in the great expansive opening and closing images (rolled among the mountains by the winter sea; the ocean, the great water, the full moon). This is a mythic structure of the circular journey "back home" to unity, that as such has nothing to do with religious belief in immortality, resurrection, and so on.

One should not be surprised to find this same circular pattern—which the Middle Ages and Renaissance, after Innocent III, called *ingressus-progressus-egressus*—in Johnson's poem on King Charles, because Johnson believed the dead king, like Arthur, would also triumphantly conquer through death. Let me recapitulate by looking again at the first two stanzas:

> Somber and rich, the skies
> Great glooms, and starry plains;
> Gently the night wind sighs;
> Else a vast silence reigns.

> The splendid silence clings
> Around me: and around
> The saddest of all Kings,
> Crown'd, and again discrown'd.

As I have noted above, the development is from the expanse of the infinite spaces to the figure of the broken king. The two are then tenuously linked together in a nexus which corresponds to the central point in Herbert's stanza and Bossuet's peroration:

> Armor'd he rides, his head
> Bare to the stars of doom;
> He triumphs now, the dead,
> Beholding London's gloom.

We are in between the infinite and the finite with the conflation of the *universal* "great glooms" of the first stanza and the *concrete* "London's gloom" of this stanza. The final stanza of the poem completes the circle by its *egressus*, without any mention of the contingent king, back to the infinite screen of the heavens:

> Yet, when the city sleeps,
> When all the cries are still,
> The stars and heavenly deeps
> Work out a perfect will.

It is entirely possible that Johnson had read Bossuet's sermon, and it is certain that he knew Herbert's poem, but it is doubtful if he was consciously imitating either; it is rather more likely that this structure is a kind of sphragis stamped by the pervasive agency of the heuristic myth on the psyche of every poet aware of the latent tragedy in a contingent being that is driven to aspire to the absolute. All three passages are the expression of that fundamental structure discussed in chapter 1. As final corollary to the discussion thus far, one should point out the convergence not only of literary, religious, and poetic myth in these various texts but their convergence as well with what may oxymoronically be called "historical myth." For Bossuet's sermon is titled "Oraison funèbre de Henriette-Marie de France, reine de la Grande-Bretagne," Herrick's "sweet Maria" and wife of the discrowned Charles Stuart. As Bossuet promised that the infinite would embrace her who was reverenced in the Gallican Church as a sainted widow, so also Johnson two centuries later would promise "triumph" and the "sublime" to him whom the Anglican Church still celebrates with the feast of King Charles— the "Glory of all Martyrologies," said Bishop King in his "A Deepe Groane."

I have noted that Johnson's poem was much admired by Yeats. From the *Autobiography*: "I shall remember all my life that evening when Lionel Johnson read or spoke aloud in his musical monotone, where meaning and cadence found the most precise elocution, his poem suggested 'by the Statue of King Charles at Charing Cross.' It was as though I listened to a great speech. Nor will that poem be to me what it was that first night." "That poem" has a pattern identical with a more celebrated poem by Yeats himself. Again, the evolution is from the awesome vast expanses to the fragile and contingent:

> Once more the storm is howling, and half hid
> Under this cradle-hood and coverlid
> My child sleeps on.

This is "A Prayer for My Daughter" and, as such, a supplication that the infinite will not crush the finite. As a "prayer" for the "triumph" of the child, one may not be entirely surprised that the poem reduplicates the fulfillment structure of our earlier texts with its movement from infinite to finite and then back out to the infinite. (The structure of the first three lines is the condensed structure of the whole first stanza.)

> Once more the storm is howling, and half hid
> Under this cradle-hood and coverlid
> My child sleeps on. There is no obstacle
> But Gregory's wood and one bare hill
> Whereby the haystack and roof-levelling wind,
> Bred on the Atlantic, can be stayed;
> And for an hour I have walked and prayed
> Because of the great gloom that is in my mind.
>
> I have walked and prayed for this young child an hour
> And heard the sea-wind scream upon the tower,
> And under the arches of the bridge, and scream
> In the elms above the flooded stream;
> Imagining in excited reverie
> That the future years had come,
> Dancing to a frenzied drum,
> Out of the murderous innocence of the sea.

This is certainly less explicit than Johnson, and it is certainly less naive than Herbert, and—if naiveté and piety are convertible, as the German mystic, Peter Wust, said—probably this poem is less expressive of faith in its power as prayer: nevertheless, the same pattern is imposed, though here figurally and thematically as in the Tennyson passage and not pictorially as in Herbert. But it is the same, and all the more clearly so by the repetition of the everyday, commonplace, temporal setting, "I have walked and prayed," at the end of the first and the beginning of the second stanza. The development is from howling storm, roof-leveling wind, to the casual contingency of a father thinking about his cradled infant, and then out again to the screaming wind and frenzied drum: infinite-finite-infinite.

If even the frailest little girl (who is also, however, a *reine dépossédée*) can stand before the great universal storm and not be utterly engulfed, or *as* engulfed, yet saved, then the human person, so the myth suggests, may not be entirely isolate in the cosmos.

> Ist nicht so, gejagt und dann gebändigt,
> Diese sehnige Natur des Seins?
> Weg und Wendung. Doch ein Druck verständigt.
> Neue Weite. Und die zwei sind eins
>
> [*Sonnette an Orpheus* 1.xi]

As Yeats and Rilke both suggest, there is some reason or, if not reason, some instinct for hope; otherwise, "Wherefore those prayers to the moon?" (Stevens's "Annual Gaiety"), wherefore "a prayer for my daughter"?

"Not so fast," as Crashaw says when interrupting his own narrative of Teresa rushing off to what she regarded as her martyrial marriage with the absolute. The myth has not yet been verified as fact; perhaps can never be so verified. To desire salvation for one's daughter is not to save her. Indeed, the ultimate irony of the skeptic is Goldmann's comment on the words of Pascal: "To desire God is indeed to possess him." Goldmann notes, "It is a movement which, because it is eternal and instantaneous, never goes forward." So we remain caught in an endless hermeneutical spiral in which the myths of metaphysics confirm the structured myths of poetry. But neither can go beyond its mythic status: that achievement is left at best to shaman and mage. For present purposes that is as it should be. It is the equivalence of these myths that matters here.

To the question of philosophers as diverse as Gilbert Ryle and Merleau-Ponty—"Am I my body?"—common sense and self-reflection both respond by saying, "Yes, I am, *but* . . ." This instinctive "but" necessarily prefaces the hesitant but nevertheless certain realization that there is something "more" to me than body—

proving Donne correct when he wrote of bodies: "They are ours, though they are not wee." This elusive "more" can be called by any name one wishes—soul, spirit, psyche, "a small blue thing," and so on—and it and the body somehow constitute that reality one points to by declaring "I." Thus man is, and can say, "I am": *sum*. But the heuristic myth suggests he knows himself to be more than merely this unsponsored ego; he is a body and a "something more"—as Rilke attests, a duality destined "to be one." He is therefore a "sursum" (and here we rejoin Pico della Mirandola), an "I am" that overflows beyond the limbs, beyond the limns that limit him. If this is so, then this quality of breaking out of the enclosure and into something transcendent should somehow be expressed in those lines that most move us. And it seems to be so—as the following passages suggest. (I shall take up in chapter 4 a wider range of variations on this new pattern.)

Let me look at some lines from a poet now demeaned as out-moded by contemporary poets and critics—with the notable excep-tion of James Wright. The poem is "Dining Room Tea" by Rupert Brooke. The theme is the poet's glimpse of something "timeless" in the most quotidian event. Here is neither the unsoldered fellowship of Arthur's passing nor the compulsive fellowship of "Sunday Morning"; it has a less portentous ambience than those. It is as banal a situation as that of a man musing in a thunderstorm over his sleeping child—but by that fact, since all poems are one poem, "musing upon the [dispossessed] king my brother's wreck." Friends are gathered in careless security when

> . . . suddenly, and otherwhence,
> I looked on your magnificence.
> I saw the stillness and the light,
> And you august, immortal, white,
> Holy and strange.

The prevalent line is "end-stopped," and the operative device is "enjambment." Each repeated line marches steadily to its terminus, which is stressed, and breaks against it. The limns are experienced. But the barrier suddenly is cracked by the necessity of unstressing "white" and letting the speech flow over (sursum) immediately to the stressed, "Hōly and strange." Again, it is the alluring and ter-

rifying absolute, the unlimited, to which man seems to be missioned; and he now recognizes that mission because in its figural
analogues—as here—he seems to find peace.

Similarly, in "Dust"—a minor exercise in metaphysical wit
whose ancestral poem is Carew's "To My Mistress in Absence"—
Brooke relentlessly stops each of six stanzas with a stressed masculine only to break step in stanza 7 with a feminine ending that
arabesques immediately into stanza 8. Stanza 6 typifies the organization of all the preceding stanzas and is presented here only in
illustration of that overall pattern which is about to be violated as
two earthly lovers, contingent and finite, feel the presence of the
transcendent, dead lovers who have been coursing through the universe in search of one another—all in verification of Jonson's "even
ashes of lovers find no rest":

> Nor ever rest, nor ever lie,
>   Till beyond thinking, out of view,
> One mote of all the dust that's I
>   Shall meet one atom that was you.
>
> Then in some garden hushed from wind,
>   Warm in a sunset's afterglow
> The lovers in the flowers will find
>   A sweet and strange unquiet grow
>
> Upon the peace . . .

Sursum is surprise: we are not surprised *by* joy; the joy *is* surprise.
That something should break out of its limits shocks and delights,
because man is the being that transcends his limns: again,
"L'homme passe *infiniment* l'homme." Thus, a theory of enjambment will generally entail a theory of poetic surprise and, with
certain qualifications, that will also be a theory of human transcendence. It is with some implications of this notion of surprise
that I want to close this chapter.

I have already noted that Leonard B. Meyer's theory of musical
meaning is based on something akin to surprise. In *Emotion and
Meaning in Music* he says, "Affect or emotion-felt is aroused when
an expectation—a tendency to respond—activated by the musical
stimulus situation, is temporarily inhibited or permanently blocked."

The question that must be asked, however, is why surprise is delightful; why does the inhibition or blocking of expectation produce pleasurable emotion? For all his insight, Meyer's psychological explanation does not provide much of an answer. We certainly experience anger or bitterness when frustrated, but on the other hand we usually experience joy and satisfaction when not frustrated. In a later work Meyer returns to the problem and clarifies his notion of surprise, not by relying on standard psychological theories of frustration but by drawing upon the resources of that discipline now known as Information Theory. The crux of the argument is the following statement: "Information is measured by the randomness of the choices possible in a given situation. If a situation is highly organized and the possible consequents in the pattern process have a high degree of probability, then information (or entropy) is low." That is, to the degree one can predict what is coming, to that degree one already knows the "message" and to that degree is not learning anything completely new. And since knowledge is pleasurable, in an artistic composition there would be therefore no or little "affect or emotion-felt."

Now, it is certainly true that "all men naturally desire to know" and that knowing what comes naturally is pleasurable. *But*, is it the pleasure of acquiring knowledge that one experiences, say, in the startling coda to Stevens's "Snow and Stars"?

> Let him remove it to his regions,
> White and star-furred for his legions,
> And make much bing, high bing.
>
> It would be ransom for the willow
> And fill the hill and fill it full
> Of ding, ding, *dong*.

There is no "high degree of probability" that "the bluejay suddenly / Would swoop to earth" (Stevens's "The Sense of the Sleight-of-Hand Man") or any such degree that "Snow and Stars" would conclude on a dissonant instead of the traditionary and rhyming "ding, dong, ding." But our delight in this totally unexpected resolution has nothing to do with the conveyance of "information," no matter how broadly defined. Rather, if one were to do a phenomenological analysis of the emotional response to Stevens's poem, one would probably compare that response to the effect produced by the "punch line" to a good joke.

Howard Nemerov in "Bottom's Dream" has written a useful study on the affinities of poems and jokes. But in the end, however much one enjoys the essay and the entertaining parallels, one is left with only a vague perspective on the original problem: what makes the joke funny; what makes the poem pleasurable; or ultimately— for this is the issue—why is a narrative of anticipated surprise essentially pleasurable and essentially human? For Freud, in several places, but particularly in "Jokes and Their Relation to the Unconscious," the joke represents the conquest of inhibition by a release of repressed psychic energy. Theodore Reik has written two treatises elaborating Freud's insight. He observes, "The first reaction at hearing a joke is a kind of unconscious fear or shock." Unfortunately, common experience discloses this as a mere *ipse dixit* which also waffles the issue by category mistake, since "fear" and "shock" are not, as Reik intends here, convertible terms. To the statement, one must reply "shock," yes; "fear," not necessarily. Reik then continues:

> It is as if a latent anxiety, which lives in all of us, had suddenly become intensified. The joke has touched upon certain taboos, forbidden ideas that exist in our unconscious and awaken the temptation to break through the inhibition that our cultural pattern considers valid. This temptation is at first rejected in the form of fear at the thought expressed in the joke. Then we realize that the fear is superfluous and we enjoy the joke.

But the entire argument is vitiated by the fact that the jokes Reik proffers are what in common parlance we would call "dirty jokes," just as many of Freud's were "ethnic jokes." Moreover, if jokes touch upon taboos, one would expect that the ultimate taboo—at least for Lévi-Strauss—incest, would be the subject of a whole genre of jokes, whereas in fact most people would have difficulty in recalling ever having heard a single story on this theme.

Reik's explanation may clarify *an element* of the perennial sophomore's pleasure at something like "The members of the nudist camp could barely make ends meet," or an element of the more educated response to the information that Whistler had suggested that a play by Oscar Wilde be called "The Bugger's Opera." But Reik does not explain the nature of the essential pleasure as such. If one takes the simplest "joke," like the mere statement, "Shelley's 'To a Skylark' is written in pterodactyls," or, "Confessional poetry is plathological," nothing could be more sexually neutral. And as with the reaction to the coda of Stevens's poem above, one immediately knows how irrelevant Freud's and Reik's theorizings are to clarifying that experience. One may take a more complex joke, such as the following, and again the commonsense judgment will be that virtually nothing in one's pleasurable response stems from impulse escaping the psychic censor. The following is from the standard repertoire of an academic storyteller, though I abbreviate considerably—which of course reduces somewhat the listener's suspense. "An Indian chief had three squaws who were coming to term at the same time: the first squaw went into the tepee and delivered a five-pound baby boy on a buffalo hide; the second delivered a five-pound baby boy on an antelope hide; the third squaw went into the tepee and delivered a ten-pound baby boy on a hippopotamus hide. When the chief went into the tepee, he said . . ." I am artifically extending the suspense by postponing the punch line and putting it into a footnote.[4] Let me give a third example, which is not a joke as such but which induces a comparable kind of delight. John Hollander in *Vision and Resonance* is discussing "music" in poetry:

> the music of poetry is one not of musical sounds, nor of the repertory of sounds that a particular language succeeds in segregating from the clamor of possibles; and thus it is that what one reads, there on a page arranged in verse, hearing and vision joined in words, is music. *Ut pictura musicaque poesis*: the poem is song and picture.

In reading this unquestionably serious judgment about the nature of poetry, one is delighted at the recognition of this totally unexpected syllabic echo of Stevens in "Peter Quince at the Clavier."

---

4. The son of the squaw of the hippopotamus is equal to the son of the squaws of the two adjacent hides.

That delight, as in all of the instances I have supplied, has nothing to do with either information acquired or impulse vented. It has to do with the experience in the reader or listener of an aspect in his own psychic makeup which he recognizes as not under the control of the conscious rational faculty, the experience of something that is utterly unconstrained and unconstrainable, utterly free.

There are people who may study the above lines or the above "jokes" until they are "blue in the face" and "completely embarrassed" at their obtuseness in not being able to grasp what is "funny." (Both of those responses are combined in Hopkins's phrase, "gaze out of countenance.") There is no way they can force the joke (or the poem, since Hopkins is explicitly referring to an aesthetic experience) to communicate. Force and compulsion are in what classically is called the domain of "matter," the domain where everything is predictable because everything is physically linked, "part outside of part." This is the domain that corresponds in classical philosophy to the exercise of *ratio* (ratio = measure = meter = matter), to the exercise of Blake's "Rational Demonstration," to the exercise of logical, discursive knowledge—the domain where things can be "proved." One cannot prove a poem or a joke; one either "gets it" or one doesn't: again Hopkins, "Where a glance master more may than gaze." Classically, this latter is the domain of "spirit," the domain where come into play these synonymous polarizations: *intellectus* as opposed to *ratio*, *Chokmah* as opposed to *Binah*, *prajna* as opposed to *vijnana*, *finesse* as opposed to *géometrie*, *Vernunft* as opposed to *Verstand*. This is the domain where one leaps the gap between premise and conclusion without the "middle term," without having the joke "spelled out."

Now, we are delighted at this unmediated recognition of a principle of utter unconstraint that transcends the limits of our everyday, harried, pressured exterior. We recognize in this uncontrollable outburst the highest reality "within" ourselves (all spatial metaphors are deceptive), a principle of free spontaneity, of "spirit," which responds to the principle of free spontaneity, of "spirit," "embodied" in the poem or joke. This is what in the preceding discussion I have called the principle of infinity and unity "residing" in the finite and the fragmentary, which constitutes man as the nexus, the combination of both elements. That principle of infinity and unity in man reaches out to, or better, is drawn out by the principle of infinity and unity exterior to man. The experience of this drawing out (ecstasy) is the only *indicator* (by definition there can be no proof) of the reality of something "transcendent," a term I shall clarify further in chapter 4.

PART TWO: PHENOMENOLOGY

III: *Canon*

As I mentioned in the preface, the chapter titles of this book are intended to pay homage to Stevens by way of "The Comedian as the Letter C." But Stevens could as well have called that poem "The Tragedian as the Letter T." According to the heuristic myth, man is not just the creature whose efforts to embrace the absolute, to close his arms about it, and thus effect the circle of perfection are doomed to comic failure;[1] he is also the "poor, bare, forked animal," the tormented creature who is cruciform, who is drawn at once to the horizontal multiple and the vertical unity, and whose tragic fate is, in Heidegger's words, "to stand at the crossing of the paths of existence in a state of permanent decision."

This "crossing of the paths" is the medieval Pythagorean glyph "Y"—Pope's "Samian letter"—the trunk of which represented the indecisive years of childhood, while the fork represented the adult options *aut Deo/aut mundo*. Chapman gives a less medieval and thus a less theologically grounded reading of this figure in one of the "Virgils Epigrams," subtitled "Of this letter Y":

> This letter of Pythagoras, that beares
> This forkt distinction, to conceit prefers
> The forme mans life beares. Vertues hard way takes
> Vpon the right hand path: which entrie makes

---

1. Stevens's letter "C" is a symbol of "the breaking of the circle," which I shall discuss in greater detail in chapter 10. Though in the *Letters* he explained the "C" in terms of its audible echoes in the poem, it is clear from his other Kabbalistic meditations on the sacred alphabet that the letter "C" is a figurative emblem of the same order as "A" and "Z" in "An Ordinary Evening in New Haven": "It is the infant A standing on infant legs, / Not twisted, stooping polymathic Z."

(To sensuall eyes) with difficult affaire:
But when ye once haue climb'd the highest staire,
The beautie and the sweetnesse it containes,
Giue rest and comfort, farre past all your paines.

Pythagoras's "Y" is a correlative of the vital-fatal "X" of Stevens's "Motive for Metaphor." Because man is the paradox of living-death, of absolute-contingent, he is tormented by this "X"—which stands "for the unknown."

Since the chiasm is the pattern I shall examine first, however briefly, it is worth pausing over the fuller import of Stevens's poem. The last two stanzas are:

> Desiring the exhilaration of changes:
> The motive for metaphor, shrinking from
> The weight of primary noon,
> The A B C of being,
>
> The ruddy temper, the hammer
> Of red and blue, the hard sound—
> Steel against intimation—the sharp flash,
> The vital, arrogant, fatal, dominant X.

Northrop Frye in an essay titled after the poem offers a common misreading: "What Stevens calls the weight of primary noon, the A B C of being, and the dominant X is the objective world, the world set over against us." This is excessively reductive, particularly for Stevens, the arch-welder of antinomies. Rather, what is being contrasted here is the monistic "A B C" world, the prose world of the humorless abecedarian I discussed in the last chapter, for whom everything has to be "spelled out"; it is the world of Yeats's "prosaic light of day" ("primary noon"). That world in Stevens's conception is about to be dissolved by the making of metaphor, by the fusing of polarities (red-blue, solidity-fragility, steel-intimation) on Mulciber's forge, on the anvil of Los. What results from this making of metaphor is the fascinating but mysterious poem, the mime of man ("X"), which both heightens and briefly appeases man's sense of his own duality as a paradoxic being, as a combination, in Berdyaev's metaphysic, of slavery and freedom, of death and life, of fatal and vital—for which the poetic analogues are countless, for example,

the mariner possessed by "death in life," Browning's pontiff (bridge
building is to make priestly metaphor) inquiring "Do I live, am I
dead?," Tennyson's "idle tears" (the tears of *otium*, of "easeful"
death), "O death in life," and lastly the doubly tormented, and
doubly chiastic, figure of Malbecco:

> Yet can he neuer dye, but dying liues,
>   And doth himselfe with sorrow new sustaine,
>   That death and life attonce vnto him giues.
> And painefull pleasure turnes to pleasing paine.
>   [*FQ* 3.10.60]

Not because it is a dominant structure—being more decorative
than architectural—but because it happens to be a key to many of
the poems that follow, I begin with a summary discussion of the
chiasm. For present purposes, I read that figure as primarily representative of the intersection of the infinite and the finite, and of
man's confusion as the conjunction of both; it is secondarily representative of the intersection of female and male, also with its attendant confusions—nexus and sexus, as Henry Miller intimates. For
both of these representations one may think of the sexually charged
descriptions of Desdemona, Juliet, and Christabel—"moist...,
hot, hot, and moist"; "Blubb'ring and weeping, weeping and
blubb'ring"; "dreaming fearfully, Fearfully dreaming"—or of the
sexual bewilderment of the servant of the Lord Love in Robinson's
"Eros Turannos":

> She fears him, and will always ask
>   What fated her to choose him;
> She meets in his engaging mask
>   All reasons to refuse him;
> But what she meets and what she fears
> Are less than are the downward years,
> Drawn slowly to the foamless weirs
>   Of age, were she to lose him.

And this chiasm recalls the torment of another victim of love,
Donne in "Twicknam Garden":

> Blasted with sighs, and surrounded with teares,
> Hither I come to seek the spring,
> And at mine eyes, and at mine eares,
> Receive such balmes, as else cure every thing.

It is the confusion of Hodgson's "Eve," who stands,

> Wondering, listening,
> Listening, wondering.

All of these personae are in transit between innocence and experience, as is also, and more explicitly, the speaker in Blake's "The Angel":

> And I wept both night and day,
> And he wiped my tears away,
> And I wept both day and night,
> And hid from him my heart's delight.

This conflict of innocence and experience is certainly reflected in the chiastic patterns embodied in several of Shakespeare's sonnets. The following representative samples are from Sonnets 28 and 96 respectively:

> How can I then return in happy plight,
> That am debarr'd the benefit of rest?
> When day's oppression is not eas'd by night,
> But day by night, and night by day, oppress'd,
> And each, though enemies to either's reign,
> Do in consent shake hands to torture me.

> Some say thy fault is youth, some wantonness;
> Some say thy grace is youth and gentle sport;
> Both grace and faults are lov'd of more and less;
> Thou mak'st faults graces that to thee resort.

The same tension prevails in Marvell's "The Fair Singer," where he observes that he could have "fled from One but singly fair" and that even the first encounter with a harmonized duality (a prelapsarian idealization) was "sweet":

That while she with her Eyes my Heart does bind,
She with her voice might captivate my mind.

But the sweetness is dissipated as he is no longer harmoniously captivated (a harmony conveyed by the above parallel structure) but instead is ensnarled by the tormenting chiasm:

But all resistance against her is vain,
Who has th'advantage both of Eyes and Voice,
And all my Forces needs must be undone,
She having gained both the Wind and Sun.

Since the chiasm is a figure of great antiquity, shaping the Hebrew mentality according to N. W. Lund and functioning classically as a device suggesting completeness or closure and, in the Petrarchan tradition, as a convention of variety, it would perhaps be naive to read any intensely personal torment into Marvell's agonizing over his mistress's tyranny. Nevertheless, some ontological nerve is being touched here; so true is this that even in chiasms from the palmary exponents of préciosité there seems to be a kind of tragic echo. As with the Browning lines cited in the preceding chapter, the following from Crashaw's "Weeper" seem almost by their structure alone to engender this mood of tragedy:

No where but here did ever meet
Sweetnesse so sad, sadnesse so sweet.

This may be stylistic cliché, but it affects one with the same piercing note as Milton on Ceres' quest.

This is equally true of sonic chiasms, which Kenneth Burke was the first to explore extensively—and again Milton is the exemplar: thus Dagon, a being whose duality is utterly monstrous ("upward Man / and downward Fish") was dreaded

in *G*ath and *A*scalon,
And *A*ccaron and *G*aza's frontier bounds.
[*PL* 1.465–66]

This sonic motif brings out both Satan's duplicity and the confused plight of any fallen angel when seeking to penetrate the citadel of unity:

> What strength, what art can then
> Suffice, or what evasion bear him safe
> *Th*rough the *st*rict *S*enteries and *St*ations *th*ick.[2]
>
> [2.410–12]

This kind of orchestration further explains the present chapter title: "canon" here is not to be understood merely as the formulation of certain standards; it is also intended to be understood in the musical sense of a contrapuntal melody that derives from the dominant theme—in the two examples above, a sonic chiastic structure reflecting the duality, deception, or confusion expressed in the rhetorical statements. And since Milton is writing about the supreme act of duplicity, one would expect this sonic structure to be employed repeatedly—and indeed it is, as in the much-quoted lines expressive of Satan's foul distemper:

> So farewell Hope, and with Hope farewell fear
>
> [4.108]

So speaks the "artificer of fraud; and was the first / That practis'd falsehood under saintly show"; that is, so speaks the first creature consciously aware of his own dual nature: not just the father of lies but the father of Everyman. (For good reason did Chesterton opine that the double entendre was the "original sin.") So, too, with scores of other such structures in *Paradise Lost*: the flaming volleys and vaulted fire (4.213–14), the cloud and Pillar and Pillar and Cloud (12.203, 208), representative of the confused wanderings of the children of Israel.

---

2. This modulation of the chiastic motif (ABCBA) is called "pedimental" after the architectural design and is homologous with the classical hysteron proteron. These are fairly common structures in *Paradise Lost*, as the following fragments indicate:
Sidonian Virgins paid thir Vows and Songs . . . [1.441].
Surer to prosper than prosperity
Could have assur'd us . . .[2.39–40].
If thence he scape into whatever world,
Or unknown Region, what remains him less
Than unknown dangers and as hard escape . . .[2.442–44].
His back was turned but not his brightness hid . . . [3.124].
That Mountain as his Garden Mould . . . [4.226].
Left to his own free will, his will though free . . . [5.236].
The flaming Seraph fearless . . . [5.875].
And earth be chang'd to Heaven, & Heav'n to Earth . . . [7.160].

"Those who cannot read Greek should read nothing but Milton and parts of Wordsworth: the state should see to it"—*sic* Matthew Arnold, whose own wrestlings with the daimon of duality have been insightfully explored by Dwight Culler. But my use of Arnold's pairing of Milton and Wordsworth is only partially based on the more or less standard thematic resemblances of the fall from Eden transmuted into the excruciatingly self-conscious Wordsworthian mythos of descent from youthful Nature-ecstasy to prematurely geriatric torpidity; or, again, of Satan as self-deluding hero in the cosmic arena and the "hero" of *The Prelude* as self-deluding in the private arena of his own imagination.[3] Rather, the pairing is based on figural affinities, of which the following is one of the most exemplary.

> when like a roe
> I *bounded* o'er the *mountains* by the sides
> Of the deep rivers, and the lonely streams,
> Wherever nature led: more like a man
> Flying from something that he dreads, than one
> Who sought the thing he loved. For nature then
> (The coarser pleasures of my boyish days,
> And their glad animal movements all gone by)
> To me was all in all.—I cannot paint
> What then I was. The *sounding* cataract
> *Haunted* me like a passion.

3. The texts, of course, are suggestive, not probative, and would certainly include the following juxtaposings:
> ... And so I dare to hope,
> Though changed, no doubt, from what I was...
> ... Not for this
> Faint I, nor mourn nor murmur; other gifts
> Have followed... ["Tintern Abbey," 65 ff.].
> ... yet not for those,
> Nor what the Potent Victor in his rage
> Can else inflict, do I repent or change,
> Though chang'd in outward lustre... [*PL* 1.94–97].
> ... more like a man
> Flying from something that he dreads, than one
> Who sought the thing he loved... ["Tintern Abbey," 70–72].
> I fled, but he pursu'd (though more, it seems,
> Inflam'd with lust than rage) and swifter far... [*PL* 2.790–91].

Almost like Herbert's "Easter Wings," this is a kind of visual structure, here reflecting Wordsworth's growing ambiguity concerning the relation of self to external world. From oneness with his own being and oneness with reality he is descending to a state of conflict, the final phase of which shall be the intellectual and imaginative annihilation of the external in the name of the utter autonomy of the internal—and concomitantly the birth of modern poetry out of the death of Wordsworth's own poetry. This trajectory, even more manifest in Arnold, is from authentic unity to the inevitable experience of duality and the resolution of that duality, not by an ascent to a higher unity but by a descent to what may be described as a monadic condition. In the "Tintern Abbey" passage the parenthetic insertion has a parallel structure expressive of the original harmony of his dual nature—what I have called, with regard to the similar parallel structure in Marvell above, a prelapsarian ideal. But the fact that this parallel structure (coarser pleasures-animal movements) is enclosed by the visual chiasm points up the gradual collapse of that harmony in the face of the heightened consciousness of duality accompanying adolescence; lastly, the fact that this is a parenthesis expressing contempt and disdain for the authentically unified state of innocence indicates Wordsworth's literally demonic effort at self-deception, an effort to convince himself, like Satan in hell, that his present divisiveness is preferable to his original unity.

Since I have already looked briefly at parenthetical statements, and will do so in more detail shortly, one need only note here how, again, each pattern reflects another, how each succeeding "myth" reduplicates its predecessor. But, it should be emphasized again, our interest is engaged by this passage from "Tintern Abbey," not primarily because we are morbidly concerned with Wordsworth's gradual disintegration but because his personal myth is the final refraction of the kind of mythic structure embodied here, as that mythic structure is itself a secondary or tertiary refraction of the paleomythic structure, that is, the structure of the heuristic myth which seems to be incised in man's central being, incised in what John of the Cross called "el profundo centro." Lastly, to indulge a parenthesis here, it may be observed that John of the Cross's poems have the same relationship to his turgid Scholastic commentaries on them that Wordsworth's postecstatic cogitations have to his innocent childhood experiences.

I turn now, not without some hesitation because it has been the subject of deadly debate, to the last chiastic pattern in this discussion:

> "Beauty is truth, truth beauty,"—that is all
> Ye know on earth, and all ye need to know.[4]

Without getting into the welter of glosses, voluminous if not always luminous, this passage has inspired or motivated, I would offer a clarification consonant with the overall thesis being established here. The structure is chiastic, indicative, again, of man's congenital confusion about the relationship of polarities; the structure is also rhopalic after the fashion of the "decrescendo" analyzed in chapter 1. The direction is from three terms to two terms, that is, from some separation of the poles to a closer linkage of them; from the triadic (beauty-is-truth) to the dual (truth-beauty), and then to the singular *unity*, which is the real goal. But the latter proves to be impossible of attainment. Hence the break: "—." To merge truth-beauty (one may conceive the latter as a kind of portmanteau term) into perfect oneness requires the leaping of that gap: it requires the greatest of "one's grand flights" beyond the domain of separability, through the medium of "easeful death" (the passing of Arthur, the martyrdom of Charles) into the domain of oneness. ("To overcome dualism would be to rise from the dead," says one of Norman O. Brown's aphorisms.) Thus, in the most exact sense, "all we know *on earth*" is that we can bring opposites together (on the vital level by what is called copulation, and on the poetic level by what is called metaphor) in a kind of momentary satisfying conjunction; however, we cannot fuse them into a real and permanent union until we are no longer "on earth" but—to use traditional language— "in heaven."

This kind of progression runs through Cusanus, for whom triads engendering unities is an obsessive theme. But the Keatsian pattern

---

4. The punctuation of the text has been much controverted. It should be clear from the reading I have adopted—that is, on my own "intrinsicest" grounds—why the present form seems preferable.

is precisely forecast by Marsilio Ficino in his *Platonic Theology* where, tracing the steps the creature must ascend, he notes approvingly that according to Pseudo-Pythagoras the human soul is conceived as "one and many," the angelic as "one-many," and God as simply "one": "animam *unum et multa*; angelorum *unum multa*; Deum denique *unum*." These correspond to the threefold *scala ad unitatem* in all of Keats's major poetry, a threefold structure which Earl Wasserman so brilliantly discerned. This is similar to the underlying structure, I shall suggest in the ninth chapter, of Marvell's "To His Coy Mistress." The poem is not, as Eliot believed, an Aristotelian syllogism but a Burkean "dialectical pyramid," or, to make use of another Kabbalistic figuration from the sacred alphabet, a Platonic "lambda."

From Keats's death as "life's high meed" to Cummings's death as "no parenthesis" provides the transition to my first fully developed structural pattern. In Chapter 2, I referred to the poignancy of the parenthetic phrase in the following passage with its suggestion that, on the one hand, man is either a sob or sigh of the great breath that all primitive religions identified with the "sky god" or, on the other hand, "God is a great sigh lying unspeakable in the depths of the soul" (Thomas Münzer).

> Perhaps the self-same song that found a path
>   Through the sad heart of Ruth, when, *sick for home*,
> She stood in tears amid the alien corn.

In reading this and similarly designed phrasings, one has the sense that this almost casual interjection somehow, suddenly, and surprisingly exposes a hitherto hidden reality. (I am talking specifically now about an aural phenomenon which cannot be verified save, as Hopkins told Bridges, by reading it "with the ears.") If one takes the poem without the parenthesis, there is simply the visible, public scene, not much different from that of Wordsworth's reaper. But if the passage is read with stress on the parenthesis, the effect is epiphanic: like getting the joke, though on a more profound level. In one brief, sobbing instant the very depth of being-in-exile is revealed. Again, the structure is that of the authentic, concealed interior (the personal dimension of which may be called the "infi-

nite") unexpectedly made manifest through the quotidian exterior
(the "finite").

This is unquestionably so of this parenthesis in Yeats:

> When you are old and gray and full of sleep,
> And nodding by the fire, take down this book,
> And slowly read, and dream of the soft look
> Your eyes had once, and of their shadows deep;
>
> How many loved your moments of glad grace,
> And loved your beauty with love false or true;
> But one man loved the pilgrim soul in you,
> And loved the sorrows of your changing face.
>
> And bending down beside the glowing bars
> Murmur, *a little sadly*, how love fled
> And paced upon the mountains overhead
> And hid his face amid a crowd of stars.

Nothing better bespeaks the weariness of age than this casual im-
plosion of atrophied passion and faded memory. This is how it will
be, the brief phrase suggests; even anguish and despair will slowly
flicker out.

Perhaps as revelatory is the parenthesis in Yeats's "An Old Song
Re-sung":

> Down by the salley gardens my love and I did meet;
> She passed the salley gardens with little snow-white feet.
> She bid me take love easy, as the leaves grow on the tree;
> But I, *being young and foolish*, with her would not agree.
>
> In a field by the river my love and I did stand,
> And on my leaning shoulder she laid her snow-white hand.
> She bid me take life easy, as the grass grows on the weirs;
> But I was young and foolish, and now am full of tears.

In the first stanza our interest is aroused because there is yet hope
for the speaker who is still being drawn in two directions, toward
satisfaction of impulse and toward responsiveness to the beloved;
there still exists a tension, however diminishing, between interior
disposition and outward experience. But in the last stanza the tension disappears, as does the parenthesis, and the persona is con-

firmed in univocity; eros is suppressed, and he is left alone and loitering in the world of gross factuality.

Yeats's most heavily parenthetic poem is "A Prayer for My Daughter," a poem on the importance of "natural naturalness," on the importance of perfect equilibrium and interassured paradoxicality in woman, who should be at once "flourishing" and "hidden," "beautiful" and "charming," "merry" and "querulous," and so on. As evident in the following passages, the parenthetic phrase or clause is the best vehicle for expressing this inner-outer harmony and balance.

> May she be granted beauty and yet not
> Beauty to make a stranger's eye distraught,
> Or hers before a looking-glass, for such,
> Being made beautiful overmuch,
> *Consider beauty a sufficient end,*
> Lose natural kindness and maybe
> The heart-revealing intimacy
> That chooses right, and never find a friend.
> . . . .
> My mind, *because the minds that I have loved,*
> *The sort of beauty that I have approved,*
> *Prosper but little,* has dried up of late.
> . . . .
> She can, *though every face should scowl*
> *And every windy quarter howl*
> *Or every bellows burst,* be happy still.

So, too, with that even longer parenthesis in Robinson's "Mr. Flood's Party," which I have cited earlier; here the poet himself makes explicit that the duality being underscored is that of the formal Mr. Flood, a kind of sixty-year-old pub man, and the sore-at-heart Eben—and the whole duality, as John Ciardi first noted, plays on the ebb and flood, the dual tide of human existence. It is this kind of parenthetic structure, though here more subtly evinced, which accounts for the unquestioned pathos of the following from "Il Penseroso":

> Or bid the soul of Orpheus sing
> Such notes as, *warbled to the string,*

> Drew iron tears down Pluto's cheek
> And made Hell grant what Love did seek.

Certainly, one is here moved by the old sweet mythos, but on a deeper level we are also moved by this pattern expressive of a hidden dimension, of a reality obscured by the visible drama, a pattern that again puts us into the fundamental human stance, defined heuristically above, as beings whose inner worth (spiritus = breath = sob) emerges casually, unwittingly, and sometimes almost imperceptibly through the public mask or screen.

What is this inner worth? It may be characterized as one's very being, one's infinite value, one's authentic self: what I voice when I say, "I give you my word." Such a declaration means that my very substance stands behind, within, what I utter and outer: this "word," however fleetingly, is my self—with Hopkins, "What I do is me." Thus, John Donne speculates in a mood of total openness ("watch not one another out of fear"):

> I wonder, *by my troth*, what thou, and I
> Did, till we lov'd?

To pledge one's troth is to give one's word, is to give one's self. But this parenthetic insertion, apart from its sexual application, has a richer significance than those above. The phrase is not merely an oath; it is also a locative: where does he wonder this? *By my troth*: next to the beloved who literally is his "word," his troth—"our two loves be one." To glimpse the continuity of this structural tradition—a continuity perhaps more revelatory than the mere material linkage of imagery from poem to poem—then one should reflect on the fact that this beloved who is elsewhere the "dreame" of all "beauty" (though Donne uses "beauty" pejoratively, not unlike Eliot's "Get the beauty of it hot") is also the *troth* of John Donne. For, one might say without levity, and taking seriously Anaxagoras's maxim, "Everything is everything," that it is in the metaphor of poetry and the consummation of sexual union that beauty is troth, troth beauty.

My present concern, however, is with the parenthetic structure as such and its affecting quality as another expression of the inscape of human existence—as in the following brief extract from Carew's "Elegie":

> Can we not force from widdowed Poetry,
>> Now thou art dead (Great Donne) one Elegie
>> To crowne thy Hearse?

By now the structure should speak immediately to the listener, but to verify its effectiveness discursively one would emphasize the concealment of the poet literally in the hearse, and imaginatively through the typically Donnean play on the surname, which in its own deeper meaning here expresses both the consummation of the poetic tradition and the consummation of the poet's marital bond with the muse (again, Eliot, and again pejoratively: "Well, now that's done")—all of this being reminiscent of the concealment and the consummation in Donne's own parenthesis on his death:

> As West and East,
>> In all flatt Maps (and I am one) are one,
>> So death doth touch the Resurrection.

So unconsciously, so inadvertently does the listener assimilate the parenthetic sigh into his aesthetic response that even in passages where there is nothing overtly melancholy the structure alone may generate such a mood. The concluding lines to Stevens's "Sunday Morning"—which I shall discuss from differing points of view in subsequent chapters—are almost a paradigm of the utterly neutral and are in that sense totally "ambiguous," to use Stevens's own word, with every affirmation balanced by a corresponding negation. Yet, there is something heroically pessimistic about the entire coda, and a factor in that aura of pessimism must be the brief, "sobbing" parenthesis:

> Deer walk upon our mountains, and the quail
> Whistle about us their spontaneous cries;
> Sweet berries ripen in the wilderness;
> And, in the isolation of the sky,
> *At evening*, casual flocks of pigeons make
> Ambiguous undulations as they sink,
> Downward to darkness, on extended wings.

That sob is the outburst of the lachrymae rerum; it is the sigh of "creation in travail" which Vaughan in "Rom. Cap. 8 ver. 19" and Arnold in "Geist's Grave" identified with the mysteriously plaintive sounds of the animal and vegetable world about us. It is the same sigh of "despairing—spare" ("The Golden opes, the Iron shuts amain") that Milton breathes when recalling Lycidas:

> Batt'ning our flocks with the fresh dews of night,
> Oft till the Star that rose, *at Ev'ning*, bright
> Toward Heav'n's descent had slop'd his westering wheel.
>
> [29–31]

It is easier to experience aurally the effect of the parenthesis as the sigil of the infinite in the finite, of the reality in the epiphenomenon, through more extensive passages, as in the quotation from Robinson above, or in the following seemingly trivial observation by an admirer of Donne—where one may note also the chiastic male-female polarization:

> The Marigold, *whose Courtiers face*
> *Echoes the Sun, and doth unlace*
> *Her at his rise, at his full stop*
> *Packs and shuts up her gaudy shop,*
> Mistakes her cue, and doth display
> [Cleveland, "Upon Phillis walking...," 27–31]

This next, even more extended parenthesis illuminates not so much the infinite *in* the finite as the longed-for correlation of the two:

> Bright star, would I were steadfast as thou art—
>   Not in lone splendor hung aloft the night
> And watching, with eternal lids apart,
>   Like nature's patient, sleepless Eremite,
> The moving waters at their priest-like task
>   Of pure ablution round earth's human shores,
> Or gazing on the new soft-fallen mask
>   Of snow upon the mountains and the moor—
> No—yet still steadfast, still unchangeable,
>   Pillowed upon my fair love's ripening breast,

> To feel for ever its soft fall and swell,
>   Awake for ever in a sweet unrest,
> Still, still to hear her tender-taken breath,
> And so live ever—or else swoon to death.

Here both structure and statement support the theme of the unchangeably changeable, the ecstatic stasis, the infinite finite, "the life that is fluent in even the wintriest bronze." This paradox is intensified, though on a different level, by the fact that it is the opulently attractive, almost Shakespearean imagery of the parenthesis that depicts the realm Keats is rejecting, and the trite imagery of the conclusion that depicts the state to which he professedly aspires. There is thus on the biographical plane a hint of the poet's possibly unrecognized willingness to sacrifice his art to the fulfillment of his passion for Fanny Brawne.

In the following from Stephen Spender the parenthesis clearly stands for the concealed-revealed truth:

> Not palaces, an era's crown
> Where the mind dreams, intrigues, rests;
> The architectural gold-leaved flower
> From people ordered like a single mind,
> I build.

Here the parenthesis reveals the hateful reality—obscured in most pre-Romantic poetry—of the despot's palace which imposed a tyrannic artificial order on free men as it imposed a tyrannic artful order on the free profusion of nature; it thus exposes, as did Joseph Warton on Versailles or Blake on London, the falsity of the neoclassic ideology, an ideology, one might say, which valued the facade over the interior, the mask over the self, and by that fact manifested itself as a totalitarian, that is, as an antiparenthetic, world view.

Dylan Thomas's "The Hunchback in the Park" plays on the untouched splendor of reality and the world of imagination where for a brief moment the hunchback dwells erect and handsome, like everyman dreaming his crooked heart is straight:

> And the old dog sleeper
> Alone between nurses and swans
> (While the boys among willows

Make the tiger jump out of their eyes
To roar on the rockery stones
And the groves were blue with sailors)

Made all day until bell time
A woman figure without fault.

And if with archetypal criticism one wants to invoke those secondary strata I discussed in chapter 1, then perhaps this might do: the old dog sleeper is Jesus at the beginning of Mark's Gospel "polarized" in the desert ("alone"), ministered to by angels and accompanied by animals ("between nurses and swans"), or that later Jesus, bones broken, dreaming on the death that touches resurrection which would follow upon the dying-consummation of union with his bride, the purified world "without fault"—*sine macula.*

Charlotte Mew, pathetic victim of her own idiosyncratic vision—and much admired by the equally agonized Theodore Roethke—is almost the poet par excellence of the parenthetic exclamation; and few other poems express as touchingly as hers the muted strain of a dualized creature whose sense of infinitude only fleetingly breaks through the screen of the finite. The passages should require no commentary.

Because all night you have not turned to us or spoken,
   It is time for you to wake; your dreams were never very deep:
I, *for one*, have seen the thin bright, twisted threads of them
   dimmed suddenly and broken.

                         ["Beside the Bed"]

 You would have scoffed if we had told you yesterday
Love made us feel—*or so it was with me*—like some great bird.
                      ["To a Child in Death"]

It is not for a moment the Spring is unmade today;
These were great trees, it was in them from root to stem:
When the men with the "Whoops" and the "Whoas" have carted the
   whole of the whispering loveliness away
Half the Spring, *for me*, will have gone with them.
                     ["The Trees Are Down"]

His heart, *to me*, was a place of palaces and pinnacles and shining
towers

["I Have Been through the Gates"]

In a characteristically profound essay, "L'Effet de sourdine dans
le style classique de Racine," Leo Spitzer discussed something very
similar to our parenthetic structure. The word *sourdine*, a cognate of
surd, does not have its English musical meaning of "mute" or
"muffle"—though as a muted trumpet it is mentioned in Marvell's
"Upon Appleton House"—but rather is to be translated as
"modulate," as a pianist modulates by playing the pedals. Spitzer
described such structures as "the determinants which define the
situation and posit its values." His "situation" is what I have earlier
called the quotidian exterior, the public posture, whereas the defining "determinants" of "value" are the authentic interiority, the
hitherto concealed dimension of depth.[5] Of the many examples
Spitzer supplied, I will cite only two, the first from *Phèdre*, the
second from *Britannicus*.

> C'est bien assez pour moi de l'opprobre éternel
> D'avoir pu mettre au jour un fils si criminel,
> Sans que ta mort encor, *honteuse à ma mémoire*,
> De mes nobles travaux vienne souiller la gloire.
>
> [4.2]
>
> Et que derrière un voile, *invisible et présente*,
> J'étais de ce grand corps l'âme toute-puissante.
>
> [1.1]

---

5. Such "determinants" are well brought out in the two following passages from *Paradise Lost*:

> So spake th' Apostate Angel, *though in pain*,
> Vaunting aloud, *but rackt with deep despair* . . . [1.125–26].
> . . . Into this wild Abyss,
> *The Womb of nature and perhaps her Grave,*
> *Of neither Sea, nor Shore, nor Air, nor Fire,*
> *But all these in thir pregnant causes mixt*
> *Confus'dly, and which thus must ever fight,*
> *Unless th' Almighty Maker them ordain*
> *His dark materials to create more Worlds,*
> Into this wild Abyss the wary fiend
> Stood . . . [2.910–18].

The best extended treatment of such Miltonic parentheses is Leslie Brisman's sensitive and
judicious *Milton's Poetry of Choice and Its Romantic Heirs*.

The "soul" behind the "veil" is almost the definition of this structure, of which Spitzer further remarks that its aesthetic effect is to "produce a tension." The tension, of course, can only be between the various polarizations and their analogues that I have been discussing. Curiously, all of this is almost the very language of the New Criticism, for which Spitzer would later express considerable disdain (the present essay dates from 1931), and makes quite clear that in its theoretical foundations the New Critics may have been more firmly grounded in the ontic-antics of poets than are many of those who have dismissed the New Criticism as a mere method of close reading yoked to a drearily mechanical calculus of verbal strategies. As a contemporary of Racine had noted in his own prose-poem: "Il y a du plaisir à voir deux contraires se heurter" (*Pensées*, 135).

Hopkins was described by Dylan Thomas as one of the major influences on the poets of his generation; and it should not be surprising that Hopkins is among the most cited poets in this book. I take my two final examples of the significance of parenthetic structures from him. In "In the Valley of the Elwy," the parentheses—again, seemingly casual, incidental, even mere ballast in the verse—may in fact be the essential clue to fully comprehending the poem.

> I remember a house where all were good
>> To me, *God knows*, deserving no such thing:
>> Comforting smell breathed at very entering,
> Fetched fresh, *as I suppose*, off some sweet wood.
>
> That cordial air made those kind people a hood
>> All over, as a bevy of eggs the mothering wing
>> Will, or mild nights the new morsels of Spring:
> Why, it seemed of course; seemed of right it should.
>
> Lovely the woods, waters, meadows, combes, vales,
> All the air things wear that build this world of Wales;
>> Only the inmate does not correspond:
>
> God, lover of souls, swaying considerate scales,
> Complete thy creature dear O where it fails,
>> Being mighty a master, being a father and fond.

The first quatrain expresses the kenotic descent from the infinite ("God") to the finite ("I"), from absolute certitude ("knows") to contingent tentativeness ("suppose"). And the whole poem is centered on those two different orders of existence, which Hopkins's religious tradition would, broadly speaking, have denominated the "supernatural" and the "natural." This central focus is maintained in the next quatrain: the realm of the "of course" is the natural, entropic, flowing realm of time; the realm of the "of right" is the supernatural realm of eternal and divine decree. The chiastic structure (absolute-contingent/contingent-absolute) encoded in the complete octave betokens therefore—as noted earlier in this chapter—a "conflict" between these symbolic extremes: God knows-I suppose/of course-of right.

The sestet is devoted to the nature of this conflict and to its resolution. In the first tercet the unsullied physical beauty of the Welsh countryside is equated with the divine totality (a common equation in Hopkins), and man is identified with the fractious and fragmented—the terms are cognate and, again, correlatives of the contingent finite. (I shall discuss the cymatic-corpuscular nature of lines 9 and 10 in chapter 9.) Only a principle of perfect mediation could resolve this conflict between creature and creator, infinite and finite, a principle which Hopkins would have defined as "incarnation." By incarnation, the natural is identical with the supernatural, it is "in balance" with it in the starry "scales"; or, in the precise language of the concluding tercet, the Old Testament God of the natural order, the mighty master who draws man by all the cords of Adam, is identical, is in balance with the New Testament Father, after whom all paternity in heaven and earth is named, and who is loving and fond. The very pattern of the coda expresses an axiom of Scholastic theology: not chronologically but ontologically, *gratia praesupponit naturam*—the supernatural presupposes the natural, as the father presupposes the master, as New Testament presupposes Old Testament.

My last illustration is possibly even more cogent than the preceding ones because it seems to be more in violation of almost all standard critical norms. In the above examples, the parenthetic utterances were more or less obviously related contextually to the body of the statement. It does not seem to be so with Hopkins's "Spring."

Nothing is so beautiful as spring—
    When weeds, in wheels, shoot long and lovely and lush;
    Thrush's eggs look little low heavens, and thrush
Through the echoing timber does so rinse and wring

The ear, it strikes like lightnings to hear him sing;
    The glassy peartree leaves and blooms, they brush
    The descending blue; that blue is all in a rush
With richness; the racing lambs too have fair their fling.

What is all this juice and all this joy?
A strain of the earth's sweet being in the beginning
    In Eden garden.—Have, get, before it cloy,

Before it cloud, *Christ, lord,* and sour with sinning,
Innocent mind and Mayday in girl and boy,
    Most, *O maid's child,* thy choice and worthy the winning.

The parentheses appear to be arbitrary, completely unintegrated with the rest of the poem, and as is not unusual with what is on the surface inexplicable they have generally been misunderstood or written off as flaws. But apart from their deeper function as structures of the primordial sigh at the heart of reality, it *is* this very arbitrariness that now underlines their purpose. In the structural sense their unpredictability serves to bring out most sharply the unpredictability of this eruption of the infinite through the finite—all, not too unlike the oath of John Donne. From that viewpoint they are what Herbert, Vaughan, and their tradition called "spiritual ejaculations," spontaneous prayers or invocations that were to punctuate all the activities of a good man's life and thus spiritualize the temporal. *That* is the primary explanation of their presence in this poem.

    But from a more conventional critical perspective, however arbitrary the phrases seem to be, they may still be organically integrated into the overall organization of the poem—that organization being another variation on the kenotic pattern explicated earlier. The octave moves from an absolute statement about spring— "*nothing* is *so* beautiful"—to the description of the playful, utterly contingent newborn lambs; while the sestet moves from the indeterminate past to the particular present—from earth's being in the beginning to Mayday in girl and boy. The first parenthetic outburst calls upon the *Kyrios Christos*—on which W. Bousset has written the classic study—the *causa exemplaris* and absolute ruler of the universe, and thus relates directly to the absoluteness and undefinability at the beginning of both octave and sestet. The second outburst, "O maid's child," calls upon the newborn Jesus who is also the *agnus Dei* and, as such, the mediating link (racing lambs) that binds together the closing line of each of the two parts of the whole poem.

Now, I do not want to suggest that Hopkins in this poem was composing either a *summa theologica* or a *summa sociologica*, but such is the ubiquitousness of these structural formats that they must be recognized as undergirding many of our models for comprehending the universe. For Bousset the *Kyrios Christos* is the theocratic deity (Hopkins's "Christ, lord") with affinities to Pauline doctrine who displaced the eschatological "Son of Man" (Hopkins's "maid's child") with affinities to Johannine doctrine: the institutional God thus displaced the God of the people. The broad lines of this thesis seem to me accurately drawn, though it has been contested by the Catholic L. Cerfaux and the Protestant O. Cullmann. What Hopkins may be said to be doing in this little poem through its structure (which the heuristic myth suggests may be the structure of the mind as well as the structure of the universe) is fusing those two traditions. By further extension, and now in the language of Weber and Troeltsch, the structure of Hopkins's poem may thus also be said to represent a synthesis of *Gesellschaft* and *Gemeinschaft* and of church and sect.

In any case, returning to the poem itself, all three structures in the sonnet—octave, sestet, parentheses—are isomorphic with the overall, total structure, and that structure is in turn isomorphic with the infinite-finite pattern of "Easter Wings" and of the other poetic texts treated in the preceding chapter.

IV: *Commerce*

Heidegger has said that even a child asks, "Why is there anything at all, rather than nothing?" But the child, even though the best philosopher, like the old philosopher in Rome, arrives at no answer, except that there is not any reason why there should be anything at all. The poet takes that "anything at all" and finds in its very arbitrariness, in the delight of its irrational eruption—as in the exclamations of Hopkins in the previous chapter—if not an answer, at least a fitful assuagement. In the rough map outlined in chapter 2, I described one of the basic strategies for expressing this surprise at the momentary inbreaking of meaning into chaos, and conversely of the finite into the infinite, under the heading "enjambment."

The theoretician of enjambment is John Hollander, who seems to have been fascinated by this structure from the time of his 1959 essay, "The Metrical Emblem," to his *Vision and Resonance* of a decade and a half later. In this book he maintains his earlier judgment that enjambments in English poetry "are clearly different" in their functions: "the uses to which they are put are as divergent as any verbal acts." Now, certainly it is true in principle that the uses to which enjambments are put are as divergent as any verbal acts, since at least initially one must interpret the function of any given enjambment in terms of its accompanying lexical statement. Nevertheless, by this kind of evenhanded relativism, Hollander seems to have been led to ignore one of the most salient and one of the most recurrent uses of this metrical technique, to ignore precisely that verbal act describing that human experience which most frequently (or with sufficient frequency to suggest a general conclusion) and most understandably employs enjambment. He ignores the *topos* that almost "naturally" goes hand in hand with this *figura*, a *topos* that the very expression "hand in hand" serves to reveal. For, as I noted earlier, when one examines what happens in any effective enjambment, the pattern will generally reduce to something as simple as that a sequence of steadily end-stopped lines is suddenly broken by a line that overflows into the succeeding line or stanza. Since poetic structure is, at the least, a kind of pictogram of poetic statement, one would therefore expect enjambment to occur when assaying that situation in which, after repeated frustration, the human subject suddenly experiences the overcoming of limitations and an expansion into something beyond those limits.

Geoffrey Hartman, when discussing the beginning stanzas of Wordsworth's "Resolution and Independence," refers to this kind of expansiveness and its structural format. What Hartman calls Wordsworth's "slight hemming" is "expressed by the repeatedly end-stopped lines." In the second stanza, Hartman continues, "with the picture of the hare, the mood overflows and is close to breaking down the end-stopped line." A remarkable echo of Wordsworth's theme and structure is Yeats's "The Indian upon God":

> I passed along the water's edge below the humid trees,
> My spirit rocked in evening light, the rushes round my knees,
> My spirit rocked in sleep and sight; and saw the moorfowl pace
> All dripping on a grassy slope, and saw them cease to chase
> Each other round in circles.

Now, the usual term for what Wordsworth and Yeats are experiencing is "transcendence," a word which though traditionally used in the context of religious myth, even in Kant and Emerson, has been taken up by such avowed makers of nontheistic myths as Heidegger, Bloch, Horkheimer, and Marcuse to express one's capacity—and I repeat my earlier definition—to go beyond the limbs that limit one and to enter into the realm of "the other."

It would be difficult to read this description and not immediately advert to the preeminent human experience of "going beyond," of "overflowing," in human sexual union—or, in Wordsworth, to what another of his students, Frederick Garber, calls the "nuptial metaphor" of man and nature. This sexual bonding I will try to

show, is one of the most prevalent and one of the most rich contexts
of enjambment (though certainly *not* the only) for poets in the
English-language tradition.[1]

My first example is a *locus classicus* for many reasons:

> Beyond a mortal man impassioned far
> At these voluptuous accents, he arose,
> Ethereal, flushed, and like a throbbing star
> Seen mid the sapphire heaven's deep repose;
> Into her dream he melted, as the rose
> Blendeth its odor with the violet.

A pause is demanded either explicitly by the punctuation or im-
plicitly by the syntax at the end of each of the first four lines; there
is no pause tolerable on either basis at the end of the line which
describes the consummation of the union itself; rather, by placing
the comma after "melted" the reading is controlled entirely by the
enjambment: "Into her dream he melted, as the rose blendeth its
odor with the violet." This is the expression of what I have called
man's nature as a "sursum," as a being whose essence is to transcend himself—as above, by breaking out of the constraints of the
external facade and into the inner self of another.

Keats provides a solemnly transparent and passionately earnest
depiction of this sexual union. It is precisely the kind of depiction,
with its explicit imagery and blatant exposition of private desires,
that Byron in his letters complained so vehemently about. More to
Byron's taste for the covert and oblique would have been the even
more detailed and articulated—but still ambiguously veiled—sexuality of Shakespeare's Sonnet 151, where the enjambments are the
central pillar on which is erected the whole triumphant affair:

> Love is too young to know what conscience is;
> Yet who knows not conscience is born of love?
> Then, gentle cheater, urge not my amiss,

---

1. This may also explain what otherwise seems a howling non sequitur, why anent stanza
18 of Milton's "Nativity Ode" Tillyard observed that "something of sex" at that point enters
the poem—though it is equally mysterious why this casual observation has been so often
puzzled over by critics. Unless every time one reads about snakes' or dragons' tails one thinks
"phallus," the judgment makes no sense—unless it is that the first two lines of the stanza are
enjambed: "And then at last our bliss / Full and perfect is."

> Lest guilty of my faults thy sweet self prove:
> For, thou betraying me, I do betray
> My nobler part to my gross body's treason;
> My soul doth tell my body that he may
> Triumph in love; flesh stays no farther reason,
> But, rising at thy name, doth point out thee
> As his triumphant prize. Proud of this pride,
> He is contented thy poor drudge to be,
> To stand in thy affairs, fall by thy side.
>> No want of conscience hold it that I call
>> Her "love" for whose dear love I rise and fall.

But whether explicit or oblique, sexual love is the fundamental medium of transcendence. And this explains why in all great world religions—a fact often obscured by priestcraft and asserted by poetry—sexual union is the fundamental sacrament, is, as Saint Paul said echoing contemporaneous mystery cults, "the great mystery," the *Mysterium Magnum* of Jacob Boehme's mystic nuptials. As Keats affirmed this directly and in astral imagery, and Shakespeare indirectly and in the language of moral philosophy, so Browning did also—though in images drawn from the Bible. In "Popularity," out of a total of thirteen stanzas only one is "run-on"—a traditional term for enjambment which expresses with nice exactitude the sexual and syntactic event. It is a remarkable passage even for Browning who is a master of these metrical structures, a passage in which he is less preoccupied with naked narration or critical exculpation—though the obvious intent of the whole poem is *apologia*—than with responding to the "supreme theme." He thus seems to lose himself in his figures and so eclipse his purely expository ends:

> Enough to furnish Solomon
>> Such hangings for his cedar-house
> That, when gold-robed he took the throne
>> In that abyss of blue, the Spouse
> Might swear his presence shone
>
> Most like the center-spike of gold
>> Which burns deep in the bluebell's womb

> What time, with ardors manifold,
> > The bee goes singing to her groom,
> Drunken and overbold.

This is a stunning achievement, and one cannot imagine much more being added: we have the sexual union, the archaism, "what time" (the bee, not the grey-fly), that tempers the otherwise too blatant phallic ensheathing, the play on the fusion of polar colors, the chiastic male-female/female-male patterns, the kenotic descent from those imperial bowers to the industrious bee; and probably innumerable other devices that set off flaringly the central enjambment.

The image of the bee is standard (for example, Herrick's "The Bag of the Bee," Cleveland's apiary tour de force, "Fuscara," or Karl Shapiro's "A Cut Flower"), but the enjambment is not.[2] Browning is certainly not consciously imitating an equally enjambed and more sexually replete poem, Carew's "A Rapture"; it is rather that both poets are responding to the common stimuli of the same experience:

> Then, as the empty bee, that lately bore
> Into the common treasury all her store,
> Flies 'bout the painted field with nimble wing,
> Deflow'ring the fresh virgins of the Spring,
> So will I rifle all the sweets that dwell
> In my delicious paradise, and swell
> My bag with honey, drawn forth by the power
> Of fervent kisses from each spicy flower.
>
> > > > > > > > [55–62]

One might consider as well the following from Browning's "In a Gondola," where, although the poem is cast in conversational idiom

---

2. However, it might be worth noting that the two poets most identified with the use of bee imagery rarely employ it in this conventional, explicitly sexual context. Abstracting from other considerations, e.g., Dickinson's idiosyncratic intellectual formation, Plath's father-obsession, or even from the mere fact that male bees sting, it is likely that this particular sexual image is too cluttered with the detritus of male aggressiveness and domination (even in Cleveland's "Fuscara" where there is no "deflowering," the bee "preys," "perches" like a hawk, etc.) to be congenial to the woman poet—and this notwithstanding the ultimate subjection of male to female in all bee-loud glades.

and the enjambment is therefore less surprising, the pattern nevertheless is very affecting:

> The moth's kiss, first!
> Kiss me as if you made believe
> You were not sure, this eve,
> How my face, your flower, had pursed
> Its petals up; so, here and there
> You brush it, till I grow aware
> Who wants me, and wide ope I burst.
>
> The bee's kiss now!
> Kiss me as if you entered gay
> My heart at some noonday,
> A bud that dares not disallow
> The claim, so all is rendered up,
> And passively its shattered cup
> Over your head to sleep I bow.
>
> [49–62]

One of the earliest sting songs in this tradition of osculatory
enjambment—as Lévi-Strauss's coinage might have it—is Thomas
Lodge's "Rosalind's Madrigal," in which the first two lines of each
stanza are enjambed. The first stanza sets the pattern and initiates
the theme:

> Love in my bosom like a bee
>   Doth suck his sweet;
> Now with his wings he lays with me,
>   Now with his feet.
> Within mine eyes he makes his nest,
> His bed amidst my tender breast;
> My kisses are his daily feast,
> And yet he robs me of my rest.
>   Ah, wanton, will ye?

However, my concern is not with the conventional theme of "love's
sting," "honied thigh," and so on, but with the kiss itself, in all its
forms, as the primary act of transcendence and with its embodiment in enjambment. One of the richest examples of this "kiss of
transcendence" is Milton's clock poem, "On Time."

Fly, envious *Time*, till thou run out thy race,
Call on the lazy leaden-stepping hours,
Whose speed is but thy heavy Plummet's pace;
And glut thyself with what thy womb devours,
Which is no more than what is false and vain,
And merely mortal dross;
So little is our loss,
So little is thy gain.
For when as each thing bad thou hast entomb'd,
And, last of all, thy greedy self consum'd,
Then long Eternity shall greet our bliss
With an individual kiss;
And Joy shall overtake us as a flood,
When everything that is sincerely good
And perfectly divine,
With Truth, and Peace, and Love, shall ever shine
About the supreme Throne
Of him, t'whose happy-making sight alone,
When once our heav'nly-guided soul shall climb,
Then all this Earthy grossness quit,
Attir'd with Stars, we shall for ever sit,
Triumphing over Death, and Chance, and thee O Time.

Here the first ten lines are all more or less heavily end-stopped; at the eleventh line, which may be regarded as the "eleventh hour," the moment of transcendence, of enjambment, is signaled. (For a similar use of enjambment, one may compare lines 148–55 of the *Intimations* Ode.) Time, we are told, shall cease upon the honied middle of the night, as the temporal "overflows" into the eternal; or rather, Milton emphasizes, eternity shall overflow and encompass time. The broken fragments of the contingent time-bound world— even to the metronomic, "So little is our loss, / So little is thy gain"—are subsumed into the absolute totality, are "eternized." After this "individual kiss" (which with Hardison, and Brooks and Hardy, I read as "kiss for the individual soul") has transformed time, the rest of the poem is heavily enjambed, so that the structure of the entire work is designed out of the relation of time to eternity, of the fragment to the whole, of the broken to the continuous; and the final consummation of the poem may be regarded as beyond

time, as zero-time: "*O* Time." For the modern reader this poem
takes on added weight because its burden of time, moving as slowly
as the heavy plummet, is the burden of the man with the blue
guitar, "heavy in cold chords / Struggling toward impassioned
clouds." But unlike Milton, for whom eternity's "individual kiss" is
identical with the ideal state of Stevens's "impassioned clouds," the
"buzzing of the blue guitar" never produces fulfillment. Where
Milton's "lazy leaden-stepping hours" are absorbed into the peace
of eternity, Stevens's "lazy, leaden twang" is only fictive music
which never resonates the eternal diapason.

In the following from Charlotte Mew, whose conversational
idiom owed much to Browning and whose metrical license may
remind one of Milton's poem above, we have as in "Popularity" the
same overflowing sexuality as well as a kind of kenotic descent—
but here, descent from the land of the living to the state of what in
Milton is "entombed." In a passage from her neglected "Madeleine"
sequence, in which almost all of the preceding twenty or so lines
have been end-stopped, the poet muses:

> I wonder was it like a kiss that once I knew,
>> The only one that I would care to take
> Into the grave with me, to which if there were afterwards, to wake
>> Almost as happy as the carven dead
>> In some dim chancel lying head to head
> We slept with it, but face to face, the whole night through.

Similarly, it is the "kiss" of love that engenders the only enjambment in Keats's sonnet "To Fanny."

> I cry your mercy—pity—love!—aye, love!
>> Merciful love that tantalizes not,
> One-thoughted, never-wandering, guileless love,
>> Unmasked, and being seen—without a blot!
> O! let me have thee whole,—all—all—be mine!
>> That shape, that fairness, that sweet minor zest
> Of love, your kiss,—those hands, those eyes divine,
>> That warm, white, lucent, million-pleasured breast,—

This is a sonnet by the seasoned and mellowed Keats; but even in
a considerably more immature effort, "On an Engraved Gem of

Leander," dating from spring, 1816, it is the kiss that again breaks
the regular end-stopped lines:

> Come hither all sweet maidens soberly,
>   Down-looking aye, and with a chasten'd light
>   Hid in the fringes of your eyelids white,
> And meekly let your fair hands joined be;
> As if so gentle that ye could not see,
>   Untouch'd, a victim of your beauty bright,
>   Sinking away to his young spirit's night,
> Sinking bewilder'd 'mid the dreary sea:
> 'Tis young Leander toiling to his death;
>   High swooning, he doth purse his weary lips
>   For Hero's cheek, and smiles against her smile.
>   O horrid dream! see how his body dips,
>   Dead-heavy; arms and shoulders gleam awhile:
> He's gone; up bubbles all his amorous breath!

The first poem I know of in which this theme and pattern occur
is Nicholas Breton's "A Report Song." The only strong enjambment, and one that dramatically breaks the metrical pattern, is in
the fourth verse, the verse on kissing:

> Shall we go dance the hay, the hay?
> Never pipe could ever play,
> Better shepherd's roundelay.
>
> Shall we go sing the song, the song?
> Never Love did ever wrong,
> Fair maids, hold hands all along.
>
> Shall we go learn to woo, to woo?
> Never thought came ever to,
> Better deed could better do.
>
> Shall we go learn to kiss, to kiss?
> Never heart could ever miss
> Comfort, where true meaning is.
>
> Thus at base they run, they run,
> When the sport was scarce begun.
> But I waked, and all was done.

But one may consider as well the comparably strong enjambment in "A Country Song," attributed to Philip Sidney, where again after a fairly regular sequence of end-stopped lines the kiss brings on the first sharp break in that overall pattern:

> So may you never die,
> But pulled by Mira's hand,
> Dress bosom hers, or head,
> Or scatter on her bed:
> Tell me, if husband spring time leave your land
> When he from you is sent,
> Wither not you, languished with discontent:
> Tell me, my silly pipe;
> So may thee still betide
> A cleanly cloth thy moistness for to wipe;
> So may the cherries red
> Of Mira's lips divide
> Their sugared selves to kiss thy happy head.
>
> [46–58]

This is equally true of the stanza from Cleveland's "To the State of Love" (40–52), which contains what is probably his most notorious image: only these first two lines of the stanza are enjambed.

> Now to the melting kiss that sips
> The jelly'd Philtre of her lips.

So, too, with that derivative Donnean, Charles Cotton, in "The Visit"—again, after a steady pattern of end-stopped lines:

> Near to her maiden bed I drew,
>   Blessed in so rare a chance as this;
> When by her odorous breath I knew,
>   I did approach my Love, my Bliss;
> There did I eagerly pursue
>   My hopes, and found, and stole a kiss;
>   Such as perhaps Pygmalion took,
>   When cold his ivory love forsook.

I would cite also an early sonnet of Tennyson; but I do somewhat diffidently, since in his other sonnets from this period the enjambment is usually controlled by the larger demands of the sonnet form rather than by its scanty "plot"—here centered on assorted idealized kisses.

> O Beauty, passing beauty! sweetest Sweet!
>> How can'st thou let me waste my youth in sight?
> I only ask to sit beside thy feet.
>> Thou knowest I dare not look into thine eyes.
> Might I but kiss thy hand! I dare not fold
>> My arms about thee—scarcely dare to speak.
> And nothing seems to me so wild and bold,
>> As with one kiss to touch thy blessed cheek.
>
> Methinks if I should kiss thee, no control
>> Within the thrilling brain could keep afloat
>> The subtle spirit. Even while I spoke,
> The bare word KISS hath made my inner soul
>> To tremble like a lutestring, ere the note
>> Hath melted in the silence that it broke.

"'Kiss' rhymes to 'bliss' in fact as well as verse," Byron reminds us; and perhaps that is why that other onomatopoeically derived term, "buss," is now an archaism. Though it may be as Herrick wrote:

> Kissing and bussing differ both in this:
> We buss our wantons, but our wives we kiss.

In any case, the two words obviously mean the same thing and so, as in the following comic passage from *The Faerie Queene*, are embodied in the same kind of structure:

> All day they daunced with great lustihed,
> And with their horned feet the greene grasse wore,
> The whiles their Gotes vpon the brouzes fed,
> Till drouping Phoebus gan to hide his golden hed.
>
> Tho vp they gan their merry pypes to trusse,
> And all their goodly heards did gather round,
> But euery Satyre first did giue a busse
> To *Hellenore*: so busses did abound.
>
> [3.10.45–46]

These various poems all seem in their various ways to be cogent examples of what I have called the "enjambment of transcendence," because they are all concerned one way or another with the biological and psychological outpouring or overflowing ("influence" in the radical sense) of one person or reality into another—as with the first strong enjambment in "Lamia":

> For somewhere in that sacred island dwelt
> A nymph, to whom all hoofed Satyrs knelt;
> At whose white feet the languid Tritons poured
> Pearls, while on land they withered and adored.
>
> [13–16]

We may respond for a number of reasons to the depiction of such an event, but what would seem to be a large part of our specifically poetic response stems from the fact that this structure is the yantra of the attaining of fulfillment by transcending limitations. It is certainly so in the following, which also has as professed subject an act of overflowing:

> The world is charged with the grandeur of God.
> It will flame out, like shining from shook foil;
> It gathers to a greatness, like the ooze of oil
> Crushed.

It may be left to conjecture whether these religiously cathected "last oozings" also imply a sexual consummation; though perhaps one should reemphasize in this context of enjambment Lévi-Strauss's notion of the homologousness of all myths. In the light of that notion one may suggest that underlying Hopkins's image of the olive press with its overflowing oil is the traditional symbol of the olive tree as representing sexual fruitfulness (for example, the olive-tree bed of Penelope and Ulysses or the Psalmist's simile of "children like olive plants").

But there is no doubt about the sexuality in what may be regarded as an ancestral passage to Hopkins on the grandeur of God, Lovelace's "Love Made in the First Age," where we encounter again Cleveland's "jelly." I emphasize once more the fact that the eighteen lines preceding this passage are all end-stopped:

> Then unconfined each did tipple
> Wine from the bunch, milk from the nipple,
>   Paps tractable as udders were;
> Then equally the wholesome jellies
> Were squeez'd from olive-trees and bellies,
>   Nor suits of trespass did they fear.

So, too, with Crashaw, in all of whose poetry the sexual and the mystical are marvelously fused (even to that touch of *fellatio divina* in the "Hymn to Saint Teresa"), in his poem "In the Praise of Spring"—though I should add that this poem is rather heavily enjambed throughout:

>   then the fields
> (Quick with warme *Zephires* lively breath) lay forth
> Their pregnant Bosomes in a fragrant Birth.
> Each body's plump and jucy, all things full
> Of supple moisture: no coy twig but will
> Trust his beloved bosome to the sun.
>
>   [11–16]

There is a characteristically sadistic sexuality in Swinburne's structurally close parallel with Hopkins on God's superabundance:

> From boy's pierced throat and girl's pierced bosom
> Drips, reddening round the blood-red blossoms,
>   The slow delicious bright soft blood.
>
>   ["Ilicet," 73–75]

—whereas it is merely the overflowing and sanguinary inundation itself that is expressed in section 47 of Meredith's "Modern Love":

> But in the largeness of the evening earth
> Our spirits flew as we went side by side;
> The hour became her husband and my bride.
> Love, that had robbed us so, thus blessed our dearth!
> The pilgrims of the year waxed very loud
> In multitudinous chatterings, as the flood
> Full brown came from the West, and like pale blood
> Expanded to the upper crimson cloud.

With regard to a possible conflation of the sexual and the mystical in "God's Grandeur," it should be noted as tangential confirmation of this possibility that in "The May Magnificat" (the hymn of Mary celebrating her own reception of the overflowing *logos spermatikos*) the most surprising enjambment occurs in a description of the "swelling," of the pregnancy, in all of nature at springtime:

> Flesh and fleece, fur and feather,
> Grass and greenworld all together;
>   Star-eyed strawberry-breasted
>   Throstle above her nested
>
> Cluster of bugle blue eggs thin
> Forms and warms the life within;
>   And bird and blossom swell
>   In sod or sheath or shell.

The echoes of Browning's "Popularity," where the religious and the sexual are also joined, certainly are not conscious, any more than is the pattern of enjambment itself. These are simply the images and the structures that express the transcendent or, in terms of our Milton poem, express the encounter of eternal and temporal. Again, in the Hopkins passage, all polarities meld, even to the strawberry red and bugle blue, and the final ensheathement in what constitutes an epithalamium of the marriage of heaven and earth.

As I have suggested, we respond to the basic structure because it somehow represents, symbolizes, evokes something of man's very nature as sketched in the original heuristic myth. But as these various citations make clear, it is only in its contextual setting that one can *critically* verify the presence and purpose of a given pattern. Critical verification is not proof. In poetry only one poem proves another;[3] so what I am trying to do is argue from what might be called converging probabilities. By offering enough separate examples of the surprising effects of, in this instance, a particular kind of enjambment, one is led to conclude that this structure seems to

---

3. This principle is rooted in a text of Anaxagoras I have already cited: "Everything is everything"; it is in the Scholastics' "per simile simile percipiens," in Peirce's "The sense of a symbol is its translation into another symbol," in Bachelard's "L'image ne peut être etudiée que par l'image," and lastly, it is the guiding principle of much of Harold Bloom's critical achievement.

reflect some human reality, seems somehow to be congruent with what we think of as "human nature"—otherwise, there would be no basis for responding with pleasure to the structure in the first place. This pleasure is experienced immediately in the encounter with the structure, but its precise significance can be critically assessed only through the mediation of the "plot," "narrative line," "dramatic situation" of the poem itself.

As in the formal elements of all the arts, there are no quantitative devices, no methods, no technical instruments for exhaustively and definitively relating a given structure to a given plot or theme. The structure is the matrix, the die; its relatively invariant shape extrudes or forms an incalculable number of "products," all in their exterior dimension slightly modifying or diverging from the original cast but all fundamentally isomorphic with it. This explains those scores of enjambed passages that must come to any reader's mind and that are not apparently in any way indicative of what I have called "transcendence."[4] It is certainly not for me to jog memories, but one might consider for random but apposite example the tour de force of Browning's "My Last Duchess." Similarly, on a priori grounds, one might—if the variations on this structure I am analyzing were viewed as simply an *ensemble de recettes*—anticipate an abundance of enjambment in Blake's *Songs of Innocence* and very little in the *Songs of Experience*. In fact, as Alicia Ostriker, the best taxonomist of Blake's metric techniques, has pointed out, there is very little enjambment in either body of poems. But the reason for this is probably only that Blake's higher priority was to maintain the mirroring effects of the two sequences, just as Browning in "My Last Duchess" had other ends in mind to which the recurring (and

---

4. But even here one may urge a caution, because in many enjambments that seem to be purely "dramatic" in function there may be a sense of unexpected fulfillment which is itself an oblique sign of transcendence. I am thinking of Housman's "Eight o'Clock":

> He stood, and heard the steeple
>   Sprinkle the quarters on the morning town.
> One, two, three, four, to market-place and people
>   It tossed them down.
>
> Strapped, noosed, nighing his hour,
>   He stood and counted them and cursed his luck;
> And then the clock *collected in the tower*
>   *Its strength,* and struck.

therefore not surprising) enjambment had to be subordinated. Concerning the latter poem, it may be the very violation of the common reader's expectation that couplets do not run on which engenders surprise and concomitantly delight, and that surprise and delight, as I have suggested, are themselves the marks of eros surpassing itself, of human transcendence. One might carry this even further and find in this structural conflict between the demands of the artificial couplet and the demands of conversational freedom an analogue of the conflict between the hampering and artificial rigidity of the Duke (obsessed with artifacts) and the graceful ease of the Duchess—with the last two lines of the poem, both end-stopped, affirming the triumph of artifice over life, the destruction of the enjambment of freedom, and the death of the Duchess: her complete limning, her complete finitizing in the portrait.

But even when the enjambment seems to run counter to the "story line" of the poem, this collision itself engenders aesthetic delight: it is the commonplace paradox of Edmund Burke's as well as of Keats's pleasure-pain, and it is the commonplace clarification of our possible "pleasure" at the horrors in a play of Sartre or Pinter, or at the "distortions" of a Modigliani or a Dubuffet.[5] We find pleasure in the more or less unconsciously apprehended primordial structure, and this pleasure blurs or even suppresses our "pain" at the second-order narrative or depicted scene. Thus, in the following enjambment in Cummings's "Always before Your Voice," the articulated anguish is not canceled out but "counterpointed" with our pleasure at its embodying structural pattern:

> but my heart smote in trembling thirds
> of anguish quivers to your words,
> as to a flight of thirty birds.

Even here in this explicitly sexual poem, there is an encounter with the transcendent, and this transcendent is defined, allusively but firmly, as God. In one of the most renowned Sufi poems, the mystic Farid ud-din 'Attar tells of the trials thirty birds (*si-murgh*)

---

5. I take the examples from "modern" works of art precisely because, contra a number of theoreticians of whom Susan Sontag is typical, I regard "pleasure" as an intrinsic concomitant of the aesthetic response to the art of any period. The axiom is inviolable: *omnia admirabilia sunt delectabilia.*

undergo in trying to find God, whose name when discovered is
revealed as identical with theirs, "Simurgh," and who tells them to
lose themselves in him and thus they shall fulfill their true natures.
Just as in Milton the temporal becomes the eternal, so here the
creature becomes the "creator."

Nevertheless, for critical validation of this general thesis of enjambment, it is obviously a more effective tactic to argue less from
the "counterpointing" and more from the congruence of structure
and meaning. Hence, the following from Marvell's "To His Coy
Mistress," where the end-stopped lines suggest the inability of the
two lovers to break through the barriers separating them—and,
again, Milton's and Charlotte Mew's tomb image is introduced:

> then Worms shall try
> That long preserv'd Virginity:
> And your quaint Honour turn to dust;
> And into ashes all my Lust.
> The Grave's a fine and private place,
> But none I think to do there embrace.

In the next paragraph there is a sudden leap out of the prison of
time into a kind of eternal present; the barriers fall, and passion
overflows:

> Now therefore, while the youthful hew
> Sits on thy skin like morning dew,
> And while thy willing Soul transpires
> At every pore with instant Fires,
> Now let us sport us while we may.
>
> [27–37]

There is a comparable congruence of structure and meaning in
Crashaw's "Hymn to Saint Teresa," again, after a long succession
of more or less fully end-stopped lines:

> She'l offer them her dearest Breath,
> With Christ's Name in't, in change for death.
> She'l bargain with them & will give
> Them God; teach them how to live
> In him; or, if they this deny,
> For him, she'l teach them how to Dy.

The violation of established pattern created by the enjambment
signals for the first time in the poem (we are already around line 50)
that mission of Teresa, which so moved George Eliot, of "giving
them" God; and, moreover, her willingness to pour out (*influere*)
her life for them. Here, as with the example from Keats's "The Eve
of St. Agnes" and with most of the tradition, death whether sexual
or real is seen as the ultimate act of self-transcendence.

Conversely with that poem Coleridge said he wrote with
Crashaw's "Teresa" in mind, "Christabel," in which the abruptly
terminated lines, like a staccato of frustrated self-immurement,
bespeak the utter absence of transcendence in the deceptive Geraldine. It is her possession by the daimon of enslavement, it is—
current psychological talk would have it—her incapacity "to authentically relate" that is figured forth in the following:

> Nor do I know how long it is
> (For I have lain entranced I wis)
> Since one, the tallest of the five,
> Took me from the palfrey's back,
> A weary woman, scarce alive.
> Some muttered words his comrade spoke:
> He placed me underneath this oak;
> He swore they would return with haste;
> Whither they went I cannot tell—

The structural strategy—which Angus Fletcher has brilliantly
analyzed under the rubric "parataxis"—is the direct opposite of
Crashaw's above, and since the identification of the sexual and the
mystical is a commonplace of the poetic and religious tradition (and
preeminently for Coleridge who was familiar with Eckhart, Suso,
and Boehme), Coleridge's reference to "Teresa" remains baffling
unless one introduces the notion of a Bloomian "clinamen" here;
Coleridge's lines are rhythmically a swerve away from the pattern
of Crashaw's.

A more illuminating illustration of this construction—end-
stopped lines equated with imprisonment and delimitation, and
enjambment equated with transcendence and union—is offered in
Wilde's "Impression du Matin." The illustration is more illuminat-

ing because it shapes the entire poem and not merely a fragment. In this poem, to which Lord Alfred Douglas later wrote a disorganized companion piece, Wilde adds a French twist to the standard Romantic contrast between the freedom of natural activity and the enslavement of urban corruption: it is the encounter of Wordsworth and Baudelaire at some crepuscular moment (du matin) on Westminster Bridge.

> The Thames nocturne of blue and gold
> > Changed to a harmony in gray;
> > A barge with ocher-colored hay
> Dropt from the wharf: and chill and cold
>
> The yellow fog came creeping down
> > The bridges, till the houses' walls
> > Seemed changed to shadows, and St. Paul's
> Loomed like a bubble o'er the town.
>
> Then suddenly arose the clang
> > Of waking life; the streets were stirred
> > With country wagons; and a bird
> Flew to the glistening roofs and sang.
>
> But one pale woman all alone,
> > The daylight kissing her wan hair,
> > Loitered beneath the gas lamps' flare,
> With lips of flame and heart of stone.

The woman is an avatar of Geraldine, a clinamen of Saint Teresa. And one can see why for Wilde and his fellow Rhymers "la musique avant toute chose" was axiomatic: here, the melodious moan of transcendence harmonizing the first four stanzas and the pulsing pizzicati of imprisoned eros ("heart of stone") in the last. In the language of Milton's "On Time," one might say that the poem expresses the obdurate rejection of the eternal by the temporal.

Wilde's narcissistic harlot is, as Donne would put it, "betrothed unto" the temporal, and unless "enthralled" by the eternal "never shall be free." From Donne's holy sonnets I take one of my last examples of the "power" of enjambment, a power which Donne may be both responding to and employing in the resolution of what was for him the excruciating historical and theological dilemma of allegiance to richly painted Romanism or to lamenting and mourning Protestantism. (Since the issue is far more significant than mere ecclesiastical controversies, Donne's anti-Romanist polemics are not entirely relevant to his resolution of the dilemma.)

The familiar lines are:

> Batter my heart, three person'd God: for you
> As yet but knocke, breathe, shine, and seeke to mend;
> That I may rise, and stand, o'erthrow mee, and bend
> Your force, to breathe, blowe, burn and make me new.

A good deal of heavy-handed explication has been devoted to the entire sonnet, particularly among the second generation of New Critics for whom the mention of "three" set off triadic tics—more lately replicated in the quest for the historical Trinity in "God's Grandeur." Itrat Husain's early study of Donne's theology never took the poetry seriously, and Robert Jackson's recent *John Donne's Christian Vocation* garbles the poem in an effort to pile one New Critical ingenuity upon another. Both the dismissal and the distortion are peculiar because the poem is central not merely to Donne's philosophical-religious views but to the philosophical-religious views of the entire era, and by extrapolation to those views in any era in which the subject-object, or here, the absolute-contingent relationship, is the ultimate metaphysical issue. The broader question relates to the perennial dilemma of—some random but apt examples—the primacy of lamp or mirror, whether man "half perceives and half creates," whether beauty is ever present "and but the beholder wanting," and lastly, whether one can define genius as Coleridge did in the *Biographia* (15) as "possessing the spirit, not possessed by it."

Again, the traditional parallel of mystical and sexual union must be put into service in any discussion of what I have called the absolute-contingent relationship. And, as opposed to the "Protestant" univocal position Coleridge embraces in the last quotation, one may legitimately invoke the "Catholic" Pope (whose admirers, Byron in particular, Coleridge once contemptuously grouped with "other ignoramuses") in *Eloisa to Abelard*:

> All then is full, possessing and possest,[6]
> No craving Void left aking in the breast.
>
> [93–94]

The contrast Donne draws is between a being that merely patches and polishes (one may think of the stock figure of the tinker after Herrick and Wordsworth) and a being that recasts and utterly transforms (one may think of Blake's Los). Or, to give this central problem more contemporary bearing, one may think of the contrast—a leitmotiv of Stevens—between the philosopher who merely theorizes about reality, who merely "pinches and pokes" it (Cummings's "La Guerre II"), and the poet who seeks to transform it utterly. Claudel has said the last word on such philosophers—it is indeed almost the last word in *Le Soulier de satin*—and proleptically on the Benthamism of none other than Claude Lévi-Strauss:

A quoi cela sert-il de tant regarder et de se promener éternellement en amateur avec un pot de couleur à la main, faisant une retouche ici et là?
Et quand une chose est finie de rembailer son petit fourniment de rétameur pour aller ailleurs bricoler?
Il n'y a qu'une chose nécessaire, c'est quelqu'un qui vous demande tout et à qui on est capable de tout donner.

In Donne's personal dilemma the contrast is between, on the one hand, the Lutheran doctrine of "imputation"—sexually played on in *Elegie* 19 with astonishing bravura, and partially endorsed by Milton in *Paradise Lost* (12.408–10)—whereby man is not intrinsically changed when he is "justified" but is merely cloaked, as it were, in the merits of Jesus; and on the other hand, the Catholic doctrine that the soul is modified in its very substance by "sanctifying grace," so substantially modified in fact that the soul is *quoddammodo* God while at the same time it retains its own personal identity. Thus the *Roman Catechism*, finished in Donne's era,

---

6. Also to be brought into evidence is Stevens's "superman" of "Montrachet-le-Jardin," who is the pale mimic of the "speechless, invisible gods": "The super-man friseured, possessing and possessed." This total reciprocity, this perichoretic harmony, is the very definition of Shelley's untranslatable coinage, "epipsychidion."

explicitly affirmed that, "While retaining their own substance, those who delight in God do assume a certain and properly divine form, and they may be regarded as Gods rather than as men."

In the most general language possible, the opposition that distressed Donne is between a relationship of continuity and a relationship of "rupture," an opposition exemplified in the present century by the controversy between the Lutheran Anders Nygren affirming the antagonism of eros and agape and the Catholic Martin D'Arcy affirming their mutuality. And on this mutuality, the one startling enjambment in the first half of Herbert's "The Church-Floore" casts a particularly brilliant ray of theological and poetic light.

> Mark you the floore? that square & speckled stone,
>   Which looks so firm and strong,
>   Is *Patience*:
>
> And th'other black and grave, wherewith each one
>   Is checker'd all along,
>   *Humilitie*:
>
> The gentle rising, which on either hand
>   Leads to the Quire above,
>   Is *Confidence*:
>
> But the sweet cement, which in one sure band
>   Ties the whole frame, is *Love*
>   And *Charitie*.

In this last stanza, the allusion is to the Pauline *caritas aedificat*, an allusion which is then extended into the second part of the poem with its reference to "puffing" death, because the parallel phrase to *caritas aedificat* in Saint Paul is *scientia inflat*. But more pertinent to the eros-agape-enjambment synapse is the fact that this last stanza of the first part, the eschatological stanza, relating how the whole edifice is tied together, breaks the previously established pattern of the single "natural" virtues, patience, humility, and confidence, all embodied in end-stopped structures; while the transcendent, "supernatural" dual virtues of love and charity are embodied in the structure of enjambment. Thus, in accord with the Catholic tradition, Herbert shows eros overflowing into agape.

If one were to summarize these opposing traditions in poetic terms, one could say that the opposition is between Catholic metaphor and Protestant simile—and therefrom depend two radically different world views. Because those two world views are the matrices for some of the textual analyses that follow, it may be helpful to sketch further consequences implicit in the dilemma Donne's sonnet seeks to resolve. The underlying issue in that sonnet opens up three possible options—though the first, having no religious bearing for Donne or for Western religions in general, need be only glanced at: namely, that the contingent, finite self is utterly absorbed and lost in the absolute and infinite. This is the position embraced by much of the German idealist tradition, by Althusser's Marxian "antihumanism," and by Hinayana Buddhism. Second, the contingent self remains essentially separated from the absolute, a view that has been formulated philosophically in this century by Ernst Bloch with his sharp separation of the "penultimate" from the "ultimate," and a view that has been sustained in terms of classical Protestantism by Karl Barth in his early attacks on the philosophic notion of the *analogia entis*, a notion which affirms some link, however seemingly tenuous, between contingent and absolute. Thus Barth, in the first edition of his famous commentary on the Epistle to the Romans, observed that though men "may be capable of conceiving infinity, it is an infinity limited by our finitude, and thus nothing more than an infinite finitude." The third option relies on the *analogia entis* and affirms that the contingent self is paradoxically merged with the absolute, while (and this heightens the paradox) nevertheless remaining contingent—Milton's *"individual* kiss." This is the philosophic position that Marcuse's *Negations* reads into Hegel's concept of "totality," and it is the traditional Catholic and Eastern Orthodox religious position. Lastly, it is the position, I am suggesting, that Donne affirms in this sonnet—as he does also in the sixth Sermon in his affirmation that "Grace is the soule of the soule."

For the "true-blue Presbyterian" ("Hudibras") whom Donne is contesting, the finite is so imprisoned, so end-stopped, that it cannot become the infinite; it cannot truly experience the enjambment of transcendence and transformation; it can only be breathed upon, as one would breathe upon a piece of metal to polish it; thus, it can only be shined or mended. For the Catholic, the infinite is so "omnific"—to use a term from Milton who was also, Walter Clyde Curry showed years ago, tormented by this problem—that when it draws man out of himself, although he is made utterly "new," he does not lose his old finitude. As the emphatically Catholic coda to Herbert's "Artillerie" has it: "I am but *finite*, yet thine *infinitely*."[7] It is the same rejection of Lutheran imputation, of this mere "mending" of the soul, that one recognizes in Herbert's use of the verb "anneal" in "The Windows" and in the coda to his poem "Giddinesse":

> Lord, mend or rather make us: one creation
>   Will not suffice our turn:
> Except thou make us dayly, we shall spurn
>   Our own salvation.

The enjambment here is again that of transcendence and transformation, and it stands in marked contrast to the end-stopped condition of self-immurement in the preceding stanza:

> Surely if each one saw anothers heart,
>   There would be no commerce,
> No sale or bargaine pass: all would disperse,
>   And live apart.

"Commerce" on the rudest level is mere trade. It is also a traditional term for sexual union—as we have noted, the locus of transcendent experience. But even more, in the present context, it is a term for the union of the infinite and the finite; as such, it is used in the prayer which Herbert probably recited at Christmastide and which begins, "O admirabile commercium" ("O wonderful intercourse") in celebration of the marriage of heaven and earth. *But*, Herbert's and Donne's poems tell us, along with all of those considered ear-

---

7. But Herbert, true wayfarer on the Anglican *via media*, seeks to adopt both positions in "Aaron," as does Milton (a more vagrant wanderer) in *Paradise Lost* 3.290–94. As to the coda of "Artillerie," both Poulet in *Metamorphosis of the Circle*, and Nicolson in *The Breaking of the Circle* refer to Traherne's "My soul a Spirit infinit!"; but this affirmation has nothing in common with Herbert's, which relates to the action of "grace" in the soul. Traherne is voicing a commonplace based on Aristotle's "anima est quoddammodo *omnia*." More worthy of attention in the passage from "Artillerie" is the metaphor of warfare, which closely parallels the imagery of the central section of Donne's sonnet.

lier, none of this intercourse, on both the sexual and the religious plane, will take place if man rejects the realm of enjambment.

In neither Herbert nor Donne does the prayer conclude with a petition to be utterly absorbed by the infinite: rather, while seeking to be transformed into the infinite, each wants to retain his own finitude. The parallel between mystical union and sexual union holds true again. Indeed, Erich Fromm has taken as cornerstone of his understanding of human love the principle that as one loses oneself in the *beloved* one comes to a fuller sense of oneself as *lover*. Since this paradox is essential to my overall thesis, I will discuss it more fully now—and again will draw upon the witness of both the religious and the poetic traditions.

There is no need to take up to what degree the insistence on this paradox represents what has been, infelicitously, called "Judeo-Christian hedonism"; the fact is that such insistence is integral to the central Western vision of man's relation to the "other," whether sexual or mystical. As Buber observed, "The 'I' is indispensable to any relationship"—a statement which catachrestically confirms Simone Weil's idiosyncratic counterassertion in *La Connaissance surnaturel*, "To say 'I' is to lie." Thus, to return to the terminology of Donne's and Herbert's enjambments, the finite is not lost in the infinite ("My mind dropped like a hailstone into God's infinite ocean and melted and joined with Him": Sankara); rather, to the degree that the finite is ingathered into the infinite, it becomes more truly finite.

This is precisely the paradox Hopkins is wrestling with in his comment on the *Exercises* of Ignatius Loyola:

Suppose God shewed us in a vision the whole world inclosed first in a drop of water, allowing everything to be seen in its native colours; then the same in a drop of Christ's blood, by which everything whatever was turned scarlet, *keeping nevertheless* mounted in the scarlet *its own colour too*.

From the viewpoint of the mystical *conjunctio*, the resultant drop, fusing the blue and the scarlet, which we have already encountered in Browning's and Hopkins's enjambed lines above, would be the "violet sweet" of Hopkins's hyphenated Deus-homo or the "purple

patches" of all poetic centos. Employing a different kind of color
imagery, Hopkins makes the same point as his comment on the
Exercises in that Metaphysical marvel, "The Blessed Virgin Compared to the Air We Breathe." (One might consult for the sexual
aspect of the mystical parallel Carew's "A Prayer to the Wind to
Touch All His Mistress.")

> Again, look overhead
> How air is azured;
> O how! Nay do but stand
> Where you can lift your hand
> Skywards: rich, rich it laps
> Round the four fingergaps.
> Yet such a sapphire-shot,
> Charged, steeped sky will not
> Stain light. Yea, mark you this:
> It does no prejudice.
> The glass-blue days are those
> When every colour glows,
> Each shape and shadow shows.
> Blue be it: this blue heaven
> The seven or seven times seven
> Hued sunbeam will transmit
> Perfect, not alter it.
> Or if there does some soft,
> On things aloof, aloft,
> Bloom breathe, that one breath more
> Earth is the fairer for.
>
> [73–93]

As air is to objects, the infinite is to the finite. But Hopkins goes
even further here than he did in his comments on the Ignatian
Exercises.[8] The infinite doesn't "alter" the finite, it makes the finite

8. I am citing Loyola and Hopkins, Jesuits both, and one might counter with the axiom of
that great reviler of Jesuitry, "Le fini s'anéantit en présence de l'infini" (*Pensées*, 233). But
what seems at best mystical hyperbole here was for the French school of spirituality, according to its lyric historian, Henri Bremond, almost invariably interpreted orthodoxly. The
shadow of the Monophysites hovers indifferently over Gallicanists, Jansenists, and Jesuits,
but for all, though in differing degrees, *anéantir* did not mean literally "annihilate"; rather, it
was the other side of the dialectic of purification, the destruction of carnality. The language
is, again, that of *kenosis*.

more finitely perfect: "Earth is the *fairer* for." Thus, not only is the self not extinguished in the absolute ("keeping... its own colour too"), but when conjoined to the absolute, the self becomes more truly itself (its own color becomes richer, fuller, and so on).

In confirmation of this assumption and in what is almost a gloss on the mystical axiom, *homo magis Dei quam sui ipsius* (man is more of God than of himself), Stevens inquires at the end of "The Idea of Order at Key West" as to why "the glassy lights, / The lights in the fishing boats... / Mastered the night... / Fixing emblazoned zones... / Arranging, *deepening*, enchanting night." As the light arranges the night, it also deepens it: the light makes the dark "more" dark, makes it more *itself*. When mastering the contingent (the word "mastered" in Stevens is an ancestral manmark from Hopkins), the absolute fecundates and enriches this very contingency and individuality. In Hopkins's Scotist shorthand, its thisness becomes more *this*, while at the same time becoming utterly and totally *that*. This is also a conclusion of psychology from James on religious experience to Maslow on peak experiences—indeed, both are echoing Meister Eckhart, whom Harold Bloom shrewdly calls a "speculative psychologist," that when one is drawn out of his being (ecstasy) one discovers a deeper sense of self-identity.

Such deeper finitizing of the finite when it is "insorbed" into the infinite has been brought out in the religious and poetic tradition by the emphasis on one's proper name in relating to what Stevens calls "the great Omnium," to the nameless *Deus ineffabilis*. The unique value of the individual expressed in the "I have called you by name" of Isaiah stands in symbolic opposition to the totalitarian anonymity of the classical tradition voiced by Ulysses' "My name is Nobody." Much has been written on the significance of "naming" in the Jewish-Christian tradition (Adam, Abram-Abraham, Jacob-Israel, Simon-Peter, and so on) as a sign of transformation to a new life or to a new persona; but the emphasis has been more on the meaning of the symbolic or generic name and the power of the nominator and less on the heightened dignity and uniqueness of the nominee—this latter resulting from a failure to take seriously Max Müller's *nomina-numina* syzygy or Cornelius Agrippa's observations in *Occult Philosophy* on "the power of proper names." (One might even profitably reflect on Howard Nemerov's pun on his surname as suggesting the poet's mission: "namer of" things.)

What I would want to emphasize in the context of this discussion of the heightened personhood realized in the encounter with the "Omnium" (again, Milton's *individual* kiss) is the deeper selfness which the designating of the name confers. Thus, according to the masters of the Kabbalah *each* of the 600,000 people who fled Egypt continues to subsist individually in the universal community of Israel, and *each* has his own personal relationship with the Torah: "To none other than he, whose soul springs from thence, will it be given to understand it in this special and *individual* way that is reserved to him." According to Isaac Luria, in the Messianic age "every single man in Israel will read the Torah in accordance with the meaning peculiar to his root." And like Hopkins's "self," which retains its unique coloration when engulfed by the universal coloration of the "supernatural," Isaac Luria adds, "And thus also is the Torah understood *in Paradise.*" This latter statement evokes Jesus' promise of "salvation" to the faithful servant: "I will confess his name before my Father and before his angels." And this promise, in turn, is the inspiration for Crashaw when he calls the discalced Carmelites the

> ... thousand soules, whose happy names
> Heav'n keeps upon thy [Teresa's] score.
>
> [173–74]

The philosopher of the "proper name" is Rosenstock-Huessy— and not surprisingly, for reasons I will elaborate further in chapter 8, like Buber, also a Jew. But this topos is a constant among the poets as well. To keep this short, one may limit examples to a few poets of this century: Robinson's "If you will listen she will call . . . Luke Havergal"; or de La Mare's contemporary "judge" Samuel: "Calling me, 'Sam!'—quietlike—'Sam!'" Yeats draws the distinction more finely between what may be thought of as the Eastern notion of an impersonal absolute (Sunyata-Sunyata) "attracting" a de-selfed mortal and the "Western" notion of an ultimate reality personally addressing a human "hearer of the word":

> But something rustled on the floor,
> And *someone* called me by *my* name.

In concluding this chapter on enjambment as a structure that resonates this personal bond between infinite and finite (and all their analogues), I emphasize again that none of these patterns can be regarded either as indefectible keys for entrance into a poem or as quantifiable instruments for evaluating it. A constellation of structures is no "magical cohort," to use Bateson's phrase, nor is it a stamp of litmus paper to be attached to this or that poem in verification of its success or failure. The discovery of the significance of the structure often comes after the process of evaluation that is a much more pluriform and omnigenous activity—but an activity which itself depends essentially on an act of transcendence whereby the eros of the poem encounters the eros of the reader; being encounters being; form encounters form.

But, as I have stressed earlier, neither would I opt for quite so apparently relativizing a view as that of John Hollander, whom I quote again on enjambments: "the uses to which they are put are as divergent as any verbal acts." For a final illustration, I take one Hollander supplies from Eliot:

> Princess Volupine extends
> A meagre, blue-nailed phthisic hand
> To climb the waterstairs. Lights, Lights,
> She entertains Sir Ferdinand
>
> Klein, who clipped the lion's wings.

The "trope" is what would correspond to an "indecorous catachresis" in the classic manuals. And the poetic intent is comic (though blurred by the typical anti-Semitism), as are almost all violent reversals of conventional expectations. But this comic effect is the result of our sense of surprise, and surprise I noted earlier is a concomitant of joy because it is the state in which we experience the totally free outburst of *Vernunft* from the constraints of *Verstand*— again, other synonyms for those two polar faculties can be supplied *ad libitum*. Poems and jokes are, as detailed earlier, comparable in that both engender this sense of delightful surprise; both free us from the realm of prosaic, plodding, discursive knowledge (again, the realm of Stevens's ABC of being where we "kill the joke" by "spelling it out") and hurl us into the realm of mystery where self flashes off frame, where we leap the gap from *A* to *Z* (Stevens's

"X"), where we "get the joke" as we meet the poem immediately, intuitively.

Thus, I repeat, the elucidation of any number of examples of enjambment that do not seem to relate directly to transcendence in terms of the poem's paraphrasable content in no way controverts what has been said above. What such examples *do* do is point up the limited number of basic structures the poet has at his disposition and the vast range of narrative embodiment in which to deploy them. The obvious pedagogical parallel would be the innumerable forms ("all the forms of nature") Cézanne saw as reducible to three simple solids. A more apt parallel would be with music as understood in the finale of that poem on which Hollander has offered the classic historical, philosophical, and aesthetic exposition. From her limited store of notes, Cecilia

> Enlarged the former narrow bounds,
> And added length to solemn sounds,
> With nature's mother wit, and arts unknown before.

To assume—as precisely John Hollander does not—a limited number and univocal effect from a limited store of musical structures would be to succumb to a kind of aesthetic Benthamism, as in the malaise of the young Stuart Mill who recalled in the *Autobiography*:

> And it is very characteristic both of my then state, and of my mind at this period of my life, that I was seriously tormented by the thought of the exhaustibility of musical combinations. The octave consists only of five tones and two semitones, which can be put together in only a limited number of ways, of which but a small proportion are beautiful: most of these, it seemed to me, must have been already discovered, and there could not be room for a long succession of Mozarts and Webers, to strike out, as these had done, entirely new and surpassingly rich veins of musical beauty.

To this the only response is the Coleridgean aesthetic of Newman, whose equally decisive psychological collapse was moderated by music, and who wrote in the fifteenth University Sermon:

There are seven notes in the scale; make them fourteen; yet what a slender outfit for so vast an enterprise! . . . Shall we say that all this exuberant intensiveness is a mere ingenuity or trick of art like some game or fashion of the day without reality, without meaning? Or is it possible that the inexhaustible evolution and disposition of notes . . . should be a mere sound which is gone and perishes? . . . It is not so; it cannot be. No; they have escaped from some higher sphere, they are the out-pourings of eternal harmony in the medium of created sound; they are echoes of our home; they are the voice of angels, of the Magnificat of the Saints, or the living Laws of Divine Governance, or Divine Attributes.

There exists in poetry as in music a "law of return," which decrees that a given composition should always come back to its starting point. The basis for this "law," the heuristic myth suggests, is the helical character of any movement from unity through multiplicity and back to a higher unity. The nature of this circularity shall be examined in chapter 10. For the present, I am concerned with our apparent fascination by violations of such a law; for while there is satisfaction to be realized in the fulfillment of expectations, there is also, as I noted in the preceding chapter, the curious delight of surprise at their frustration.

Again, it should be stressed that neither a structure of fulfillment nor a structure of frustration by itself guarantees a successful poem. It is emphatically not a matter of "If P, then Q." Thus, in the following complete poems by de La Mare and W. H. Davies, it is obvious that, while one's expectations are certainly fulfilled through a development which is inexorably contrived, the poems remain first-rate examples of what Keats called "bitcherell":

> The sandy cat by the Farmer's chair
> Mews at his knee for dainty fare;
> Old Robin in his moss-greened house
> Mumbles a bone, and barks at a mouse.
> In the dewy fields the cattle lie
> Chewing the cud 'neath a fading sky.
> Dobbin at manger pulls his hay:
> Gone is another summer's day.

When primroses are out in Spring,
  And small, blue violets come between;
  And merry birds sing on boughs green,
And rills, as soon as born, must sing;

When butterflies will make side-leaps,
  As though escaped from Nature's hand
  Ere perfect quite; and bees will stand
Upon their heads in fragrant deeps;

When small clouds are so silvery white
  Each seems a broken rimmed moon—
  When such things are, this world too soon,
For me, doth wear the veil of Night.

The colon in de La Mare and the dash in Davies signal a kind of finale or *summatio*. But the poems are so predictably conformist that they arouse the antinomian instinct in the reader who longs for an anti-*summatio*, for the shattering of this studied rusticity. And that is precisely what Frost, who went to school to the Georgians, understood and achieved by the simple device of ironic closure—though it must be said that for Frost frequently such closure became as mechanical a formula, like the anticipated twist or reversal in an O.Henry story, as were the rehearsed traditionalism and bland Franciscanism of his British mentors.

But there is nothing mechanical about the following from Beckett's *Poems in English:*

        to cover
        to be sure cover cover all over
        your targe allow me hold your sulphur
        divine dogday glass set fair
        stay Scarmilion stay stay
        lay this Huysum on the box
        mind the imago it is he
        hear she must see she must
        all aboard all souls
        half-mast aye aye

        nay

Those who think that the faddists of "thanatology" are dead wrong
may applaud this precisely because of its nay-saying to death; but
here it is the structure that communicates the violence of this rebellion by its brief monosyllabic outburst against the overwhelming
multiplicity of verbal acquiescence in death that precedes the explosive negative. Beckett's poem is called "Malacoda," which may
loosely but appropriately be translated here as "anti-*summatio*"; as
such it is one of the patterns to be considered in this chapter.

The coda was described by classical rhetoricians under the heading *peroratio* and was employed by Provençal poets as the *tornata*,
or the *cauda* in relation to *frons*, by their successors under such
names as *envoi* and *commiato*; lastly, it has been brilliantly examined
by Barbara Herrnstein Smith in *Poetic Closure*. What follows shall
differ from that invaluable study by an exegesis which is concerned
less with "how poems end" (her subtitle) and more with why these
particular endings so affect the reader—concerned, in short, with
the "metaphysics" of this particular structure. I begin with a *catena
aurea* from Milton and a passage from Keats, in all of which the
coda seems to move us less by its dramatic or rhetorical reinforce-
ment of the meaning than by its function as a kind of orchestral
climax.

> As when the potent Rod
> Of Amram's Son in Egypt's evil day
> Wav'd round the Coast, up call'd a pitchy cloud
> Of locusts, warping on the Eastern Wind,
> That o'er the Realm of impious Pharaoh hung
> Like Night, *and darken'd all the Land of Nile*.
>
> [*PL* 1.337–42]

> Next Chemos, th'obscene dread of Moab's Sons,
> From Aroar to Nebo, and the wild
> Of Southmost Abarim; in Hesebon
> And Horonaim, Seon's Realm, beyond
> The flow'ry Dale of Sibma clad with Vines,
> The Eleale to th'Asphaltic Pool.
> Peor his other Name, when he entic'd
> Israel in Sittim on thir march from Nile
> To do him wanton rites, *which cost them woe*.
>
> [*PL* 1.406–14]

> With these in troop
> Came Astoreth, whom the Phoenicians call'd
> Astarte, Queen of Heav'n, with crescent Horns;
> To whose bright Image nightly by the Moon
> Sidonian Virgins paid thir Vows and Songs,
> *In Sion also not unsung*, where stood
> Her Temple on th'offensive Mountain, built
> By that uxorious King, whose heart though large,
> Beguil'd by fair Idolatresses *fell*
> *To Idols foul.*
>
> [*PL* 1.437–46]

> As when the Sun new ris'n
> Looks through the Horizontal misty Air
> Shorn of his Beams, or from behind the Moon
> In dim Eclipse disastrous twilight sheds
> On half the Nations, *and with fear of change*
> *Perplexes Monarchs.*
>
> [*PL* 1.594–99]

> thee I revisit safe,
> And feel thy sovran vital Lamp; but thou
> Revisit'st not these eyes, that roll in vain
> To find thy piercing ray, and find no dawn;
> So thick a drop serene hath quencht their Orbs,
> *Or dim suffusion veil'd.*
>
> [*PL* 3.21–26]

Or one may note this long passage, where each succeeding coda functions like a musical leitmotiv signaling fulfillment of "the law of return":

> Round he surveys, and well might, where he stood
> So high above the circling Canopy
> Of Night's extended shade; from Eastern point
> Of Libra to the fleecy Star that bears
> Andromeda far off Atlantic Seas
> *Beyond th' Horizon*; then from Pole to Pole
> He views in breadth, and without longer pause
> Down right into the World's first Region throws
> His flight precipitant, and winds with ease

Through the pure marble Air his oblique way
Amongst innumerable stars, that shone
Stars distant, *but nigh hand seem'd other worlds,*
Or other Worlds they seem'd, or happy isles,
Like those Hesperian Gardens fam'd of old,
Fortunate Fields, and Groves and flow'ry Vales,
Thrice happy Isles, *but who dwelt happy there*
He stay'd not to enquire: Above them all
The golden Sun in splendor likest Heaven
Allur'd his eye: Thither his course he bends
Through the calm Firmament; but up or down
By centre, or eccentric, hard to tell,
Or Longitude, where the great Luminary
Aloof the vulgar Constellations thick
That from his Lordly eye keep distance due,
Dispenses Light from far; they as they move
Thir Starry dance in numbers that compute
Days, months, and years, towards his all-cheering Lamp
Turn swift their various motions, or are turn'd
By his Magnetic beam, that gently warms
The Universe, and to each inward part
With gentle penetration, though unseen,
Shoots invisible virtue even to the deep:
So wondrously was set his Station bright.

[*PL* 3.555–87]

Or as a Thief bent to unhoard the cash
Of some rich Burgher, whose substantial doors,
Cross-barr'd and bolted fast, fear no assault,
In at the window climbs, or o'er the tiles:
So clomb this first grand Thief into God's Fold.

[*PL* 4.188–92]

Up he rode
Follow'd with acclamation and the sound
Symphonious of ten thousand Harps that tun'd
Angelic harmonies: the Earth, the Air
Resounded, (thou remember'st, for thou heard'st)
The Heav'ns and all the Constellations rung,
The Planets in thir stations list'ning stood,

> While the bright Pomp ascended jubilant.
> Open, ye everlasting Gates, they sung,
> Open, ye Heav'ns, your living doors; let in
> The great Creator from his work return'd
> Magnificent, *his Six days' work, a World*:
>
> [*PL* 7.557–68]

> So rose the Danite strong
> Herculean Samson from the Harlot-lap
> Of Philistean Dalilah, and wak'd
> *Shorn of his strength.*
>
> [*PL* 9.1059–62]

> Still was more plenty than the fabled horn
> Thrice emptied could pour forth at banqueting
> For Proserpine returned to her own fields,
> *Where the white heifers low.*
>
> [*The Fall of Hyperion* 1.35–38]

It is certainly no accident that the Milton passages are among the
most renowned in *Paradise Lost*. And while by an indulgence in
labored eisegesis one might read a dramatic function into these
codas (particularly that from book 4), their primary impact seems to
derive from the "musical" pattern itself, a pattern which is affecting
because it intensifies and fitfully allays the multiplicity-unity
polarization. But as I have already acknowledged, the distinction
between the "orchestral" and the "dramatic" is artificial, an *ens
rationis*, since the "dramatic" is but another representation of the
"orchestral," though it is largely through the analysis of the former
that we validate forensically the existence and function of the latter.
Again, to paraphrase Stevens, one structure explains another structure and another structure, which ultimately "explains" the central
structure.

For instance, the following coda, in addition to—or rather in
correlation with—its "orchestral" function, may be seen as under-
lining the violent character of the satanic rebellion:

> that fixt mind
> And high disdain, from sense of injur'd merit,
> That with the mightiest rais'd me to contend,
> And to the fierce contention brought along

Innumerable force of Spirits arm'd
That durst dislike his reign, and me preferring,
His utmost power with adverse power oppos'd
In dubious Battle on the Plains of Heav'n,
And shook his throne

[*PL* 1.97–105]

The dramatic effect is not unlike that in the following from *Hyperion*:

So far her voice flowed on, like timorous brook
That, lingering along a pebbled coast,
Doth fear to meet the sea; but sea it met,
And shuddered.

[2.300–03]

Here, too, the coda emphasizes the shocking nature of the encounter.

It is tragedy itself, defined as the overwhelming of the finite by the infinite (or of their respective mimes), that is brought out in the following:

But drive far off the barbarous dissonance
Of Bacchus and his Revellers, the Race
Of that wild Rout that tore the Thracian Bard
In Rhodope, where Woods and Rocks had Ears
To rapture, till the savage clamor drown'd
Both Harp and Voice; *nor could the muse defend
Her Son.*

[*PL* 7.32–38]

The ineffectualness of the muse, the principle of harmony, in the face of the chaotic is the greatest of all tragedies.

Stanley Fish has based an entire theory of Miltonic metaphor on the kinds of brief codas exemplified in the following passages:

His spear, to equal which the tallest Pine
Hewn on Norwegian Hills to be the Mast
Of some great Ammiral, *were but a wand.*

[*PL* 1.292–94]

> There lands the Fiend, a spot like which perhaps
> Astronomer in the Sun's lucent Orb
> Through his glaz'd optic Tube *yet never saw*.
>
> [*PL* 3.588–90]

The dramatic function of the coda in this passage from *Endymion* has a considerably less cosmic sweep than the preceding but again suggests the intrusion of a totally new order of activity—or passivity.

> And shaping visions all about my sight
> Of colors, wings, and bursts of spangly light;
> The which became more strange, and strange, and dim,
> And then were gulfed in a tumultuous swim:
> *And then I fell asleep.*
>
> [1.568–72]

A more fascinating coda, because it is essential to the architecture and thus to the understanding of one of the great lyric utterances, is in Milton's "On the Morning of Christ's Nativity":

> That glorious Form, that Light unsufferable,
> And that far-beaming blaze of Majesty,
> Wherewith he wont at Heav'n's high Council-Table,
> To sit the midst of Trinal Unity,
> *He laid aside.*

Saint Paul's "kenosis" has traditionally been translated as "self-emptying," and this coda by its brevity and by its position expresses powerfully the stripping away entailed in the act of the "sky god" in taking on himself the form of a servant, the *descendit de caelis* of the infinite into the mortal clay of finitude. It might be noted in passing that the contempt Milton displays for the *condition charnelle*—"darksome house"—represents another aspect of that heritage of the "schismatiques" which tormented Donne and contrasts with the "mean house" of the "Catholiques" as represented by Hopkins in "The Caged Skylark" where "mean" signifies, not "darksome" and despicable, but rather "intermediate"; it is the "middle" dwelling where man briefly, like Bede's bird, tabernacles himself between the first heavenly dwelling (Wordsworth's "God, who is our Home") and the ultimate "paradise."

Milton's coda is architectonic because the entire prologue stands to the rest of the poem as these four lines stand to the phrase, "He laid aside." The movement is from the solemn and ordered pattern of the introductory stanzas, representative of the eternal harmony of the absolute, to the irregularity of the stanzas in "The Hymn" itself with its emphatic temporal character. This movement, I have suggested in chapter 1, is the movement of all lyric poetry, and it may best be defined as "kenotic"[1]—a term first used in a poetic context by the great interpreter of Pascal and Rilke, Romano Guardini, in a study of "The Windhover" translated by Geoffrey Hartman. The elevation of the particular to the universal is the path of tragedy where historical, that is, factual, temporal verisimilitude dominates. The lyric takes the opposite trajectory: the historical, the temporal, is subjected to the "higher" laws of the paleostructure. Thus Dryden's "old Timotheus" is the singer of tragedy, and "divine Cecilia" is the singer of lyric:

> He raised a mortal to the skies;
> She drew an angel down.

I turn now to another variant that might be labeled the "coda of sincerity." The first example is the well-known "perfect pathos" Keats heard in the last two lines of the following:

> She dwelt among the untrodden ways
> Beside the springs of Dove,
> A Maid whom there were none to praise
> And very few to love:

---

1. Nowhere is this kenosis better described than in "Lamia" (1.146–70). In the beginning of the poem Lamia is a Uroboros figure, the perfect poem which like the religious sacrament "works what it says," in which the words spoken truly transform reality. But the sacrament is not for the minister; it is for others, *propter nos homines*. And so Lamia in Crete (Eden) can really help Hermes, but she cannot help herself. Lamia *In Crete* is the Christ who compared himself to the serpent and who, according to the theologians, is the archetypal sacrament: "He saved others, himself he cannot save." Lamia *In Corinth* is poem, most beautiful, most moving, most touching of poems, but still only poem, and hence ultimately ineffectual. Real are the sacraments of gods; unreal are the poems of men—as Stevens in anguished discovery cried out to the unattainable muse of sacramental music: "Unreal." In this is the explanation of the seeming contradiction that Lamia at the end of her kenosis on Crete is described as being "nothing but pain and ugliness," while seven lines later she is "a lady bright, / A full-born beauty new and exquisite." The anguish of all poetry is that the most splendid and radiant poem in this world is, compared to the perfect sacramental poem of the ideal world, nothing but ugliness and pain.

A violet by a mossy stone
  Half hidden from the eye!
—Fair as a star, when only one
  Is shining in the sky,

She lived unknown, and few could know
  When Lucy ceased to be;
But she is in her grave, and, oh,
  The difference to me!

The pathos derives not from the exclamatory tone of the statement—we have encountered that earlier, "Half-hidden from the eye!"; rather, it derives from the sudden dissolution of the elaborate intricacies of the first ten lines with their exaggerated oxymoronic quality—literally a preposterous aggregate of contradictions—the sudden dissolution of this whole world of artifice in favor of the world of seemingly simple, spontaneous declaration.[2] It is a break *away* from the aesthetic narrowly defined and *toward* the ethical, also narrowly defined—both definitions supplied by Kierkegaard. And it is the collision of these two rival realms, rival, as Keats said, "from Plato to Wesley," with the resultant triumph of the second that arouses this sense of pathos. Put banally, it is the conflict of art and life, with life suddenly emerging as victor. But, beyond all that, the very paradox of this collision engenders in the reader an even more refined poetic experience homologous with the sought-after experience of Keats's "beauty is truth," the aesthetic *is* the vital, art *is* life.

The structure is not unlike that in the following passages, respectively from Arnold, Sassoon, and MacDiarmid:

I struggle toward the light; and ye
Once-longed-for storms of love!

2. It is likely that Wordsworth realized it was the collision of this sequence of paradoxes with the concluding direct statement that generated the remarkable effect of the poem because, as is commonly noted, the present poem differs from the original by inserting an additional paradox and by deleting two stanzas of plain, unembellished description. F. W. Bateson cleverly argued for a psychological motive in these revisions to accord with his larger thesis that the "Lucy" poems are the symbolic destruction of the incest-breathing Dorothy, with the paradoxes canceling each other out and thus "according a momentary credibility to a non-rational reality." I think the structural explanation above provides a stronger reason for the emendations.

If with the light ye cannot be,
I bear that ye remove.

I struggle toward the light—but oh,
While yet the night is chill,
Upon time's barren, stormy flow,
Stay with me, Marguerite, still!

["Absence"]

At dawn the ridge emerges massed and dun
In the wild purple of the glowering sun
Smoldering through spouts of drifting smoke that shroud
The menacing scarred slope; and, one by one,
Tanks creep and topple forward to the wire.
The barrage roars and lifts. Then, clumsily bowed
With bombs and guns and shovels and battle gear,
Men jostle and climb to meet the bristling fire.
Lines of gray, muttering faces, masked with fear,
They leave their trenches, going over the top,
While time ticks bland and busy on their wrists,
And hope, with furtive eyes and grappling fists,
Flounders in mud. *O Jesu, make it stop!*

["Attack"]

Something—but what? Poetry's not written for men
And lies always beyond all but all men's ken.
—Only fools—countless fools—are deceived by the claims
Of a Menella Bute Smedley and most other names.

So when this book is revised for reissue
Let us have you included lest somebody should miss you.
Here with your peers—Spoof, Dubb, and Blong,
Smiffkins, Pimple, and Jingle. *Oh Lord! how long?*
["On the Oxford Book of Victorian Verse"]

The Arnold and the MacDiarmid (the latter evoking Browning's "Popularity") are somewhat truncated, with no great loss, however, since the earlier lines merely erect more expansively the screen against which the coda is projected.

In the following intensely rhythmic sonnet of Brooke with its swelling metrical pulsations, and in the "curtal" sonnet of Elinor

Wylie, one must attend to the entire poem because here the coda less manifestly violates the overall pattern; nevertheless, the structure emerges, and it affects the reader in much the same way and for the same reasons as in the poems above.

> Breathless, we flung us on the windy hill,
> Laughed in the sun, and kissed the lovely grass.
> You said, "Through glory and ecstasy we pass;
> Wind, sun, and earth remain, the birds sing still,
> When we are old, are old...." "And when we die
> All's over that is ours; and life burns on
> Through other lovers, other lips," said I,
> "Heart of my heart, our heaven is now, is won!"
> "We are earth's best, that learnt her lesson here.
> Life is our cry. We have kept the faith!" we said;
> "We shall go down with unreluctant tread
> Rose-crowned into the darkness!..." Proud we were,
> And laughed, that had such brave true things to say.
> *And then you suddenly cried, and turned away.*
>
> ["The Hill"]

> This is the bricklayer; hear the thud
> Of his heavy load dumped down on stone.
> His lustrous bricks are brighter than blood,
> His smoking mortar whiter than bone.
>
> Set each sharp-edged, fire-bitten brick
> Straight by the plumb-line's shivering length;
> Make my marvelous wall so thick
> Dead nor living may shake its strength.
>
> Full as a crystal cup with drink
> Is my cell with dreams, and quiet, and cool....
> Stop, old man! You must leave a chink;
> How can I breathe? *You can't, you fool!*
>
> ["Sanctuary"]

A further consideration of this structural format may help resolve the problem of the precise significance of the last line of "The Chimney Sweeper" and "Holy Thursday" in Blake's *Songs of Innocence*. Since for present purposes the poetic strategy in each poem may be regarded as pretty much the same, I will quote only the latter:

'Twas on a Holy Thursday, their innocent faces clean,
The children walking two & two, in red & blue & green,
Grey-headed beadles walk'd before, with wands as white as snow,
Till into the high dome of Paul's they like Thames' waters flow.

O what a multitude they seemd, these flowers of London town!
Seated in companies they sit with radiance all their own.
The hum of multitudes was there, but multitudes of lambs,
Thousands of little boys & girls raising their innocent hands.

Now like a mighty wind they raise to heaven the voice of song,
Or like harmonious thunderings the seats of Heaven among.
Beneath them sit the aged men, wise guardians of the poor;
Then cherish pity, lest you drive an angel from your door.

The opposing views concerning this coda were summarized by Hazard Adams and have been more recently brought up to date by E. D. Hirsch, with the former endorsing the effectiveness of the line and the latter like Stanley Gardner criticizing it as a blot on the poem. As a rule the endorsers read the poem in relation to Blake's entire vision and see the last line as "foreshadowing" (Gleckner) the world of experience. Terms like "irony" (Erdman and Bloom) and "satire" (Frye) recur among these readers, so it should be hardly surprising that—without professing certitude about who fished the murex up—I would also incline toward that same viewpoint: irony or satire is almost the definition of the structure being analyzed in this chapter. Hence, Hopkins writing about his imitation of Milton in "Tom's Garland" stated that he wanted "the coda for a sonnet in some sort 'nello stilo satirico.'"

Blake may have sung this song at the Mathews salon, and one can readily imagine the shock among his listeners if, as seems not unlikely, he suddenly were to cast the last line as a kind of recitative. Without any preparation, they would have been hurled *out of* the elaborate artifice of the body of the poem—as cunningly constructed as that of the "Lucy" poem above—and *into* the world of direct address, *out of* the world of "overhearing" and aesthetic distancing and *into* the world of immediate and present reality. But again, the collision of those two traditionally antagonistic worlds—baldly, contemplation and action—would engender an even richer experience of the surprising nexus of polarities.

The paradox is intensified by the fact that, if the governing mood of "Holy Thursday" is ironic, that does not mean the coda itself must be read ironically; rather, it is only if it is read as simple moral injunction that the overall irony of the poem is realized. Blake's poem is not merely an attack on the smug patrons of the charity schools but also is an attack on all those, past and present, who, rather than being harrowed by the plight of the impoverished, insulate themselves against that plight by mouthing pious saws (saws = sage = wise guardians). They are the people trapped in "The Net of Religion" who we are told (*The Book of Urizen*, pl. 25, 22) dwell in "a soft repose! / Inward complacency of Soul" (*Jerusalem*, pl. 23, 14–15). Blake may have had in mind Matthew Prior's "Prologue to the Orphan," with its nasty closure which treats the condition of the poor as occasion for amusement:

> For the distressed, your pity we implore:
> If once refused, we'll trouble you no more,
> But leave our Orphan squalling at your door.

Given this kind of complexity in Blake's closures, one may wonder whether their critics may not be victims of a very narrow notion of organic development that demands clear-cut transitional devices and that makes little allowance for the shock of sudden reversals. One glossator has said of the last line of "The Chimney Sweeper," "Doing one's duty here means primarily going up chimneys without having to be forced": this, of a poem that Swinburne singled out for its perfect combination of "inner" and "outer" music—the "outer music" presumably being the simple pictorial description of the visible scene ("a picture of wonderful beauty," Wickstead) and the "inner music" being the omnipresent latent irony which the coda signals.

As for the alleged poetic "irrelevance" (Hirsch) of Blake's codas because of their admonitory direct address to the listener, it is strange that there is little condemnation among the critics of a similar "relapse" into preachment in the following:

Glory be to God for dappled things—
　For skies of couple-color as a brinded cow;
　　For rose-moles all in stipple upon trout that swim;
Fresh-firecoal chestnut-falls; finches wings;
　Landscape plotted and pieced—fold, fallow, and plough;
　　And all trades, their gear and tackle and trim.
All things counter, original, spare, strange;
　Whatever is fickle, freckled (who knows how?)
　　With swift, slow; sweet, sour; adazzle, dim;
He fathers-forth whose beauty is past change:
　　Praise him.

Again, we have a poem as replete with the most extreme paradoxes
as Blake's "Holy Thursday" or Wordsworth's "She dwelt..." and,
again, the sudden shattering of that heavily stylized pattern by a
prose statement, here, as in Blake, by an imperative: "Praise him."[3]
Sermonizing, perhaps, whether ironic or not, is commendable in
Jesuit priests but not in prophets against empire.

　This coda design may also illuminate our understanding of the
concluding stanza of "Ode to a Nightingale." Though it is the
penultimate stanza that has generally been the object of most critical debate, it is the final stanza that has been most often either
dismissed with relatively little attention or misconstrued altogether
as merely a kind of *envoi* expressing the poet's return to isolation
and emptiness. My immediate focus is the repetition of the word
"forlorn," the governing term in the stanza and by my reading the
most dramatic point in the poem—though totally ignored in Slote's
study on drama in Keats and analyzed fully, though conventionally, only in Brooks's *Modern Poetry and the Tradition*. This repetition is usually regarded as merely a bridge construction of no more
significance than any other transitional device. Even in the detailed
"distillations" of E. C. Pettet, the function of the repetition goes
unexplained, though it admittedly entails "some shift in meaning."

　In unpacking that "shift," it may be suggested that the same
relationship prevails here between the last stanza and the body of
this poem that prevailed in all the examples of coda above: the

---

3. It is odd that Hopkins's remarkably skilled French translator, Gérard Leyris, misreads
the last line as a simple exclamation rather than as an imperative: "Louange au Père!"

stanza breaks the entire preceding aesthetically distanced structure and propels the reader (and the poet) out of the world of imaginative fabrication and into the world of "reality." The coda signals, furthermore, not merely a return to the condition in the first stanza of the poem, a state of reflective solitude, but a breaking of the *poetic* frame altogether. To clarify that observation, a brief recapitulation of the poem is called for. Its larger theme is the sacrifice of self as a path to union. Simplistically: the *persona* is ascending the three-rung *scala ad unitatem* mentioned in the previous chapter. On the rudest physical plain, through wine one becomes temporarily unified with oneself and with others; similarly, though putatively in a more permanent fashion, through "poesy," which leaves one with "no identity," one achieves a kind of union; and thirdly, through death as the ultimate act of self-abnegatory fulfillment one attains lasting union. But in the last stanza this pattern is broken by a conscious and explicit adversion to *the act of writing* the word "forlorn."

Let me illustrate this by two examples. A seriously flawed poem by a flawed poet reads:

> There thou does lie, in the gloom
> Of the autumn evening. But ah!
> That word, *gloom*, to my mind
> Brings thee back, in the light
> Of thy radiant vigor, again.
>
> ["Rugby Chapel"]

A flawed poem by a surer poet reads:

> Surely some revelation is at hand;
> Surely the Second Coming is at hand.
> *The Second Coming!* Hardly are those words out
> When a vast image...
>
> ["The Second Coming"]

The poems are flawed here because the author is *describing* the *process* of his thought; he is literally engaged in the act of discursive reasoning, that is, he is in the prosaic realm of complete and total self-consciousness, and he explicitly informs us of that fact. It is as though he said: "I write a word or phrase; it sets off a chain of reflections; I point out that the reflections are triggered by the word or phrase; and lastly I discuss the reflections themselves." The process is utterly abecedarian, as I have used that term in earlier chapters.

Let me transpose to Keats: "in faery lands *forlorn.*" Suddenly, it is as though the poet looked at the paper in front of him, saw the word he had just written, became conscious of it both as entailing his action and as a lexical item, "forlorn"—"that word which I just wrote with this pen on this paper at this table reminds me of something; what is it? It reminds me of a bell . . . 'to toll me,'" and so on. The entire sequence is identical with the allegedly neurotic self-consciousness displayed in the physical gestures of Richard Nixon, a self-consciousness with which both Garry Wills and Norman Mailer have had much sport: for a brief space the gesture (read *the poem*) flows spontaneously, but suddenly Nixon (read *the poet*) becomes aware of his arm outstretched, his hand suspended "out there" ("perilous seas *forlorn*"); it is scrutinized by the mind's eye; the command is sent from the brain, passes through the neurons, the muscles are stimulated, and the arm drops stiffly to his side ("*forlorn*, the very word"). Now, if man is "a hand and a language," the stunning achievement of Keats is to show us the process of their separation by a hampering and constraining self-consciousness. Precisely what he wants to convey by the second "forlorn"—as Yeats and Arnold certainly did not by their repetitions—is this reenslavement by a self that was *almost* eclipsed in the pursuit of lasting union. He does not *tell* us self-consciousness has returned now that he has rejected the ultimate act of abnegation, the richness of dying. Instead, self-consciousness shapes and informs the entire last stanza just as it shapes and informs the clumsy Nixon gesture. Again, one may define the entire process (from union and forgetfulness of self to isolation and heightened self-awareness) as declension from the vital and mysterious X of poetry to the ABC discursiveness of prose.[4] And fi-

---

4. If as I suggested in the previous chapter metaphor grammatically means fusion and figuratively means union with the transcendent, whereas simile implies rupture or disjunction, then it is certainly significant that the rich metaphoric structure of the body of the poem is also reversed by the coda which contains the poem's *only* simile—and a highly stereotyped one at that: "like a bell."

nally, as in the codas earlier, it is the discordant concourse of these two structures, loosely the poetic and prosaic, the oblique and direct, that intensifies the reader's specifically aesthetic experience.

One may test the validity of this last judgment by examining in its light such presumably defective closures as the eleventh stanza of "On the Death of a Fair Infant Dying of a Cough" (which should be compared to stanza 101 of "Perle"),[5] the last four lines of "Mr. Flood's Party" (so outrageous to Yvor Winters), the last four stanzas of Yeats's "Among School Children," the "anticlimax" (Harper) of the fourteenth book of *The Prelude*, Iseult's strange tale concluding part 3 of Arnold's otherwise surprisingly powerful "Tristram and Iseult," "The Conclusion to Part the Second" of "Christabel," which from Byron on almost invariably has been read autobiographically, and finally, the "lumps of futurity" (Lewis) in the last two books of *Paradise Lost*, the unadorned style of which, by contrast to all that precedes in the poem, I would read as expressing the clear, untrammeled *Heilsgeschichte* ever present in the mind of God the Father.

Before moving away from Keats, and on to some more explicitly ironic closures, I will refer in passing to a coda that might be compared to the final phase of Louis Martz's "poetry of meditation." I do this primarily in the interests of clarifying my own larger theme but also to support any theory of the discontinuous continuity of the tradition. The comparison is between the elegiac wistfulness of Keats and the stoically muted despair of Stevens:

> Then in a wailful choir the small gnats mourn
> Among the river sallows, borne aloft
>   Or sinking as the light wind lives or dies;

5. Milton's poem, like "Perle" (where the poet is to the Dreamer as Milton is to the bereaved mother), may be no more about a child's death than Stevens's "The Man Whose Pharynx Was Bad" is about sore throats: all in their fullest dimension are poems about the frustration of the ultimate creative effort. It is the failure of poetry as such, its inevitably Lamia-like character, that Milton laments in "Lycidas" (45–49), in a passage reminiscent of the "blasted primrose" of the "Infant" poem. Furthermore, if Milton's "Infant" poem is also a lament for a previously written, unsuccessful poem, the otherwise excessive hyperbole, "til the world's last end," is recognizable as simply a traditional vaunt that his immortal achievement is yet to come. And there is little doubt that he viewed *Paradise Lost* as a sacrament in the fullest theological sense.

And full-grown lambs loud bleat from hilly bourn;
  Hedge-crickets sing; and now with treble soft
The red-breast whistles from a garden-croft;
  And gathering swallows twitter in the skies.

                                        ["Ode to Autumn"]

Deer walk upon our mountains, and the quail
Whistle about us their spontaneous cries;
Sweet berries ripen in the wilderness;
And, in the isolation of the sky,
At evening, casual flocks of pigeons make
Ambiguous undulations as they sink,
Downward to darkness, on extended wings.

                                        ["Sunday Morning"]

If, as all theoreticians of modern physics tell us, the observer both
modifies the reality observed and is modified by it, Stevens here is
so modified as he modifies Keats and makes clear that the accent of
acquiescence in fate has been modulated in our time to an accent of
resigned hopelessness.

Both the Keats and the Stevens closures are meditative; and
though Keats is not mentioned in Martz's historical study, Stevens
he rightly places in this tradition, with closures that might be called
applicative or recollective. It is a favorite device of Stevens—and,
significantly, much more frequent in the later more reflective
poems—so I mention without comment some of them: "The Well
Dressed Man with a Beard," "Les Plus Belles Pages," "Theory,"
"Poesie Abrutie," "Late Hymn from the Myrrh-Mountain," "Imago," "A Primitive Like an Orb" (12), "Reply to Papini," "Questions Are Remarks," "Study of Images I," "A Quiet Normal Life,"
and the last poem in the collected poems, "Not Ideas about the
Thing but the Thing Itself."

I have been saying that the relation of the coda to the body of the
poem is, by definition, ironic. The irony may be dramatic (and also
slightly comic for reasons to be considered in chapter 6):

                I found
        A thing to do, and all her hair
          In one long yellow string I wound

> Three times her little throat around,
> *And strangled her.*
>
> ["Porphyria's Lover"]

Or, as in the coda by a great admirer of Browning, it may be merely emphatic:

Strong gongs groaning as the guns boom far,
Don John of Austria is going to the war;
Stiff flags straining in the night-blasts cold
In the gloom black-purple, in the glint old gold,
Torchlight crimson on the copper kettle-drums,
Then the tuckets, then the trumpets, then the cannon, *and he comes.*

["Lepanto"]

That differs, equally, from the following coda by an admirer of Chesterton where the coda is so abrupt as to create the effect of burlesque—which of course was precisely Auden's intent.

> He was my North, my South, my East and West,
> My working week and my Sunday rest,
> My noon, my midnight, my talk, my song;
> I thought that love would last for ever: *I was Wrong.*
>
> ["Song: Stop All the Clocks"]

Since all of these codas have an element of caprice about them, since they relate to some final consummation which is vaguely anticipated but still unknown, and since they bespeak the reversal of seemingly inevitable occurrences, it is entirely understandable why they would be the favorite stylistic device of the least "outlandish" ("The British Church") religious poet in the literature, George Herbert. As one cannot say of Donne, whose Christianity, often bizarre and recherché, vacillated between Rome and Geneva; as one cannot quite say of Hopkins, whose Christianity was heavily Italianate and idiosyncratic (whereas, *contra* W. H. Gardner, his poetry is not), one can say of Herbert that the revolutionary poetry is in the traditionary piety, a piety nurtured on the *via media* of an Anglicanism that the young John Henry Newman recognized as predating the Reformation by several centuries. In the context of the discussion in the preceding chapter relating to the crucial issue of "Protestant" imputation versus "Catholic" transformation (what I have called "Protestant simile" versus "Catholic metaphor"), Herbert as we have seen reconciles both in the coda to the deceptively simple "Aaron":

> So holy in my head,
> Perfect and light in my deare breast,
> My doctrine tun'd by Christ, (who is not dead,
> But lives in me while I do rest)
> Come people; Aaron's drest.

But he is "dressed" not merely in the sense of being garbed in the Lord Jesus, of having "put on the Lord Jesus" and, thus, of appearing *like* Jesus, but also in the sense that he *is* Jesus himself—as he says in the third stanza:

> Onely another head
> I have, another heart and breast.

This is a much more precise articulation of the Anglican *via media*, embracing both Rome and Geneva, than Donne *may have* attempted in the coda of the sixth holy sonnet, where he prays to God to

> Impute me righteous, thus purg'd of evil,
> For thus I leave the world, the flesh, the devill.

I emphasize "may have attempted," because everything depends on the significance attached to the first "thus": whether it is to be taken as adverb or conjunction. In the first instance, *how* he is purged is after the fashion of imputation, that is, not purged fully at all; the second instance would render an interpretation that may be paraphrased, "impute me righteous, and hence I will be purged of evil and will leave the world," and so on. In the "Batter my heart" sonnet, Donne as we have seen endorses Catholic metaphor; in the present sonnet he straddles the issue, though like Herbert in "Aaron" he may indeed have been trying to embrace both Catholic metaphor and Protestant simile. Whereas in Elegie 19, for what can only be called private ends, he approves the Protestant doctrine.

Embedded in this Anglican tradition of the *via media* is a sense of the arbitrariness of grace on the personal level and, on the historical level, of the confounding of destiny at the eschaton, the cosmological coda to the poem of creation. This arbitrariness is expressed with remarkable concision in the double coda of Herbert's "The Water-Course":

Who gives to man, as he sees fit, $\begin{cases} \text{Salvation.} \\ \text{Damnation.} \end{cases}$

Here the ambiguity as to the referent of "he" (God? man?) brings out what later thinkers would, in expanding the image of the *via media*, call the "bridge church" function of Anglicanism. The "he" refers to man as being in the Catholic tradition *capax Dei*, and in the Protestant as incapable of anything relating to salvation. But here the *via media* swerves toward the Protestant side. The bridge may link the two churches, but for Herbert in this poem the traffic is away from Rome.

Herbert's codas, which all students have remarked,[6] are the poetic instrument for expressing his Anglican sense of personal and historical apocalypse. One need only glance at such representative poems as "Affliction," "The Church-Floore," and "The Collar" and at the pattern of each stanza of "Vertue." Redemption in this theological tradition is a wholly gratuitous act; it cannot be guaranteed or predicted; it comes freely as a gesture of the divine condescension—precisely as in that poem originally called "The Passion" but wisely retitled "Redemption."

> Having been tenant long to a rich Lord,
>   Not thriving, I resolved to be bold,
>   And make a suit unto him, to afford
> A new small-rented lease, and cancell th'old.
>
> In heaven at his manour I him sought:
>   They told me there, that he was lately gone
>   About some land, which he had dearly bought
> Long since on earth, to take possession.

6. Thus: Valentine Poggi's "final twist," and Arnold Stein's "dismissal of structure." This use of coda may also in part explain the kinship of two so seemingly different poets as Herbert and Stevens, and the interest of a critic like Helen Vendler in both.

I straight return'd, and knowing his great birth,
  Sought him accordingly in great resorts;
  In cities, theatres, gardens, parks, and courts:
At length I heard a ragged noise and mirth

  Of theeves and murderers: there I him espied,
  Who straight, *Your suit is granted,* said, & died.

This coda stems from the same kind of vision embodied in South-well's "The Burning Babe," only the plot is reversed: in Southwell, Jesus after speaking at some length leaves the startling last word to the persona of the poem: "And straight I called unto mind that it was Christmas day."

Once again the poetic myth converges with the religious myth. I referred at the beginning of this chapter to the "antinomian in-stinct" that is left dissatisfied in the reader when encountering the bland, lockstepped regularity of the Georgian poets. The unex-pected codas of Herbert and Southwell and Donne, like the doc-trine of the historical (*not* Browning's) Johannes Agricola—the Ref-ormation spokesman for radical Antinomianism—convey to us the impossibility of predicting the action of the infinite or of "bargain-ing for" a relationship with it. (Southwell, Donne, and Herbert, to be sure, were no more antinomians in the formal sense than was Thomas Aquinas.)

Since this theme of arbitrariness has become central to the tradi-tion, and is central to the present argument, it merits further treat-ment here before I return to another aspect of coda in the next chapter. And because, as M. H. Abrams has shown, it was the theological doctrine, as strongly emphasized in Herbert, that was the matrix of this notion of the capriciousness of salvation (or among the Romantics, of the gratuity of poetic inspiration), I will treat the matter from the religious side as well as from the aesthetic.

I take my "text" from a mystic who blended much of the Jewish and Christian spiritual tradition and who paradoxically lived in-stinctively out of the Torah and explicitly out of these very poems of George Herbert we have been considering. Simone Weil's *attente de Dieu* is an expression of that wise passiveness expressed in the classic sacramental formula, familiar to Herbert and Donne, *nullam obicem ponere*, meaning that man cannot compel the transcendent, he can merely "place no obstacle" in the way of its action. The summation of each of these dicta is Heidegger's aphorism, "In waiting upon we leave open what we are waiting for." Thus it says in the Zohar: "So the Torah reveals herself and hides, and goes out in love to her lover and arouses love in him. Come and see: this is the way of the Torah." Here there is no ascetic "vigor," much less any Goethean "striving." The watchword is Baron von Hügel's "Never strain," and the conviction is Wallace Stevens's "There is nothing to think of. It comes of itself"—an insight that echoes Wordsworth's in "Expostulation and Reply": "of itself will come."

Stevens recapitulates a long line of predecessors. Wordsworth translated Simone Weil's *attente de Dieu* in "The Tables Turned" as "a heart that watches and receives," and both are summarized in the Keatsian mission as "watcher of the sky": with Keats, man does not discover the "new planet"; it discovers him. "THERE is NO Natural Religion," said Blake attacking a misreading of Wordsworth: the individual does not make vows; with Wordsworth, "vows were made for me." Indeed, one could do an important study on the total gratuity of union with the transcendent by merely tracing the use of the word "unaware" in the apocalyptic moments of the great Romantics. Thus salvation comes to the mariner when he sees the water serpents and blesses them "unawares"; so, too, for the boy of Winander, enlightenment would enter his mind "unawares," as does also the leech gatherer manifest himself, while Keats's Madeline is a "missioned spirit, unaware."

Both Coleridge's and Wordsworth's poems are about sailors and wanderers, and Keats's about a journey to union; all three affirm with another *viator* of Stevens ("The sail of Ulysses"), who confirms Blake on natural religion: "There is no map of Paradise." The testimony is massive and continuing and perhaps best exemplified by Hopkins who in "The Starlight Night" is tempted to think that union is the result of some kind of bargain with the deity (much like the "moral causality" of the sacraments in Hopkins's loved Scotus for whom grace comes *ex pacto Dei*). But he immediately corrects his momentary relapse into pawnshop soteriology (or more nicely, what theologues call Irenaean-Anselmian ransom theory): "it is all a purchase, all is a *prize*. / Buy then! *bid* then!" Hopkins, like Herbert, ends up in the arbitrary world of Stevens's "cadence" (chance), of Pascal's *pari* and Mallarmé's *coup*.

As we have seen, the coda is often the expression of this arbitrariness of the transcendent. As I mentioned, for Herbert that structure is demanded by more than the aesthetics of a poem; it seems to be demanded by the nature of existence as that existence is mediated by Anglican Christianity. It clearly isn't so with Herbert's great admirer, Crashaw—and this may be not unrelated to Crashaw's conversion to a Roman Catholicism which theologically acknowledged the gratuity of salvation but in practice canceled out the doctrine by such warrants of God's mercy as the sale of indulgences, the cult of relics, and the promotion of pilgrimages to, among other shrines, Crashaw's own holy house of Loretto. With Crashaw, the coda, though as frequent as in Herbert, seems to be dictated as much by stylistic convention as by religious-poetic conviction. There are strong codas at the end of many stanzas of "The Weeper," but I quote the coda to this entire poem about a woman whose mythologized life, if it meant anything at all, clearly meant that salvation is an arbitrary act of divine condescension:[7]

> Much lesse mean we to trace
> The Fortune of inferiour gemmes,
> Preferr'd to some proud face
> Or pertch't upon fear'd Diadems.
> Crown'd Heads are toyes. We goe to meet
> A worthy object, our Lord's FEET.

The baroque is many things, not least—as Spengler following Burckhardt showed—an attempt to wrestle afresh with the interrelationship of the infinite and the finite. But in Crashaw the baroque sometimes represents the triumph of the shell (*barucca*, putative root) over the kernel, of the formulary incantation over originally intended substance. It is Huizinga who has pointed out how the accelerated pace of change in Europe at the close of the Middle Ages led to an extreme reliance on traditional rituals. In the present

---

7. The paradox itself is a convention, as is evident in Southwell's prose meditations on Mary Magdalen and in the coda to Marvell's "The Coronet":

> That they, while Thou on both their Spoils dost tread,
> May crown thy Feet, that could not crown thy Head.

context, it is almost as though, to the very degree that among the "nice tenets" of Romanists the theological doctrine of the arbitrariness of grace was obscured, the formulas embodying that doctrine were frantically repeated over and over: just as in Crashaw the coda of caprice is introduced (for example, "Teresa," 139, 150, 156) in a purely "mannerist" fashion, a term I use to mean the imitation of an imitation.

VI: *Coda*

Irony is born out of a juxtaposition: on the cosmic scale, the juxtaposition of the infinite and finite. This is "la sereine ironie" of Mallarmé's "eternal blue," which will become in half a century Stevens's "indifferent blue"—and hence no longer a subject for irony. On the historical scale, the juxtaposition is of a traditional world view and a new philosophy that calls all things into methodic doubt; and on the personal scale, the juxtaposition is of stability and "mutabilitie," a juxtaposition reinforced if not generated by the cosmic and the historic. Irony may thus almost be defined as the offspring of modernity or of that spirit and mood that we equate— chronocentrically—with modernity.

Though there will be obvious exceptions, one may further generalize these platitudes by observing that the ironic tenor will not usually characterize writers extolling or expressing a stable political-social order or a universal belief system; nor on the individual level will it usually be typical of the settled temper of middle age. From the latter derives the strength of the received wisdom that what irony Milton evinces occurs almost exclusively in the early Latin and Italian poems and in the late *Samson Agonistes*.

By way of focusing such broad and necessarily loose speculative impressions on a narrow but loose historical impression, one would therefore anticipate on a priori grounds that there will be more irony, say, in early Donne than in Spenser. I will consider Donne shortly. As for the example of Spenser, let me approach it in the light of the above comments, and in the present context of coda, by questioning Donald Cheney's interpretation of the following from *Amoretti*:

Ye tradefull Merchants, that with weary toyle,
   do seeke most pretious things to make your gain;
   and both the Indias of their treasures spoile,
   what needeth you to seeke so farre in vaine?
For loe my loue doth in her selfe containe
   all this worlds riches that may farre be found,
   if Saphyres, loe her eies be Saphyres plaine,
   if Rubies, loe her lips be Rubies sound:
If Pearles, her teeth be pearles both pure and round;
   if Yuorie, her forhead yuory weene;
   if Gold, her locks are finest gold on ground;
   if siluer, her faire hands are siluer sheene.
But that which fairest is, but few behold,
   her mind adorned with vertues manifold.

                        [Sonnet 15]

Cheney, whose readings are highly instructive, views the last line as anticlimactic or, in the present context, as "ironic," since the finale to this kind of standard list of bodily qualities would presumably have been a reference to the lady's "amarous sweet spoiles" (*FQ* 2.12.64), that is, to the external genital organs. This is certainly what any *modern* reader would probably expect, because he would almost invariably view these poems through the glass of Spenser's successors, among whom the reversal of convention became itself a new convention.[1]

Thus, what Cheney says of Spenser's sonnet is probably true of the anti-Petrarchan Carew in "In Praise of His Mistress," where the first stanza is devoted to her eyes, the second to her lips and teeth, the third to her breasts. The two concluding stanzas follow, beginning with a description of her thighs (compare *FQ* 2.3.28):

        As fair pillars under stand
          Statues two;

---

1. But it should be noted that such reversals are generally in the opposite direction from what Cheney detects in the sonnet above—as in the burlesques of Marlowe's "The Passionate Shepherd," in Shakespeare's notorious Sonnet 140, in Suckling's "The Deformed Mistress," in Herrick's "Loathesomenesse in Love," in most of the Donne poems I shall examine later, and in the many lampoons of Carew's "Ask Me No More where Jove Bestowes."

> Whiter than the silver swan
> That swims in Po:
> If at any time they move her,
> Every step begets a lover.

> All this but the casket is,
> Which contains
> Such a jewel, as the miss
> Breeds endless pains;

But the jewel in the casket is not what many of Carew's contemporaries would have anticipated. This is a Donnean poet, not a Spenserian, and hence the remarkable irony of the coda:

> That's her mind, and they that know it
> May admire, but cannot show it.

Thus, it is largely a matter of putting the poem in its proper *Sitz im Leben*. What seems to a later generation ironic may have been transparently straightforward to an earlier one. The difficulty of interpretation was unintentionally brought out in a study by Douglas Bush entitled "Ironic and Ambiguous Allusions in *Paradise Lost*," which was itself highly ambiguous in its definition of irony. Bush adjudged the reference to Psalm 24 in the following from "Epithalamion" as ironic:

> Open the temple gates vnto my loue,
> Open them wide that she may enter in.
>
> [204–05]

But there is no irony whatsoever here; there is merely allusion or at best obliqueness.[2] It would be ironic if in reply to Handel's later shrill repetition of the next line of the psalm, "Who is the king of glory?" one were to reply, "Donne's 'prince' who in prison lies"—since as I shall argue shortly Donne was alluding to sexual entrance into the beloved. If by "temple gates" Spenser implied "vulva," one would have had an obviously modern and obviously ironic structure. But even here the irony would be more striking to the secularized twentieth-century reader than to the reader of Spenser's

---

2. Similarly, there is no irony whatever in Milton's use of this same biblical tag in *Paradise Lost* 7.564–69.

age, direct heir to the allegorizing religious tradition of the Middle Ages. For the Church Fathers and the Scholastics, the reception of the "bride," creation, into the New Jerusalem was a sexual entering, even as the sexual entering of male and female through earthly marriage was identified with the triumphal reception of mankind into paradise. That earthly marriage entailed, first, a wedding bath of the betrothed (hence, the venerable antiquity—and therefore *to the modern reader*, the irony, of Stevens's pairing of "one's Sunday *baths*" with the *"weddings* of the soul"); second, it entailed an anointing in oils and perfumes and, third, a wedding banquet followed by sexual union. For the early Christian the three marital rites, derived from extant pagan cults, were thus identified with the "mysteries," that is, the sacraments of baptism, confirmation, and eucharist. Similarly, in the light of this sacred-sexual nexus, one may regard the Wife of Bath's reference to her "quoniam" as being as much a euphemism as an irony. "Quoniam" does represent a grammatical and thus also a sexual conjunction and certainly is intended to play on such bawdy cognates as coin-cunt, but its redeeming character, which raises it above the level of mere vulgarity, would have been recognized even by the unlettered in Chaucer's time from its use in the "Gloria" of the mass, where it ushers in a series of attributions of deity, "Quoniam tu solus sanctus. . . ." The Wife of Bath's reference is similar to that in *The Faerie Queene* (3.10.48) where the Satyre's frequent ringing of "his matins bell" plays on morning-rising-erection but also on the Divine Office's preparation for mass.

But for the Spenser of "Epithalamion," he is rarely ironic, and he was certainly not writing for the "modern" reader. Even when seeming to rail against his mistress he is not free of the constraints of the Petrarchan tradition, a tradition that was immune to the irony latent in celebrating, almost by a kind of *catalogue raisonné*, the beauties of an *admiranda* in whom lurked *pudendum*. This immunity is sustained by Spenser even when the tradition is beginning to disintegrate in France among poets on the periphery of the Pléiade, in Italy among the immediate successors of the *presecentisti*, and in England by Donne and by his followers.[3] Spenser's "anti-

3. One is not persuaded by various attempts (Donald Guss's primarily) to laminate Donne to the Petrarchan tradition on the basis of passages which are not particularly characteristic of either poet but common to garden-variety love poetry throughout the ages—the entire effort is like assessing Blake as a Petrarchan poet by taking into account only the juvenilia.

modernism" kept him in bondage to Petrarchan conventions, particularly in *Amoretti* and "Epithalamion," where he speaks *in propria persona*, rather than in the more innovative, impersonal, and occasionally comic "voice" of *The Faerie Queene*. Spenser quite generally, like Jonson more infrequently, writes personally and directly out of the tradition; so while one has little doubt of Spenser's intent, there is some possible ambiguity in Jonson's fifth "Celebration of Charis":

> For this beauty yet doth hide
> Something more than thou hast spied.

The "something more" is that she is "Minerva when she talks." This, too, one suspects, is a closure that would appear ironic mainly to the "modern," that is, post-Donnean reader. Probably the nearest thing to irony in *Amoretti* is the tincture of mock-heroic Louis Martz detects in some of its sonnets.

As to the sonnet Cheney adduces, there is a pertinent parallel in "Epithalamion," the very stanzaic form of which displays the domination of Petrarch:

> Tell me ye merchants daughters did ye see
> So fayre a creature in your towne before,
> So sweet, so louely, and so mild as she,
> Adorned with beautyes grace and vertues store,
> Her goodly eyes lyke Saphyres shining bright,
> Her forehead yuory white,
> Her cheekes lyke apples which the sun hath rudded,
> Her lips lyke cherryes charming men to byte,
> Her brest like to a bowle of creame vncrudded,
> Her paps lyke lyllies budded,
> Her snowy necke lyke to a marble towre,
> And all her body like a pallace fayre,
> Ascending vppe with many a stately stayre,
> To honors seat and chastities sweet bowre.
>
> [167–80]

It seems obvious that there is no irony in this standardized *descriptio puellae*, which closely follows the format of Sonnet 15. We have begun with the forehead and eyes and descended to neck and

breasts; if we descended further down that stately stair, we should
expect what in fact we do get in Spenser's less Petrarchan and more
public poems, a description of "those daintie parts, the dearlings of
delight":

> Her goodly thighes, whose glorie did appeare
> Like a triumphall Arch, and thereupon
> The spoiles of Princes hang'd, which were in battel won.
>
> [*FQ* 6.8.42]

But instead, in tandem with the traditional Sonnet 15, we ascend
up to the seat of honor—honor which has nothing to do with the
"quaint [cunt] honor" of Marvell's mistress[4]—much as we do also in
Milton's "Comus" where chaste honor is guarded, says the Lady,
by "the freedom of my mind."

To be sure, there is satire in Spenser's descriptions of corrupt
court life, and there is subtle anti-Petrarchism in the depiction of
Florimell; though, again, this is in the public narrative poems. But
as a rule the tradition overpowers and muffles whatever ironic impulse may exist: all perhaps proving that—as Byron, supreme
ironist, affirmed in a not too different context—"the cant is so much
stronger than the cunt."

By way of cautionary comment, I should observe that that
Byronic truism will be cardinal in the discussion of Donne that follows. But first, because the etiolated codas of Spenser may have
blurred the recollection of the strong codas examined in the previous
chapter, I offer the following from Habington, a poet whom George
Williamson would have described as being "on the fringe of the
Donne tradition." The poem is "To Roses in the Bosome of Castara."

> Ye blushing Virgins happy are
> In the chaste Nunn'ry of her brests,
> For hee'd prophane so chaste a faire,
> Who ere should call them *Cupids* nests.

---

4. That the broad jest is intended seems evident from the fact that an abstraction,
"honor," cannot turn to dust, whereas an organ, as part of the body assimilated to honor, can
physically deteriorate. But the jest is playful, not caustic, and thus does not shatter the
overall sexual-sacred bantering mood of the poem.

Transplanted thus how bright yee grow;
How rich a perfume doe yee yeeld?
In some close garden, Cowslips so
Are sweeter then i' th'open field.

In those white cloysters live secure
From the rude blasts of wanton breath,
Each houre more innocent and pure,
Till you shall wither into death.

Then that which living gave you roome,
Your glorious sepulcher shall be,
There wants no marble for a tombe,
Whose brests hath marble beene to me.

Though Habington on Castara, like Lovelace on Lucasta, was trying to project some light on the virtue of chastity and the virtues of
the chaste, nevertheless a strong case can be made that this coda is
trenchantly ironic. All the lofty spiritual homage expressed by
"nunnery" (presumably to be taken literally, not as in Hamlet to
Ophelia in that controverted passage or as in Faulkner on Temple
Drake), "close garden" (presumably also literally, as allusion to
hortus conclusus, a traditional title out of *Canticles* applied to the
Virgin Mary), and "cloisters"—all this apparent homage is under-
cut by the vehemence of this seemingly unforeseeable final execration, "Whose brests hath marble beene to me." From the perspective this coda offers, one can then detect hints of irony in the body
of the poem itself: "white cloysters" suggesting whited sepulchers,
"withering" into death, rather than something less defiling, for
example, "fading," or "transpiring" into death. In the sequence of
Habington's Castara poems, this poem is in the book on courtship
and thus may represent a subtle expression of his private frustration
at the sexual abstinence which his betrothed is enforcing and which
he is, out of convention, compelled to appear to be publicly embracing.

Now, one of the reasons for relegating Habington to the "fringe"
of the school of Donne would be that Williamson, who regarded
Eliot's essay on the Metaphysicals as holy writ, was intent on inflat-
ing the stock of approved minor poets like Donne himself, Herbert,
and Marvell, by intensifying prejudice against traditionally con-

temned poets like Cleveland, Lovelace, Cowley, Benlowes, and Suckling. Habington, with these others, would be an easy target if Donne could be elevated out of range to the uppermost choir of the canonical hierarchy—a process Robert Hillyer described in a passage from "A Letter to Robert Frost," which also contains its own neat coda:

> With what astonishment we witnessed Donne,
>   A poet we have always counted on,
> Whisked from his niche among the second shelves
>   And placed with Chaucer, Shakespeare,—and ourselves!

—Placed with Chaucer and Shakespeare, but not with Milton over whose "dislodgment" by the Metaphysicals Leavis, along with Eliot, Williamson, and a generation of critics, so grossly chortled: even as Leavis's recalcitrant epigones of the next generation were to chortle over the subsequent obloquy heaped on the monarchy of wit—if not on Donne himself.

These mercurial promotions and demotions are of no particular interest here; it suffices to note that with regard to Milton both his adulation in the first two decades of this century and his restoration in the most recent two, have often been based on nonpoetic, noncritical assumptions: in the first instance, on the grounds of his religious fervor, his moral intensity (Chambers had accused Donne of "ethical laxity"), his "spiritual" sublimity; and in the second instance, on the purely ethical grounds of his "genuineness" and "sincerity" ("Milton's *art* is eminently *civil*," C. S. Lewis's oxymoron, my emphasis), his seeming moneloquence, prophetic declamation, lack of ambiguity—all qualities allegedly antagonistic to those represented by Donne and exalted by the then regnant New Criticism.[5]

5. The supremely important fact for religious adulators and ethical restorers, with some subtle modulations among the latter, almost seemed to be that only Satan, Beelzebub, and their followers, along with Adam *after* the fall (respectively: Brooks, Warren, the New Critics, along with the *later* I. A. Richards), indulged in the vices of ambiguity, irony, and two-dimensional speech. There was a social-political context to all this, particularly in the United States and particularly in the sixties, when what Adorno has called "the jargon of authenticity" made "tone" and "sincerity" aesthetic values, and when riotous Vietnam War protests ludicrously took as targets "the Old Left and the New Critics" (cf. "Week of the Angry Artists," *Nation*, 20 Feb. 1967). One could only be reminded of the French anarchist ballad: "Nous dansons et nous chantons et nous dynamitons."

"Ironically"—*au pied de la lettre*—it was Cleanth Brooks who in 1951 called for the restoration of Milton on *artistic* grounds and not because "our besotted age needs Milton's moralistic vigor." But it was morality that was at issue, and Harold Bloom is right when he notes in his revised *The Visionary Company* that the critical debates of the thirties and forties, particularly with regard to Milton studies, sound today as though they had been carried on by church wardens and parsons—all fearful of discovering and exploring those subterranean depths in Milton which may loosely be described as the satanic and demonic. And a similar fear prevailed in much critical discussion of the Metaphysical poets in the twenties and thirties, with a like exclusion of the demonic, but in this case of a demonic that took the form of the sexual. Grierson, one may recall, went so far as to reject an authoritative reading because of its "radical want of delicacy."

In the preface to *Shakespeare's Bawdy* (1947), Eric Partridge scored a kindred phenomenon: "If Shakespearean criticism had not so largely been in the hands of academics and cranks, a study of Shakespeare's attitude towards sex and his use of the broad jest would probably have appeared at any time since 1918." This complaint was echoed and brought up to date by E. A. M. Colman in *The Dramatic Use of Bawdy in Shakespeare* (1974): "A glance through the Shakespearean criticism of the past fifteen to twenty years would suggest that the middle-class upbringing of many a sensitive critic has impelled him to hurry past the obscene in Shakespeare." It was out of this same claustral and emasculate intellectual climate, the universities of the twenties, thirties, and forties, that the largest body of our most influential criticism of Metaphysical poetry emerged—with the remarkable consequence that the most preposterous plays of wit were often read as univocally as the most heavy-handed, foot-stomping, prosy shrieks of Ezra Pound. The story, part of the anecdotal canon, is of C. Day Lewis—lecturing, fittingly, from none other than the chair of Keble and Arnold—in his puritan Marxist days, foundering over Marvell's imagery. The unforgettable attempt at saying something "witty," but sincere and ingenuous, concerned the conclusion of "To His Coy Mistress": "Yet there is surely something very odd about the image: if I try to visualize it, I see nothing but two lovers forever trying to squeeze

an india rubber ball through the bars of an iron gate." I shall
examine Marvell's image, which is delightfully sexual *and* sacred in
chapter 9, and so I merely want to point out now that Lewis's
misreading was of socioneurotic genesis, the collective neurosis of
the vestryman school of criticism. (Maybe an ounce of civet from
Aphra Behn's apothecary would have cured the ailment—though
perhaps better one should invoke here the ghost of Rochester on
"Monmouth the Witty.")

Only a similar numbness can explain the fact that three generations of critics had ceaselessly worried such vexatious problems as,
for example, whether this or that vigorously erotic poem could have
been written by Donne to this or that elderly dame, whether this or
that scabrous (to the vestrymen) exercise in wit could have been
written to the poet's sacramentally bonded and beloved wife,
whether Saint Lucy's Day could relate to the countess of the same
name, whether Magdalen Herbert could relate to the saint of the
same name, and so on. It would take the wit of Northrop Frye on
critics who read Shakespeare's sonnets as autobiography to do justice to this theme.

From the pietism of Walton to the literalism of Grosart, Gosse,
and Grierson (memorialized as "the three Gs"—H. W. Garrod
being the Bruckner of this mnemonic grouping), the interpretive
tradition had been fixed, and the corrections have come only in the
pioneering work of James Blair Leishman (however marred by
biographical fabrications), in Doniphan Louthan (a quickly
anathematized voice of sanity), in Empson (rejected as merely
another dualistic New Critic), and more recently in Shawcross's
notes to the poetry and in Bald's *Life*. In that older tradition, almost
every verse had to be construed autobiographically—with the attendant critical acuity reminiscent of those ingenious nineteenth-
century studies on Shakespeare as shipwright, law student, Roman
Catholic, and so on. But even the best of the New Critics beaming
in their hard Husserlian light would generally find their exegetical
key in some conjecture of Walton or Gosse, and the notion that
many of the songs and sonnets were exercises in wit, that the wit
was most engaging when most shocking—such a notion was generally lost sight of.

However, it was certainly not lost sight of in Donne's own time.

It was kept ever in mind, as in the following anonymous lines on
the epigram's coda, the ironic poems of Donne being an expansion
of this epigrammatic structure:

> The qualities rare in a bee that we meet
> In an epigram never should fail;
> The body should always be little and sweet,
> And a sting should be left in its tail.

We might now require the canniness of an Anthony Burgess or a
Thomas Pynchon with their acute sense of the dialectic of wit and
sex, of heads and tails, to elicit from these poems their pristine
meaning—though it seems to be a much younger novelist, Charles
Newman, in his lapidary *White Jass*, who has shown himself best
equipped to undertake this project of repristination. In any case,
the following is a small contribution to understanding what Alvin
Gouldner in a different context has called "the dark side" of this
dialectic.

I begin with the body of some poems before seeking a few reso-
lutions in their codas. First, one must look at some of the language
that has been glossed over or glossed incorrectly.

> I wonder, by my troth, what thou, and I
> Did, till we lov'd? were we not wean'd till then?
> But suck'd on countrey pleasures, childishly?
> Or snorted we in the seven sleepers den?
> T'was so; But this, all pleasures fancies bee.
> If ever any beauty I did see,
> Which I desir'd, and got, t'was but a dreame of thee.

Grierson read "The Good-Morrow" as a poem in which the wit "is
subordinate to the lover, pure and simple, singing, at times with
amazing simplicity and intensity"—though one cannot quite conceive the younger Donne being at any time particularly "pure,"
much less simple. Dame Helen Gardner comments on "suck'd on
countrey pleasures, childishly," with a gingerliness that is itself so
hesitant one cannot be sure of her meaning; she alludes nervously to
a possible reference to "cunt": as though that were not essential to
the wit here—as in Hamlet's "country matters"—and then univa-
lently reads "suck'd" as "suckled"; "seelily," the variant of "child-

ishly," is dismissed as repetitious, though one clear meaning of "seelily" is "genitally." It is no wonder that two decades later Clay Hunt, a good close reader but one bred in the vestryman tradition of the twenties and thirties, would describe himself as "shocked" on discovering that the first stanza was in fact about nothing but the most carnally saturated lust. Furthermore, when one recalls the orthography of the period, with *s* and *f* almost indistinguishable in script (the poems were not printed in Donne's lifetime), one ends up in this poem with a congeries of plays on country-cunt-pagan pleasures (compare, for example, the obsolescent modern equation of "farmer's daughter"); seals as both genitalia and as the brand marking the immature lovers as slaves of brute passion, not as mature "freedmen"; and lastly the crypto-identity of sucked-fucked (more pronounced in "The Flea," which may explain among the scores of extant "flea" poems, the rage for Donne's). When one looks at this congeries one sees that linguistically the poem owes less to polite speech than to the irrepressible *koine* of sex, and thematically less to Plato than to Saint Paul, where the polarization of flesh, slave, babes, lust and spirit, freedman, adult, love, is a constant theme. There is other cunning lingo and other sacred dialect in this first stanza, but enough has been catalogued here to make the point.

There is an amusing Freudian lapse as well as another misleading reference to Plato in Grierson on Donne's intermediate coda in "The Extasie," "Else a great Prince in prison lies." ("Oh Plato! Plato! you have paved the way.") Grierson read the poem as failing to exorcise completely the "unreal Platonism of the seventeenth century" and found Donne guilty of succumbing to the "dualism which he is trying to transcend." Grierson then added: "He [Donne] places them over against each other as separate entities and the lower bulks unduly." The whole vestryman school from Dame Helen Gardner up to but not including René Graziani (1968) assumed or asserted this "prince" to be the soul seeking to escape the body, whereas the surer identification of "prince" is with its slang near-homonym, "prick"—which is, no doubt, here "bulking unduly."

Such a reading would have elicited shudders of horror from these critics—as may be evidenced from the unfortunate ethnic slurs, whose superannuated nature emphasized the reactionary sexual bias of the school, the estimable Spitzer cast at the estimable Legouis when the latter merely dared to suggest that with the "prince" reference the poem was exposed as an exercise in seduction. Spitzer touted his own innocence and critical purity vis-à-vis Legouis who exuded "such gallic worldly wisdom," "such familiarity with the age-old strategems of a resourceful seducer," and so on. (It would be to indulge in equivocating to confirm my own reading by citing the dictionary definition of "prince" as "the male member of a royal family," though one might want to take more seriously the fact that in Rabelais the "male member" is *le fils du roi*.) The identification I have made is not uncommon, as in Rochester's "A Song of a Young Lady to Her Ancient Lover," where one of the "nobler parts" is identical with the slang "princycox," "princox," and other cognates of prince-prick.

This identification may also explain what seems to be an egregious flaw in what is otherwise one of Donne's most carefully crafted poems, "The Sunne Rising." After building up an elaborate equation of defective, changing love being to true and lasting love as the sun is to the two lovers' love, as schoolboys are to schoolmasters, as apprentices are to craftsmen (possibly, even, as the sauce is to the meal, amplified by playing on "saw'st," sourness, spice, time-thyme, season-seize on, and so forth, not unlike Yeats's "crazy salad" or Cummings's "Item" which ends with "exit the hors d'oeuvres")—after all of this, Donne concludes the second stanza by affirming that all kings lie in his own bed. But with a startling non sequitur, all the more startling because it is the only term that violates the basic equation of incompleteness being to perfection as time-bound love is to true love, he begins the next stanza with "She is all States, and all Princes, I." But in this particular poem, the prince is to the king precisely as schoolboy is to master, as apprentice is to craftsman, and so on, namely, another defective being seeking completion. Why did Donne not make use of the obvious term that would have suited his meter perfectly and that would have emphasized the perfect unity of the lovers, "She's all states, and all monarchs, I"? I don't want to appear excessively yantric, but that erect letter "I," set off by commas in the poem, is that same "prince" I have identified above, and that explains the use of this term rather than "monarch" here.

And if the two lovers have not yet consummated their union but are only preparing to do so ("the king *will* ride"), then from the opposite point of view the evolution from prince to king depends on the act of coition itself, on the act of "emballing," which also signifies the investment of the prince with the kingly orb and rod—as in *Henry VIII* (2.3.47–48) where the old lady tells Anne Bullen: "In faith, for little England / You'd venture an emballing." Lastly, one may note that the prince is the chief representative of the king in negotiations. Hence the parallelism of these lines regarding the prince in prison and the earlier lines concerning the "*souls* that negotiate there," "negotiate" being another word for sexual intercourse, as "plenipo" (fully potent negotiator) was also slang for the male member. Hence, also, the multiple punning in Cleveland's "The Antiplatonick":

> Like an Embassadour that beds a Queen
> With the nice Caution of a sword between.

Apart from the obvious puns, "Embassadour" plays back to "embassage," meaning "seduction," as in *The Faerie Queene* (3.9.28).

Thus the point of "The Extasie" is not to resolve "Platonic dualism" or with Spitzer, Warren, and Tillyard to define "neoplatonic mysticism"; rather, it is an "answer to the Platonicks" by tracing the process of lovemaking (not unlike Keats's process of soul-making) and so extolling the interinanimation of persons by bodily union—a terrifying prospect to the vestryman school of criticism, well summed up by C. S. Lewis, who found the possibility of a sexual resolution of the poem "singularly unpleasant."

I shall not give an extended reading of the whole of "Aire and Angels," but I regard the coda to that poem as a strongly ironic reversal hinted at, among other places, in the reference to "love's pinnace," with an even more ambitiously ambiguous play than that above on "prince." "Pinnace" here includes both male (penis) and female (a common slang term for vagina, and by metonymy, a whore). There is no question about the pinnace-female equation; there may be some about the reference to the male. In support of the latter, I would offer Herrick's "Upon Groynes" and "The Plaudite" (that is, "the clap") and would cite Carew's "A Rapture" (where one should not overlook the sexual enjambment):

> Yet my tall pine shall in the Cyprian strait
> Ride safe at anchor, and unlade her freight:
> My rudder with thy bold hand, like a tri'd
> And skilful pilot, thou shalt steer, and guide
> My bark into love's channel, where it shall
> Dance, as the bounding waves do rise or fall.
>
> [85–90]

Since the *membrum virile* was termed by Horace and others *cauda*, I want to see what light another of Donne's codas may shed on a poem that is regarded as relatively unambiguous. Almost all readings of "The Relique" assume the last three lines to be in direct continuity with the patent imagery of the poem; and the whole is regarded as the most sincere of tributes to the beloved—even the perceptive Arnold Stein regards the poem as "gay," rather than, as I would see it, morbid and mordant:

> but now alas,
> All measure, and all language, I should passe,
> Should I tell what a miracle shee was.

Since the poem mentions Mary Magdalen, and since Donne in his correspondence has drawn some farfetched comparisons of that saint with Magdalen Herbert, the conventional reading rather facilely assumes that there can be no irony in this coda because that would have affronted the alleged model or recipient of the poem. But I would reemphasize, particularly against Joan Bennett, who reads the love poems as exercises in *la vie dévote*, that this matter of a possible affront is moot. What undoubtedly would have delighted the recipient of the poem, whoever she was, *if* a she, is not the putative biographical dedication but the wit itself,[6] a wit which—as in the Habington example earlier—would have been all the more

---

6. Cowley's decree in "Ode: Of Wit," was honored, as it were, only in the breach: "Much less can that have any place / At which a Virgin hides her face"—an allusion to one of the more interesting parlor games of the period, with its own bawdy name.

exhilarating by the coda's very faintly clueing the alert reader to the fact that this exalted praise is a foil to set off more sharply the figure of this seemingly saintly woman as outrageously lust-ridden and corrupt.

In fact, our expectation—like the speaker in the poem who exposes this corruption—has been only partially cozened, as a closer examination may disclose.

> When my grave is broke up againe
> Some second ghest to entertaine,
> (For graves have learn'd that woman-head
> To be to more then one a Bed)
>   And he that digs it, spies
> A bracelet of bright haire about the bone,
>   Will he not let'us alone,
> And thinke that there a loving couple lies,
> Who thought that this device might be some way
> To make their soules,. at the last busie day,
> Meet at this grave, and make a little stay?

The length of this single sentence almost leads one to overlook that it is not a statement of fact, but a question, a question that is premised on a dubiety which runs through the entire poem, and which is revealed here by the emphasis on "think" rather than "know." The underlying context hints at the folk belief that the adultress's crimes will be disclosed after death, and the whole has a strong suggestion (second guest-ghost; woman-head, not maiden-head) of promiscuity. If so, then "device" would have both its original sense of "separated" and its secondary sense of "ruse" lurking beneath the more common meaning; similarly with "lies," meaning both "reposes" and "deceives." The guarded conclusion is that she had in life comported herself like a whore, and hence her willingness to make a "little stay," meaning "lewd interlude" as thrice repeated in "The Blossome." The substantive "stay" means "reconciliation," but it is also slang for "cuckold" and, particularly with the verb "make," points to "sty" or "stew," that is, "brothel." "Busy" and "business" both have strong sexual implications, again, as in "The Blossome": "Here lyes my businesse and here I will stay." So one might be warranted in comparing the "busie day" of

Donne with that of Shakespeare which "roused the ribald crows" (*Troilus and Cressida* 4.2.8–9), where "ribald" means not only "raucous" but also "lewd"—the latter as in *Antony and Cleopatra* (2.10.10), "the ribaldried nag of Egypt."

Under the title, "Whore of Babylon," anything Romish was identified with harlotry; but this identification would have been strengthened in Donne's own time by the fact that the brothels of London were still linked to the pre-Reformation diocese of Winchester. E. A. M. Colman, in the context of Gloucester's accusation that the bishop of Winchester "giv'st whores indulgences [in the literal as well as the technical theological sense] to sin" (*1 Henry VI* 1.3.35), cites the following from Jonson's "An Execration upon Vulcan":

> they streight nois'd it out for Newes,
> 'Twas verily some Relique of the Stewes:
> And this a Sparkle of that fire let loose
> That was lock'd up in the Winchestrian Goose
> Bred on the Banck, in time of Poperie,
> When Venus there maintain'd the Misterie.

There are interesting parallels between this and the second stanza of Donne's poem:

> If this fall in a time, or land,
> Where mis-devotion doth command,
> Then, he that digges us up, will bring
> Us, to the Bishop, and the King,
>   To make us Reliques; then
> Thou shalt be a Mary Magdalen, and I
>   A something else thereby;
> All women shall adore us, and some men;
> And since at such time, miracles are sought,
> I would have that age by this paper taught
> What miracles wee harmeless lovers wrought.

"Mis-devotion" or "Mass-devotion" both suggest continuation of the deception; the "Pope's Mass" for the Protestant sixteenth century was invariably allegorized as a whore. The woman shall be a Magdalen (another veiled whore), but he "a something else," that is, an unspeakably humiliated cuckold—Shawcross, Redpath, and others have suggested David or Jesus! Since in this anti-Petrarchan tradition all women are whores at heart, all women shall adore, but since only some men have the horns planted on them, fewer of them shall adore. The "paper," this poem, is literally a lie and therefore cannot attest to holiness, since it is of the same order as innumerable forged authentications of sham miracles for sale in countries where "mass-devotion" is practiced. Lastly, and with a view to the final stanza, it may be emphasized that miracles were defined in catechisms of the day as acts "praeter, extra, or *contra* naturam."

I am even inclined to speculate that lurking behind the "miracle" here is the most puzzled-over passage in all the prophets, perhaps in all the Bible, a passage that still defies interpretation by modern scholars, however less fascinated by it they are than were their seventeenth- and eighteenth-century forebears: "And a woman shall compass a man." Whatever it meant or means, it suggested to the common reader some reversal of relationships (between Jehovah and his people), some inexplicable, indeed in Jeremiah, some miraculous priority or ascendancy for woman, priority or ascendancy which even until recently was viewed widely as "unnatural."[7] The passage from the prophet certainly has a bearing on the coda to Cowley's "The Change," which I shall cite later in the context of Donne's "Aire and Angels." Lastly, to have done with this theme and this excursus, it does not seem likely Jeremiah has much bearing on Donne's well-known compass conceit, which Rosemary Freeman traced to a different religious source. Whatever biblical roots it may have are more likely in the phrase, "God encompasses," since throughout that elaborate metaphor the man is clearly the "prime mover." But, hence, by another spiral of meaning, the popular corruption of that quotation to "goat and compass-

---

7. If some of my readings appear rather forced—"meaning's press and screw," one might say, citing Coleridge—in countering the vestrymen, I would point to a twentieth-century, widely approved, and more or less academically respectable translation of this passage from Jeremiah which reads: "the woman must encompass the man with devotion." The moral lesson of this hermeneutical note may be that vestrymen lurk in every coign of vantage, for that latter translation was rendered by a group of ordained, celibate scholars; whereas their counterparts on the Protestant side of this sexual and exegetical divide, more simply, more accurately, maybe even more honestly, translated: "The woman woos the man."

es" may be lurking behind this same compass conceit, since in "A Valediction..." the poet must "obliquely runne" in the identical trajectory (zodiacal and terrestrial) in which "the Goat is runne / To fetch new lust" in "A Nocturnall upon S. Lucies day."

Donne concludes "The Relique":

> First, we lov'd well and faithfully,
> Yet knew not what wee lov'd nor why,
> Difference of sex no more wee knew
> Than our Guardian Angells doe;
>   Comming and going wee
> Perchance might kisse, but not between those meales;
>   Our hands ne'r toucht the seales,
> Which nature, injur'd by late law sets free:
> These miracles wee did; but now alas,
> All measure, and all language, I should passe,
> Should I tell what a miracle shee was.

If one reads "first" to mean "in the beginning" we loved faithfully, then the implied "second" suggests the conclusion that subsequently there was infidelity. That they *knew* neither what they loved nor why indicates the degree to which they had succumbed (presumably at her instigation) to the Aristotelian "abdication of reason" in the violence of a purely carnal attachment. As to "guardian angels," in the doctrine of the Schoolmen angels differed from one another as species differs from species, and here in this passage, by a difference far greater than merely the difference between male and female: that is, by that absolute difference constituted by his fidelity and her infidelity. On the other hand, the stated absence of sexual differentiation again hints at practices then regarded as "unnatural," including presumably exchange and reversal of sexual roles. Thus, the miracles are miracles not of virtue but of lust, as the latter would have been popularly defined.

As for "coming and going," Donne used the latter in "The Legacie" in our contemporary sense of "orgasm," and there is no doubt it was employed with the same meaning by Shakespeare in *Antony and Cleopatra* (1.2.66). As to "coming," it too is used by Shakespeare in the modern orgasmic sense—on this point Colman fails to disprove Partridge—in *Twelfth Night* (3.4.32–33):

Olivia. Wilt thou go to bed, Malvolio?
Malvolio. To bed? Ay, sweet heart, and I'll come to thee.

This whole dialogue is rife with Malvolio's bawdy, to which Olivia understandably gives no countenance; but the chronological reversal betrays the *entendre*: first there is the "to bed," and *then* the "I'll come."[8] Donne in the above stanza is engaging in the same kind of punning.

"Meals," too, one suspects, retains its contemporary sexual reference. Thus the "miracle" resides precisely in the fact that the ordinary and normal means of manifesting affection were never deployed, were in fact "perverted" by her unnatural passion. "Injured nature" is convertible with "unnatural"; it is the law of the flesh as opposed to the law of the spirit. The suggestion of other "unnatural" practices is equally strong: if their hands never touched the seals, we are left to assume what did. (Is the *h* to be dropped from "harmless"?) Finally, the narrative of what a "miracle"[9] she was would be the story of her instigation of these "meanes" ("The Blossome") and of her unutterably exorbitant lust—a story which is sad for the narrator-victim ("alas") and a story which would, moreover, by reason of its excesses strain the listener's credulity, as well as violate the mean of virtue and the measure of poetry.

One could extend this explication, but it would be even more tedious than the above, which should suffice to indicate how the poem can be misread by ignoring the ironic thrust of the coda. The wit of the entire undertaking resides in the ambiguity of every contributory phrase, an ambiguity apparently slanted strongly toward the convention of a sequence of praises climaxed by the aposiopetic "alas, / All measure, and all language, I should passe, / Should I tell what a miracle shee was." But to imply some kind of inenarrable exaltation here would entail a slack finale, one certainly jarring with the unconventional wit of Donne. It would, fur-

---

8. Cf. the flamboyantly rich coda to Cleveland's "To the State of Love; or, The Senses Festival":

> Then have at all, the pass is got,
> For coming off, oh name it not:
> Who would not die upon the spot.

9. "Miraculous," as adjective modifying almost any enclosure (e.g., box, cave, garden), signaled a reference to the vagina.

thermore, be quite out of harmony with the obviously ironic closure to the companion poem, "The Funerall."

So too with that gnawed and clawed bone of contention, the conclusion to "Aire and Angels": how can it be, the inquiry goes, that after a poem so lauding the total equality of the lovers, Donne can so "insolently" (Leavis) affirm:

> Just such disparitie
> As is twixt Aire and Angells puritie,
> 'Twixt womens love, and mens will ever bee.

But the reversal is exactly as stated (Jonson's "women are but men's shadows") and is intended to illuminate, first, the accepted truism that no matter how compatible the sexes are, the woman's contribution to the sexual act marks her as passive and inferior, and this inferiority is, by metathesis, a "just disparity." Thus, Donne in "The First Anniversary" (103–04) emphasizes women's inferiority both before and *after* the fall: "They were to good ends and they are so *still*, / But accessory." Leavis, less a vestryman than a Whig interpreter of poetry, would no doubt have preferred to Donne's surprising coda the following moral stereotype from Stanley's "To Celia Pleading Want of Merit":

> and thou shalt see
> That equal love knows no disparity.

Second, Donne's coda is intended to affirm the physiological reality of the woman's body surrounding the male organ as the state surrounds the prince in "The Sunne Rising" and as the sphere of air surrounds the angel—all of this making use of Donne's definition of the sexual organ as the "centrique part" in Elegie 18 and "Love's Alchemie," and also as in Cleveland's "To the State of Love," where the pun on "state" (political entity: condition) is more pronounced than it is in "The Sunne Rising":

> How would thy Center take my Sense
> When admiration doth commense
> At the extream Circumference?

[37–39]

This generates a redoubling disparity further described in Cowley's "The Change":

> So powerful is this change, it render can,
> My *outside Woman*, and your *inside Man*.

In similar fashion I would read "The Legacie," "The Anniversarie," "Twicknam Garden," "Farewell to Love," and "A Nocturnall upon S. Lucies day" (the latter being about Christian remorse and extreme postcoital physical and psychological depression) as poems in which the coda obliquely confutes all that precedes, thus setting up an irony that is all the stronger because all the more "subtile."

This treatment of Donne closes the present chapter, a closure that can be signaled by the following lines of Robert Burns, which were misread and misconstrued by Yeats in *Ideas of Good and Evil*, and further misread by Bateson in *English Poetry*—illustrating once again how the words of dead poets (certainly as in some of my exegeses above) are modified in the commentaries of the living. "An annotator has his scruples, too," says Crispin.

> The wan moon is setting ayont the white wave,
> And time is setting with me, *oh*!

VII: Culmination

In the preceding chapters I have been suggesting that just as all poems are one poem (Stevens's poem of the central poem) and all philosophical problems are one problem (footnotes to Heraclitus's "strife of opposites"), so, too, all structures are ultimately variants of one structure. That single poem, that single problem, that single structure symbolizes, defines, intensifies, and fitfully allays the ultimate mystery of man, conceived in our original heuristic myth as the intersection of the infinite and the finite, spirit and matter, unity and multiplicity. To the degree that a given poetic structure or a combination of such poetic structures illuminates the nature and momentarily relieves the strain of that mystery, to that degree the structure, in its embodiment, is connatural to man, and the poem is recognized as beautiful.

The relationship of coda to the "body" of the poem is the relationship of simplicity to complexity. In chapters 5 and 6 I have examined this relationship *as such*; that is, I have examined the nexus of the two—the synaptic point, synoptically grasped, of multiplicity *and* unity. In what follows I shall be concerned not so much with this relationship in its seemingly static condition, where one seems able to contemplate the nodal juncture itself, but with the *sequential development* through multiplicity *on the way to* unity. Obviously this is a matter of selective focus, since all of these patterns are homologous. But here as elsewhere, *il faut distinguer pour unir*. In both cases the aesthetic power is generated by the conjunction, by the collision of body and coda. In the preceding two chapters the emphasis was primarily on the coda; in this chapter the emphasis will be primarily on the body, on the fragment that presumes the whole, the plural that announces the singular, the Duessa that portends the Una.

My first type of linear complexification, "prepositional energy," takes its name from Francis Berry's *Poets Grammar*—though what I shall be doing has possibly only this title in common with Berry, whose concern is with a different kind of poetic strategy. Since it is my contention that, other things being equal, it is the poem best incorporating the greatest variety of these and similar structures which will be the superior artwork, it should come as no surprise that I cite again some familiar lines:

> The same that oft-time hath
> Charmed magic casements, opening *on* the foam
> *Of* perilous seas, *in* faery lands forlorn.

Or again:

> Adieu! adieu! thy plaintive anthem fades
> *Past* the near meadows, *over* the still stream
> *Up* the hill side.

The effect of the sequence is to suggest for a moment a closer and closer "fix" on the goal, as we reduce more and more vague approximations to what appear to be specific directions: "Where?" "There, *past* ... , *over* ... , *up*." But in fact this deliberately lapidary arrangement of locatives, which by triangulation seems to indicate a specific place, guides us to nowhere; we are still adrift and without bearings: this topos ends up being outopos, the prepositioning is pre-positioning.

> *In* the instant *of* speech,
> The breadth *of* an accelerando moves,
> Captives the being, widens.
>   ["A Primitive Like an Orb"]

For an "instant of speech," we seemed to have discovered our destination, to have captured being, only to realize on reflection that the elusive wraith has again escaped, and we are again wandering aimlessly the strange seas. Hence Stevens's last line concludes, "Captives the being, widens—and *was* there." Similarly, Blake's Thel, incarnation of amorphous velleity, can only long for the unattainable voice "*of* him that walketh *in* the garden *in* the evening time."

Rhetorically, it is almost as though we had Quintilian's *gradatio quae dicitur "klimax"*—but *without* the climax, in the ordinary contemporary meaning of that word. This staircase does not bring us to the upper room, the cenacle of union, but rather is like Charlotte Mew's "remote and quiet stair / Which winds to silence and a space of sleep / Too sound for waking and for dreams too deep"— "dreams" unlike those of Jacob "when he from Esau fled / to Padan-Aram in the field of Luz." The mood engendered is one of certitude immediately deliquescing into doubt. It is literally purgatorial in that we are aware of the poor, low stages to be surmounted, the stairs "mysteriously meant," but have no vision of the Eden at the summit. It is thus the "winding stair" of Yeats and Eliot but certainly not the *gradus ad veritatem* of Cusanus or the winding stair of Herbert in "Jordan I."

Even when the directives are less vague than in the Keats passages above, one is still left with this feeling of unfulfillment, as if one's purchase on each rung of the ladder, on each grade of the *scala sancta*, was tenuous. To the unceasing question, "Ubi sunt?" one should consider the precise accuracy of the following answers, precision and accuracy which nevertheless leave one wholly "at sea," the sea of which Sassoon writes in "Limitations"—where the enjambment of transcendence and the oscillation between positive and negative imagery may also be noted:

> Go on, whoever you are, your lines can be
> A whisper *in* the music *from* the weirs
> *Of* song that plunge and tumble toward the sea
> That is the uncharted mercy of our tears.

And the unattainable Lamia after whom *we* must all lust is glimpsed:

> Fair, *on* a sloping green *of* mossy tread,
> *By* a clear pool, wherein she passioned.

And the "Lamia" of metaphysicians

> ... might, after all, be a wanton,
> Abundantly beautiful, eager,

> Fecund,
> *From* whose being *by* starlight, *on* sea coast,
> The innermost good of their seeking
> Might come in the simplest of speech.
>
> > ["Homunculus et la Belle Etoile"]

There is also the unattainable "Lamia" of Stevens himself, whose absence is made present to us

> ... *in* the isolation *of* the sky,
> *At* evening.

Finally, Hopkins's doxological directive (with which one might compare the similar formula concluding "The Wreck of the Deutschland") to the "Lamia" of Christians:

> for Christ plays in ten thousand places,
> Lovely in limbs, and lovely in eyes not his
> *To* the Father *through* the features *of* men's faces.

That in each instance the number of phrases is three may be due to my own more or less unintended selectivity, but it may also be that the recurrence of three phrases is unconsciously an attempt by the poet (like the "intentional ternaries" of the philosopher) to convey the nature of triangulation, of location. Three is also the constituent of the simplest of all polygons, of the simplest enclosure which, like the sexual delta, can "captive being." Lastly, and for present purposes most importantly, three is the number of multiplicity par excellence, multiplicity here at the service of a unified theme, with the entire figure another expression of the almost aesthetically perfect: trinity in unity, and utter complexity in utter simplicity.

But in the prepositional sequences above the unity is not yet glimpsed; it is merely implicit or latent in the triadic structure. We have the triangulated multiplicity but not the circular unity; we do not have that "worke divine" which in *The Faerie Queene* is "partly circulaire, / And part triangulaire" (2.9.22), and in *Paradise Lost* (2.1048) is "undetermin'd square or round." And this absence may explain both the hopeful expectancy and the rueful sense of being unguided and unsponsored that these citations tend to arouse. Ernst Bloch—whose importance in any humanistic literary criticism has been well noted by Thomas McFarland—seems to me to refer to the implications of this structure toward the end of *Atheism in Christianity*, where he says, "The best of Christian mysticism can grip one powerfully with the *newness of its topos and its undying spark of utopianism*—a spark struck by something very near to us indeed, but something which has not yet fully shown itself" (original italics). It is this proximity and remoteness that is brought out in my last example from Jeffers's "Apology for Bad Dreams":

> It is not good to forget *over* what gulfs the spirit
> *Of* the beauty *of* humanity,
> The petal *of* a lost flower blown seaward *by* the night wind,
>   floats *to* its quietness.

After these brief introductory comments, I turn now to some other patterns that figure forth the hope (with Bloch), the instinct (with Stevens), or the fact (with Herbert) that every fragment presupposes a whole, that (with Cusanus) every trinity entails a unity. And I suggest again that it is the connaturality of such patterns in a given body of verse that is one of the causes of aesthetic *connaissance* (co-nascence). I begin with another familiar passage I have already cited:

> I wonder, by my troth, what thou, and I
> Did, till we lov'd? were we not wean'd till then?
> But suck'd on countrey pleasures, childishly?
> Or snorted we in the seven sleepers den?
> T'was so; But this, all pleasures fancies bee.
> If ever any beauty I did see,
> Which I desir'd, and got, t'was but a dreame of thee.
>
> And now good morrow to our waking soules.

This is clearly a movement from the fragmented to the unified or, as I shall detail in the ninth chapter, from the corpuscular to the undular. The structural evolution is usually regarded as paralleling or reinforcing the theme of carnal love evolving into spiritual love. But here, again, as in many of my earlier examples, one may maintain that the dramatic action is itself only another analogue of the experience everyman undergoes in passing, personally or symbolically, from the multiple and broken to the simple and unified. This

experience of "passing over," or journeying through complexities
and difficulties, must account in part for the memorable quality of
the following passages, which are as metrically affecting as is the
"golden section" geometrically—and for the same proportionate
reason.

> It is a beauteous evening   calm and free.

Or, again from Wordsworth, though less striking possibly because
less trammeled by multiplicity (assuming no syneresis above):

> She was a maiden city   bright and free.
> ["On the Extinction of the Venetian Republic"]

> But now the sun is rising   calm and bright.
> ["Resolution and Independence"]

> The horizon's bound, a huge peak,   black and huge.
> [*The Prelude* 1.378]

So also with the following from Thomson, Crashaw, Owen, and
Stevens respectively:

> The mighty river flowing   dark and deep.
> ["The City of Dreadful Night"]

> So spirituall   pure and fair.
> ["Hymn to Saint Teresa"]

> And sailed my spirit surging,   light and clear.
> ["Apologia pro Poemate Meo"]

> Ubiquitous concussion,   slap and sigh.
> ["The Comedian as the Letter C"]

> Become a single being,   sure and true.
> ["World without Peculiarity"]

It is a structure that gains much of its richness by juxtaposing the
heavily polysyllabic latinate with simple monosyllables, as in the
following from the first book of *Paradise Lost*:

> The dismal situation   waste and wild.
>   [60]

> Ethereal temper, massy,   large and round.
>
> [285]

This is much more effective than the following from "Lycidas" and "Comus" respectively:

> I come to pluck your Berries   harsh and crude.
>
> [3]

> I touch with chaste palms   moist and cold.
>
> [918]

The structure may even provide a key to interpretation, as in the following, also from *Paradise Lost*:

> Show'rs on her Kings Barbaric   Pearl and Gold.
>
> [2.4]

I suspect that the ordinary reading of this line, probably because one assumes a caesura after "Kings," has the adjective modifying "Pearl and Gold." The only gloss I have been able to locate is by Edward Hawkins (the "Principal Hawkins" of Newman's *Apologia*) in his modest *variorum* of 1824: "And this pearl and gold is called *barbaric*." While I don't want to force interpretations like some kind of structuralist Bentley, our present pattern indicates that the adjective modifies "Kings."[1]

All these passages share a common design with what must be the only line in "The Waste Land" one has ever heard quoted not for its psychological or sociological import but for its "music" alone:

> Inexplicable splendour of Ionian   white and gold.

This line from Eliot and the passage from Vaughan above make clear that it is not the inversion as such that most affects the reader but the complexity-simplicity collision. However, the inverted form—which itself entails a collision with an implied norm—is admittedly more common and may be regarded as providing a kind

---

1. This reading may be confirmed by the following from Book 6:

    This continent of spacious Heav'n, adorn'd
    With Plant, Fruit, Flow'r Ambrosial,   Gems and Gold. [474–75]

of grace note to the basic leitmotiv, as in the following from Tennyson, which echoes Coleridge, and from Robert Bridges:

Uplift a thousand voices   full and sweet.
["Ode Sung at the Opening of the International Exhibition"]

Go thou with music   sweet and loud.
["Christabel," 487]

With promise of strength and manhood   full and fair.
["On a Dead Child"]

I remarked above when discussing prepositional triads the emphasis on quest and (frustrated) discovery that seems to underlie
that structural format. It is the sigil of the irrepressible "Ubi?"
which denominates man as *homo viator*, whose authentic experience
(*erfahren*) can only come when he is journeying (*fahren*) from multiplicity to unity.[2] And, similarly, I would suggest that this denomi-
nation as wayfarer at least in part accounts for the unquestioned
appeal of the following lines of Wordsworth explicitly concerned
with a journey:

Earth hath not anything to show more fair,
Dull would he be of soul who could pass by
A sight so touching in its majesty,
This city.
["Composed upon Westminster Bridge"]

Here the first three lines suggest the suspense of the "long coming,"
which is fulfilled in the apocalyptic moment, in the surprising discovery of the hitherto concealed "This city."
So, too, with another poem (the eighth line reproduces the pattern above) about an equally memorable journey:

2. The medieval historian, Gerhard Ladner, regards the *homo viator* theme as derived
from that of *contemptus mundi*, the latter giving birth to such wandering figures as the
troubadors, crusaders, knights errant, etc. This, however, seems to ignore the universality of
the "wayfarer" motif, which is not confined to Christianity or to Europe but springs from
what Stevens calls "the Westwardness of things."

> Much have I travelled in the realms of gold,
>   And many goodly states and kingdoms seen;
>   Round many western islands have I been
> Which bards in fealty to Apollo hold.
> Oft of one wide expanse had I been told
>   That deep-browed Homer ruled as his demesne;
>   Yet did I never breathe its pure serene
> Till I heard Chapman speak out loud and bold:
> Then felt I like some watcher of the skies
>   When a new planet swims into his ken;
> Or like stout Cortez when with eagle eyes
>   He stared at the Pacific—and all his men
> Looked at each other with a wild surmise—
>   Silent, upon a peak in Darien.
>   ["On First Looking into Chapman's Homer"]

A few critics have been rather severe about the dreary character of this octave with its tired and clichéd imagery. But this stereotyping is precisely what is crucial. Keats's previous notions of Homer had been mired in the static figures of a dead tradition. Suddenly that tradition was cleansed, was renovated by Chapman—renovated so utterly that only the most fresh and the most "modern" imagery (Cortez not Ulysses, telescopes not Rumor) would be adequate to the new experience.

However, what is more interesting in the context of our structural analysis is that it is the octave that is end-stopped and fragmented, and thus representative of the difficulty of the voyage, and it is the sestet that is most enjambed and unified, and thus representative of attainment and peace, with the coda expressing the final shock of discovery. I would point out also (with a view to my later comments on ecstasy as the experience that transforms man from an isolated individual to a communal being, from esse to co-esse, from *Mensch* to *Mitmensch*) that when the symbolic leader, Cortez, experiences the transcendent his men experience solidarity with one another: he stared *at the Pacific*, his men looked *at each other*. This is Keats's anticipation of Husserl's "enigmatic statement" (Merleau-Ponty): "Transcendental subjectivity is inter-subjectivity." As to the specifically literary-historical problem (however poetically trivial) of Cortez-Pacific, Keats was forced to conflate the realms of gold of Tenochtitlan with the classic, and therefore pacific-horizontal, art of Homer (the wild Atlantic being Romantic-vertical). Neither Balboa nor Coronado, the other two possible candidates from among the sons of Geryon, could fuse both of these images, the calm ocean and the Eldorado of Moctezuma.

This pattern of the broken journey culminating in the surprising vision of unity must also partially explain the universal popularity of Yeats's "The Lake Isle of Innisfree":

I will arise and go now, and go to Innisfree,
And a small cabin build there, of clay and wattles made;
Nine bean rows will I have there, a hive for the honey bee,
    And live alone in the bee-loud glade.

And I shall have some peace there, for peace comes dropping slow,
Dropping from the veils of the morning to where the cricket sings;
There midnight's all a glimmer, and noon a purple glow,
    And evening full of the linnet's wings.

I will arise and go now, for always night and day
I hear lake water lapping with low sounds by the shore;
While I stand on the roadway, or on the pavements gray,
    I hear it in the deep heart's core.

I do not want to make too much of the fact that in each stanza it is *three* long lines that find their climax in the one short line of peace and fulfillment. But that these are also the broken lines, with a caesura called for in each, suggests again the plodding nature, the tediousness of the journey—which, unlike Stevens's "Page from a Tale," here culminates in the *visio pacis* of the unbroken terminal line.

This same pattern is established in a more elaborate poem by Yeats explicitly about the relation of fragment to whole:

All things uncomely and broken, all things worn out and old,
The cry of a child by the roadway, the creak of a lumbering cart,
The heavy steps of the plowman, splashing the wintry mold,
Are wronging your image that blossoms a rose in the deeps of my
    heart.

The wrong of unshapely things is a wrong too great to be told;
I hunger to build them anew and sit on a green knoll apart,
With the earth and the sky and the water, remade, like a casket of
    gold
For my dreams of your image that blossoms a rose in the deeps of
    my heart.

["Aedh Tells of the Rose in His Heart"]

Here the broken lines, which reflect not only the "broken things" but the chaos of existence itself, find their harmonic unity in the rhythmic arabesque of the last line in each stanza—and, again, of this corpuscular-undular structure I shall have more to say in chapter 9.

In the repetition in those terminal lines there may be a clue to the fascination of all poetic refrains. Over and over, almost spirally, they proclaim the unity that awaits the faithful wayfarer at the end of each stanza of his journey and ultimately at journey's end itself.[3] And that end, so the myth proclaims, is in the words of a refrain from "Perle," "grounde of all my blysse." In the light of this observation on the function of the refrain, we may consider the following superb stanzas from a poem about another voyage home:

When the breeze of a joyful dawn blew free
In the silken sail of infancy,
The tide of time flowed back with me,
The forward-flowing tide of time;
And many a sheeny summer-morn,
Adown the Tigris I was borne,
By Bagdat's shrines of fretted gold,
High-walled gardens *green and old;*

3. The exitus-reditus theme is central to all religious-philosophical speculation from Plato through Hegel and Marx. As I have indicated earlier, it is not essential to my argument whether one believes this journey symbolizes exit from the womb or exit from the *magna mater* of absolute spirit. One may define *Geworfenheit* with neo-Freudians as expulsion from the mother, or define it in Heidegger's original sense, and qualified by Marcel, as exile from being's plenitude. However, if in the light of the original heuristic myth one employs the fuller description of the circuit, *egressus-progressus-regressus*, one would have to view "regressus" not with Freud and more emphatically not with Otto Rank as *regressus ad uterum* (and hence as a pejorative) but as return to some higher state, to the utopia etched in the individual or group psyche and which seems to motivate the construction of all earthly utopias.

True Mussulman was I and sworn,
For it was in the golden prime
  Of good Haroun Alraschid.

Anight my shallop, rustling through
The low and bloomed foliage, drove
The fragrant, glistening deeps, and clove
The citron-shadows in the blue;
By garden porches on the brim,
The costly doors flung open wide,
Gold glittering through lamplight dim,
And broidered sofas on each side.
  In sooth it was a goodly time,
  For it was in the golden prime
    Of good Haroun Alraschid.

Often, where clear-stemmed platans guard
The outlet, did I turn away
The boat-head down a broad canal
From the main river sluiced, where all
The sloping of the moonlit sward
Was damask-work, and deep inlay
Of braided blooms unmown, which crept
Adown to where the water slept.
  A goodly place, a goodly time,
  For it was in the golden prime
    Of good Haroun Alraschid.

A motion from the river won
Ridged the smooth level, bearing on
My shallop through the star-strown calm,
Until another night in night
I entered, from the clearer light,
Embowered vaults of pillared palm,
Imprisoning sweets, which, as they clomb
Heavenward, were stayed beneath the dome
  Of hollow boughs. A goodly time,
  For it was in the golden prime
    Of good Haroun Alraschid.
    [Tennyson, "Recollections of the Arabian Nights"]

If the refrain constitutes the principle of unity in each stanza, and if unity is the ontological ground of multiplicity, then each stanza of this poem, like each stanza of "The Lake Isle of Innisfree" (or the whole of "Pied Beauty"), is a kind of yantra of two of the most universal symbols of the mysterious relation of the one and the many, the mighty fountain whose single source generates innumerable jets and the great-rooted blossomer whose single trunk grounds innumerable branches. That cadence is from a man named Yeats; the following is from Donne who is also writing about a voyage back to unity. The coda of "Hymne to God My God" is "Therefore that he may raise the Lord throws down," and all the poem emerges out of this initial paradox and represents the "crumbling" of that single text; the heir of this method of exposition, as John Crowe Ransom showed, is the New Criticism, and a major source, as Walter Ong showed, is Ramist nominalism. But this is not merely a model for poetry explication; it is a model for almost all formal discourse. Thus, students of medieval and Renaissance manuals on the art of preaching have noted that the generative *thema* was compared to the trunk of the tree and the *amplificatio* to the branches. As the Qur'an says, "A good word is a good tree; its trunk is firm, its branches are in heaven."

Even in poems broaching the most awesome, the most terrifying subject, one responds with pleasure to this great-rooted structure:

> Its edges foamed with amethyst and rose,
> Withers once more the old blue flower of day:
> There where the ether like a diamond glows,
>   Its petals fade away.
>
> A shadowy tumult stirs the dusky air;
> Sparkle the delicate dews, the distant snows;
> The great deep thrills—for through it everywhere
>   The breath of Beauty blows.
>
> I saw how all the trembling ages past,
> Molded to her by deep and deeper breath,
> Near'd to the hour when Beauty breathes her last
>   And knows herself in death.
>
>   [Russell, "The Great Breath"]

Russell's poem certainly represents a "swerve" via Pater and Swinburne from its most evident British forebear, Herbert's "Vertue":

> Sweet day, so cool, so calm, so bright,
> The bridall of the earth and skie:
> The dew shall weep thy fall to night;
>   For thou must die.
>
> Sweet rose, whose hue, angrie and brave,
> Bids the rash gazer wipe his eye:
> Thy root is ever in its grave,
>   And thou must die.
>
> Sweet spring, full of sweet dayes and roses,
> A box where sweets compacted lie;
> My musick shows ye have your closes,
>   And all must die.

For a poem on the omnivorous maw of death, these three stanzas, like the three stanzas of Russell, elicit a remarkably complacent mood in the listener, a mood which has nothing to do with one's acceptance or rejection of the religious faith underlying Herbert's final reversal:

> Onely a sweet and vertuous soul,
> Like season'd timber, never gives;
> But though the whole world turn to coal
>   Then chiefly lives.

The usual reading of this puzzling last stanza makes it somewhat consonant with the conclusion to Hopkins's "Windhover": namely, that in the final calcining of the world, the virtuous soul will burn more brightly and more lastingly than the degenerate. All must die, but virtue dies more brilliantly, gashes gold-vermilion in that last day. More fruitful might be a reading of Herbert along the lines of Hopkins's "Comfort of the Resurrection," where the virtuous soul is transformed from a lump of corruptible coal into the immortal diamond. The difficulty in Herbert has to do with the obvious fact that seasoned timber burns more lastingly and brightly than ordinary timber, but *burn* it does—which is small consolation for the man of virtue. But the "turning to coal" may only obliquely refer to the destruction of the world by fire; it may also refer to the actual process whereby coal is formed, a process recognized in Herbert's day as occurring in the luminescent peat bogs of Ireland. Such a reading opens up two possible interpretations. First, following Hopkins closely, the virtuous soul being more seasoned, that is, longer "aged," passes beyond carbuncular decline and literally becomes the *silex scintillans*, the living rock which is the head (chef = "chiefly") of the corner. Second, the virtuous soul remains firm and supportive of "the temple," in contrast to the dissolute soul that is like the corrupt and disintegrating wood described in Vaughan's "The Timber" and in Raleigh's "The Lie":

> Say to the court, it glows
> and shines *like* rotten wood.

I have used the word "complacency" about Russell's and Herbert's poems; that was perhaps too mild a term. Both poems have a kind of playful quality to them, an air of levity, which comes, I suggest again, from one's response to their structure, a structure in which pedestrian plodding brings one to the hoped-for destination. The public theme of each poem, the inevitability of death, is thus contradicted by the more or less concealed structure, and it is the latter which seems to dominate one's response.

Possibly it is this same recurrent structure, in a slightly different form, that makes one smile over rather than commiserate the heinous doing-in of Browning's Porphyria.

> Which done, she rose, and from her form
> Withdrew the dripping cloak and shawl,
>   And laid her soiled gloves by, untied
> Her hat and let the damp hair fall,
>   And, last, she sat down by my side
> *And called me. . . .*
> . . . .
> But passion sometimes would prevail,
>   Nor could tonight's gay feast restrain
> A sudden thought of one so pale
>   *For love of her. . . .*
> . . . .

> As a shut bud that holds a bee
> I warily oped her lids; again
> Laughed the blue eyes without a stain.
> And I untightened next the tress
> *About her neck.*

To be sure, there is the possibility that it is our startlement at the suddenness of these reversals that accounts for our amusement at this deliciously monstrous deed—so monstrous that Browning Societeers, old and new, have sought to prove no murder is here described.

But what of the strange delight one takes in Bishop King's "Exequy"? Here the enjambment does not surprise; it is too frequent for that. But the enjambed lines invariably *conclude* a statement; that is, they function structurally as the unifying summation of all the complex details that precede. Again, for reasons of brevity I quote only some representative passages:[4]

> Dear loss! since thy untimely fate
> My task hath been to meditate
> *On thee, on thee....*
> . . . .
> By which wet glasses I find out
> How lazily time creeps about
> *To one that mourns....*
> . . . .
> Thou hast benighted me, thy set
> This Eve of blackness did beget,
> Who was't my day, (though overcast
> Before thou had'st thy Noon-tide past)
> And I remember must in tears,
> Thou scarce had'st seen so many years
> *As Day tells houres.*

The second half of each of these terminal lines introduces a *new* subject, so the basic structure parallels that of the beginning of

---

4. It is a technique in many of his poems. Cf. "An Elegy upon S.W.R.," "On Two Children dying of one Disease . . . ," "An Elegy upon the most Incomparable King CHARLS the First," to cite only other poems of mourning.

Wordsworth's "Upon Westminster Bridge," and one feels safe in hazarding the conclusion that, again, part of the pleasure one takes in this poem of genuine sadness (quite unlike the Browning above) comes from one's satisfaction at the fulfillment of the structural pattern of the journey through multiplicity to unity. That of course is precisely the direction of the journey Bishop King is taking as he follows after his well-loved spouse.

I noted, in my discussion of "prepositional energy," the seeming fortuity of all my examples entailing three phrases, the preeminent number of multiplicity; it may be another matter of happy historical chance become more or less conventional practice (or of my own Cusanian selectivity) that in so many of the examples above it is the multiple that precedes the unified. "It pertains to a defect [but also to a fact] that the one can only be imitated by the many," wrote Aquinas following Aristotle, and summarized in *Paradise Lost* (8.419 ff.)—all of which is merely to say that it is only by the journey through the fragmented and chaotic that man reaches the ordered and harmonious. "Long live the weeds and the wilderness yet"—exclaimed Hopkins in his miniature of "Childe Roland . . ."[5] —not for their sake but because they are ethereal finger-pointings to what the original myth calls the concordant and peaceable kingdom.

---

5. The "anxiety of influence" relating Hopkins to Browning was glimpsed by Patmore in a letter to Hopkins (20 March 1884), and may explain Hopkins's frequent and uncharacteristically vehement attacks on Browning.

VIII: *Collision*

It is probably mere chance that in the most quoted of those Latin–Anglo-Saxon hybrids from Shakespeare, which John Crowe Ransom so genially analyzed years ago, it is frequently the rule (acknowledging once again that the rule is there is no rule) that the polysyllabic Latin precedes the monosyllabic Anglo-Saxon. Ransom, one will recall, mined everybody's favorite passages in the plays for their most attractive linguistic collisions, for example, "multitudinous sea..." and so on, "pendant boughs and coronet weeds," "pendant cradle and procreant beds." But true to his assumed modesty as major-minor writer, at once affectionate and dismissive toward his subject, Ransom didn't bother supplying reasons for everyone's liking this juxtaposition of inflated latinity and spare anglicism. But it should be apparent from the preceding chapter what those reasons might well be: the fusion of the two language families, regardless of whether the movement is from polysyllabic to monosyllabic or vice versa, symbolizes once again that basic ontological stance which posits man as the aspiring reconciliation point of finite-infinite, immanent-transcendent, multiplicity-unity.

These fusions, then, are not mere embellishments; they are among the substantive structures of English poetry. And Elder Olson, speaking for the Chicago Aristotelians, could not have been more wrong when he affirmed: "Shakespeare's profoundest touches are... profound, not as meaningful verbal expressions but as actions permitting an extraordinary number of implications, in that they are revelatory of many aspects of character and situation." On the contrary, character and situation are but other analogues, and in fact more abecedarian analogues, of the prime analogate: the

169

limned-unlimited. "The multitudinous seas incarnadine, / Making the green one red" says nothing of character and situation. What such lines do say is that men are defined as the "heavenly labials in a world of gutturals." Why should Macbeth talk that way, and why should anyone like these pyrotechnics getting in the way of what one is supposed to be really after: "action and character, which cannot be handled in grammatical terms"? (Olson again.)

Of course, such fusions do have a dramatic function, as in de La Mare's "Sam"—who I have noted is the Judge Samuel listening to the voice of another world:

> Calling me, 'Sam!'—quietlike—'Sam!' . . .
>   But me . . . I never went,
> Making believe I kind of thought
>   'Twas someone else she meant . . .
> Wonderful lovely there she sat,
>   Singing the night away,
> All in the solitudinous sea
>   Of that there lonely bay.

The melding of pretentious latinity ("solitudinous") and vulgar colloquialism ("that there") *is* operative in terms of character and situation: it points up the conflict between the imaginative insight of Sam's childhood and the pragmatic cerebration of his old age—but here again this dramatic action is merely the "lesser poem" of that "central poem" I have been assaying throughout all of this discussion. The polysyllabic and the monosyllabic also merge dramatically—but, it should not be necessary to repeat, derivative of the larger configuration—in the following line from Sassoon's "Prehistoric Burials":

> Memorials of oblivion, these turfed tombs.

Here the polarization is "situationally" of primitive man with his allegedly simple animism and modern self-reflecting man with his ratiocinative scrupulosity, a dweller in Auden's "era of mirrors."

But that poet—like Shakespeare—whom Sassoon is following across Salisbury Plain, seems to employ these linguistic fusions for their essentially poetic, that is, structural, effect, and with no apparent relation to "character" and "plot":

> with a countenance
> Of Adoration, with an eye of love.
>> [*The Prelude* 2.413]

> Redoubled and redoubled, concourse wild
> Of jocund din.
>> [Ibid. 5.378]

This is not fatuous exuberance, decorative verse, the kind of ex-crescence a more "disciplined" poet would have lopped off. It is the voice of the bard, as Wordsworth himself recognized when profer-ing the *Macbeth* passage in defense of his own practice. And it stems explicitly from the entrance of the infinite into the finite:

> that *uncertain* heaven, received
> Into the bosom of the steady lake.
>> [Ibid. 5.387]

—"Uncertain," because man is never really convinced of the reality of the transcendent until it enters into his stable, concrete, "steady" condition.[1]

It cannot be merely the randomness of history strengthened by the unique linguistic possibilities of English that has led to this pattern's constant deployment. The structure is too prevalent, be-ginning before Shakespeare and elaborated by all poets since. One recognizes it in some of the most celebrated passages of Milton:

> With hideous ruin and combustion down
> To bottomless perdition, there to dwell
> In Adamantine Chains and penal Fire.
>> [*PL* 1.45–47]

Here the style is "answerable," as the fallen angels go from the high sublime of latinity to the low bathos of Anglo-Saxon—similarly with the following passage; and "passage," it should be remem-bered, means "journey."

---

1. One may recognize in a comparable nuptial moment, that of Madeline and Porphyro, a cluster of these structural patterns; not only the enjambment but the climactic coda, "solu-tion sweet," which is itself a Latin–Anglo-Saxon, polysyllabic-monosyllabic, feminine-masculine Milton-Keats collision.

Thus roving on
In confus'd march forlorn, th'advent'rous Bands
With shudd'ring horror pale, and eyes aghast
View'd first thir lamentable lot, and found
No rest: through many a dark and dreary Vale
They passed, and many a Region dolorous,
O'er many a Frozen, many a fiery Alp,
Rocks, Caves, Lakes, Fens, Bogs, Dens, and shades of death,
A Universe of death, which God by curse
Created evil, for evil only good,
Where all life dies, death lives and Nature breeds,
Perverse, all monstrous, all prodigious things,
Abominable, inutterable, and worse.

[*PL* 2.614–26]

It would take the close reading at which John Hollander is past master to do justice to all the poetic strategies in this text. One will immediately note the complexities of the "journey" pattern in the first four lines which culminate in the brief coda, "No rest." But undoubtedly the most compelling focus for the reader is the stark Anglo-Saxon character of the line beginning "Rocks, Caves," and the heavy latinity of the concluding "Perverse, all monstrous," and so on. It is obvious that here the dominant monosyllables precede the dominant polysyllables, so that "dramatically" (using the term with all the qualifications introduced earlier) the movement may be regarded as subordinate to the theme of Satan's and his followers' fall from angelic unity to hell-bound multiplicity—a movement also underlined by the chiastic "life dies, death lives."

It is similar with God the Father, who is

Omnipotent,
Immutable, Immortal, Infinite,
Eternal King; thee, Author of all being,
Fountain of Light, thyself invisible
Amidst the glorious brightness where thou sit'st
Thron'd inaccessible, but when thou shad'st
The full blaze of thy beams, and through a cloud
Drawn round about thee.

[*PL* 3.372–79]

This return to the poly-mono pattern may be here interpreted as the latinate language of exaltation (predominantly by apophasis) gradually "shading" off to Anglo-Saxon, as the infinite becomes "clouded" by the finite.

There may, of course, appear to be something finicky about this kind of linguistic casuistry. These structures frequently function dramatically with some close correlation with meaning, and sometimes "lyrically" as patterns expressive in their own right; in the latter instance, they are more or less melodic figurations to which one responds purely for their "musical" value as "chords" of the one-many harmony—a value which is attested to by the almost universal response to the famous opening notes of Beethoven's Fifth Symphony, and less universally but much more extendedly by the "Judex crederis" motif which dominates the last part of Berlioz's *Te Deum* and which upon hearing makes one almost instinctively imagine the complementarity of corpuscular and cymatic.

For some brief poetic examples of these "chords," one may look to the "Begotten Son, Divine Similitude" of Milton (*PL* 3.384); the "superannuations of sunk realms" of Keats (*The Fall of Hyperion* 1.68); the "residuary worm" of Hopkins ("Heraclitean Fire"), which Elisabeth Schneider aptly calls "the grand style ironic"; the "circumambient gloom" of Arnold ("Mycerinus," 53), which becomes, not unfittingly, the "circumambient hocus pocus" of Robinson ("Ben Jonson Entertains... ," 166); and the "circumambient gas" excoriated and exemplified in Hulme's essays. For a more elaborate illustration, one may think of the heavily polysyllabic and undular line, "Divinely superfluous beauty" (from Jeffers's poem of that title), which brackets the predominantly monosyllabic central statement:

Divinely superfluous beauty
Rules the games, presides over destinies, makes trees grow
And hills tower, waves fall.
The incredible beauty of joy
Stars with fire the joining of lips, O let our loves too
Be joined, there is not a maiden
Burns and thirsts for love
More than my blood for you, by the shore of seals while the wings
Weave like a web in the air
Divinely superfluous beauty.

All of these may be regarded as fleeting echoes of that larger melodia of the conjoining of the finite with the infinite which Dante heard in paradise.

It is certainly true that the use of terms like "chords" and "melody" suggests Poe's "poetic principle," Pater's "condition of music," and Bremond's "poésie pure." Nor, as I made clear in chapter 1, would I shy away from such analogies; but I would offer the qualification I have been making throughout: these structural patterns are only one element among many contributing to the total aesthetic effect, even though they may be among the most specifically poetic elements—tout le reste est...

"Pure poetry," as I would use the phrase, is the poetry that by definition is "impure," that is, the poetry that represents the best collision, interplay, tension, "mix" (again, synonyms abound) of the symbols, images, figures, and so on, of the infinite-finite, unity-multiplicity reality. One of the "purest" philosophers of our time—"purest" in the sense of fidelity to "the given"—was Rosenstock-Huessy, whose proudest boast was, "I am an impure thinker." Thus, I would use "pure poetry" in a pejorative sense to characterize the efforts of the so-called confessional poets and would thus amend Robert Penn Warren's statement to apply to that kind of pure poetry: "Such poets [the confessionalists] want to be pure; but poems do not."

The classic example of *poésie pure,* as quite literally every schoolboy in France knows, is from *Phèdre*:

La fille de Minos et de Pasiphaé

This line of beauty, "denuée de signification" as Bremond said, has been for generations the central touchstone of French poetry, though J. G. Kraaft, working with an extremely sophisticated, or at least extremely complicated, critical apparatus, has recently denigrated it in his *Poésie, corps et âme*. John Hollander in *Vision and Resonance* detects some congruence of Racine's line with the following from one of Yeats's last great lyrics, "A Long-legged Fly":

There on that scaffolding reclines
Michael Angelo.

But here the weight imposed on the proper name as a complete verse simply surprises one, in a fashion not too unlike a more renowned reference:

> In the room the women come and go
> Talking of Michelangelo.

The effectiveness of Eliot's couplet comes almost entirely from its setting and its mocking quasi-sdrucciolo rhyme, as is more or less equally true of the French translation:

> Dans le salon les femmes vont et viennent
> en parlant des maîtres de Siènne.

Neither the passage from Yeats nor that from Eliot seems to me to have much in common with Racine—unlike, say, Tennyson's "This is my son, mine own Telemachus" ("Ulysses"). The impact of Yeats's derives from one's startlement at the proper name in this particular position, and the impact of Eliot's from the proper name in this particular context—though regarding the latter, one would want to include, as intensifying the effect, the structural pattern entailed in the collision of the banal and primarily monosyllabic Anglo-Saxon with the "latinate" and polysyllabic "Michelangelo."

The modern master of this kind of startlement is Browning, as in another text concerned with Renaissance painters:

> No virgin by him the somewhat petty,
>   Of finical touch and tempera crumbly—
> Could not Alesso Baldovinetti
>   Contribute so much, I ask him humbly?
> . . . .
> This time we'll shoot better game and bag 'em hot—
>   No mere display at the stone of Dante
> But a kind of sober Witanagemot.
>   ["Old Pictures in Florence"]

Or, again from Browning, where the effect seems intentionally macaronic:

> I should study that brute to describe you
> Illum Juda Leonem de Tribu.
>   ["The Glove," 49–50]

Though Browning could rhyme almost anything, including certain Carlylean place names, the tour de force of this particular "device" is from Drayton's "Endimion & Phoebe":

> And now great Phoebe in her tryumph came,
> With all the tytles of her glorious name,
> Diana, Delia, Luna, Cynthia,
> Virago, Hecate, and Elythia,
> Prothiria, Dictinna, Proserpine,
> Latona, and Lucina, most divine.
>
> [823–28]

Hardy comes a close second in "Ancient to Ancients," where without any break in the metric pattern, which he maintains at the price of chronological accuracy (just as Drayton sacrificed the normal order: goddess-unity-Cynthia; demigoddess-duality-Proserpine; witch-multiplicity-Hecate), almost the whole stanza is made up of proper names:

> Sophocles, Plato, Socrates,
>   Gentlemen,
> Pythagoras, Thucydides,
> Herodotus, and Homer—yea,
> Clement, Augustin, Origen,
> Burnt brightlier toward their setting-day,
>   Gentlemen.

I have intentionally emphasized the word "device" above because such a format can easily become a merely mechanical technique—as Tennyson *perhaps* recognized (since he would later give us such a howler as "Zolaism-abysm") in recasting the thirty-seventh stanza of "The Palace of Art" (1832):

> Isaiah with fierce Ezekial,
>   Swart Moses by the Coptic sea,
> Plato, Petrarca, Livy and Raphael,
>   And eastern Confutzee.

A decade later this more sensibly became:

> Below was all mosaic choicely plann'd
>   With cycles of the human tale
> Of this wide world, the times of every land
>   So wrought they will not fail.

And when it is a manifestly self-conscious device, the effect is of heavy irony, as in John Updike's "The Dance of the Solids": "Like starch and polyoxymethylene"; or, in this passage Walter Ong has explicated from "ME" by the British poet Adrian Henri:

> Bela Bartok Henri Rousseau
> Rauschenberg and Jasper Johns
> Lukas Cranach Shostakovich
> Kropotkin Ringo George and John

Most of these proper names have about them an alien or outlandish air, and as with Spenser's and Milton's use of such names, there is no doubt that this exotic quality contributes to the reader's fascination. But, again, none of the passages above seems to me to have much in common with Racine's line where, in fact, there is nothing any more strange about using the proper name of Phèdre's mother than in using the name of Phèdre herself.

Certainly, one reason the line of Racine is so moving is that it concludes a singularly melancholy passage and evokes, as one of Bremond's critics said, "le mystère de l'écoulement des choses":

> Tout a changé de face
> Depuis que sur ces bords les dieux ont envoyé
> La fille de Minos et de Pasiphaé.

One thinks immediately of the nostalgia of Yeats's "All's changed now," in a similarly paradoxic landscape where the fluid waters meet the solid earth; one may also be reminded of another classical and paradoxic setting where are glimpsed the shapes of deities or of mortals or of both; add to this the paradox of Phèdre herself as half-sister to the paradoxic minotaur, and one has imagery and theme harnessed in the service of the strain of dualities, and thus a passage fraught with tragic vibrations. Nevertheless, no matter how much all of these factors may move one, they do not do so as *poésie pure*, as formal elements considered, so far as possible, apart from subject matter.

In *The Overreacher*, Harry Levin discussing this line comes close to exposing its structural fascination: "The introduction of strange vocables into a familiar rhythmical framework may be the sort of magic that functions best within circles of remote association." Unfortunately, the important truth Levin's statement embodies is not confirmed—because there is neither "strangeness" nor "remoteness" by a consideration of some other lines on Pasiphaë. Thus, one may contrast the tepidity of Pope's translation from Chaucer ("The Wife of Bath's Prologue") with the richness of the original:

> But what pleas'd him was the *Cretan* Dame,
> And Husband-Bull—Oh monstrous! fie, for shame!
>
> [385–86]

whereas Chaucer to great effect achieves a kind of monumental solemnity by inverting almost syllable by syllable the structure of what would be Racine's line: "Of Pasiphaë, that was queene of Crete." Both Chaucer's and Racine's structure is entirely lost in Robert Lowell's *Phaedra*:

> Friend, this kingdom lost its place,
> when Father left my mother for defiled
> bull-serviced Pasiphaë's child. The child
> of homicidal Minos is our queen!

It is indicative both of his exceptional poetic "ear" and of his congenital sense of the tradition that Robert Penn Warren's references to this myth in the beginning of *Brother to Dragons* employ a strong Latin–Anglo-Saxon collision and conclude in the very accents of Racine:

The bull plunged. You screamed like a girl, and strove.
But the infatuate machine of your invention held.
Later, they lifted you out and wiped your lips in the dark palace.
We have not loved you less, poor Pasiphaë.

Here the latinity reflects artificiality, the crafty fabrication of Daedalus's technology, while the Anglo-Saxon bespeaks the blind, brute lust of the doomed wife of Minos. Lust itself is seen by

Jefferson, the speaker in Warren's drama, as half-curse, half-blessing, as innocence and guilt. And the culminating line expressing these paradoxes, and très voisin de Racine, is the most plangent and moving of all those I am citing from poets in English: "We have not loved you less, poor Pasiphaë."

Levin's "magic" formula is helpful, however, for something like Davenant's "To the Lady Bridgett Kingsmill; sent with Mellons," where even his twentieth-century editors are not completely certain about all of the "remote associations":

> Nor th'Abbot Tretenheim, nor Rhodigine,
> Nor the Jew Tripho, though they all defend
> Such dreames.
>
> [6–8]

Unfortunately, this is still not very much akin to the Racine passage or to those from Chaucer and Warren. But the following from Cleveland's "The Authour to His Hermaphrodite," where there are no strange vocables and possibly to the seventeenth-century reader no particularly remote associations, is quite homologous with Racine's lines:

> But stay I've wak't his dust, his Marble stirres,
> And brings the worms for his Compurgators.
>
> [33–34]

It is clear, then, that I would maintain at least part of the explanation for the power of the line from Racine is its movement from relative simplicity to climactic complexity.[2] And it should be noted that the line Hopkins singled out in his famous admonition to Bridges, "read it . . . with your ears," is cast in precisely this structural pattern:

> She had come from a cruise, training seamen—
> ["The Loss of the Eurydice," 13]

---

2. It is a structural format to which almost every English translator of Dante has paid homage in translating a line that has some similarity to that of Racine: "Guardaci ben! Ben son, ben son Beatrice" (*Purgatorio* 30.73). The first of the following translations is Longfellow's, and the second, sanctioned by Ezra Pound, is Laurence Binyon's: "Look at Me well; in sooth I'm Beatrice!" "Look on me well; I am, I am Beatrice."

This structural explanation is even more obviously apt for some additional canonic illustrations of *poésie pure*. The first is from du Bellay:

> Telle que dans son char la Bérécynthienne
> ["Antiquitez de Rome" 6.1]

And as with Pope's translation of Chaucer, one may contrast the power, and therefore the justly earned renown of the original, with the muffling of effect—and hence critical indifference—in Spenser's translation of du Bellay in "Rvines of Rome":

> Such as the Berecynthian Goddess bright
> [6.1]

The second is not in the canon and is from an author I shall identify later; the third is from Villon, and the fourth from Vigny:

> Celle qui fût Héaulmiette

> Voire, où sont de Constantinobles
> ["Ballade, a ce propos en vieil françois"]

> Lis ce mot sur les murs: "commémoration,"
> ["La Bouteille à la mer" 23.7]

In all of these, though to a greater or lesser degree, what I have called the "chord" of the one-many harmony is immediately recognizable, with the effect in Vigny enhanced by the consonant repetitions, particularly of *m*, which binds together the total pattern—just as it does in its equally famous cousin, "The moan of doves in immemorial elms."[3]

The linguistic maneuver which these various examples of "pure poetry" embody is not directly paralleled in any of the English

---

3. It is not difficult to evade Ransom's commonsense strictures on those who believe certain sounds themselves—here the sound "m"—to be intrinsically beautiful. Sound only communicates in a pattern—which, however, need not be lexical—entailing some kind of variation; this is true even of a single sound, like the gradual muting of the one extended note opening Wagner's *Rienzi*.

poets cited above, except Warren, but it is virtually the stylistic
signature of a poet almost contemporary with du Bellay:[4]

> Vse him as if he were a Philistine.
>> [*The Jew of Malta*, 993]

> He is not of the seed of Abraham.
>> [Ibid., 995]

> And on my knees creepe to Ierusalem
>> [Ibid., 1571]

> Was it not thou that scoftes the Organon,
> And said it was a heape of vanities?
> He that will be a flat dicotamist,
> And seen in nothing but Epitomies.
>> [*The Massacre at Paris*, 392–95]

> But thou art sprung from Scythian Caucasus.
>> [*The Tragedie of Dido*, 1566]

This latter suggests a more memorable passage, the prologue to
Tamburlaine:

> Weele lead you to the stately tent of War,
> Where you shall hear the Scythian Tamburlaine.

One of the two most admired passages in all of Marlowe also follows this basic pattern:

> Is it not brave to be a King, Techelles?
> Vsumcasane and Theridamas,
> Is it not passing braue to be a King,
> And ride in triumph through Persepolis?
>> [*Tamburlaine*, 756–59]

Harry Morris, author of a useful study on Marlowe as poet, has
commented: "The strangeness of syllables in unaccustomed jux-

---

4. It is also a signature of that most unmarlovian poet, Emily Dickinson, as in what is
certainly her most quoted simile: "And neigh like Boanerges" (585). This and the following
examples are numbered after Johnson's edition: "When upon a pain Titanic" (175); "Will not
cry with joy 'Pompeii'" (175); "On a Ball of Mast in Bosporus" (716); "What care the Dead
for Chanticleer" (592, and cf. 140). Examples abound: Nos. 152, 151, 560, 501, 688, 536.

taposition accounts for the beauty of the famous lines on kingship."
But as with Levin's "magic," there is no particular reason why
unaccustomed syllabic juxtaposition should engender a sense of
beauty—nor at this point in the play are we "unaccustomed" to
these particular "syllables." If, however, one define the beautiful as
that which is congruent with man's "nature," and that nature as the
nexus of unity-multiplicity, of infinity-finitude, then one does have
at least part of an explanation of the unquestioned appeal of these
lines, as of the other passages I have characterized as representing
my concept of "pure poetry."

The magnificence of Marlowe's mighty line, at least in *Tamburlaine*, cannot be unrelated to the fact that so many lines end in a
complex polysyllable, usually a proper noun.[5] Similarly, one may
note in the other plays the frequent terminal placement of such
names as Mephistophilis, Gaviston, Mortimer, Abigail, and Eper-
noune. That other equally celebrated passage in Marlowe is from
Doctor Faustus:

> O, Ile leape vp to my God—who pulles me downe?—
> See, see, where Christs blood streames in the firmament.
>
> [1431–32]

The structure itself should require no elaborate comment now. But
I think it a telling point that it is a French critic, bred in the
tradition of *vers donné*, Marcel Thiry in *Le Poème et la langue*, who
has spoken the mot juste concerning this passage by characterizing
the climactic polysyllabic "firmament" as the expression of a "longueur infinie," the "infinie" of the original heuristic myth. There is
a similar structure, suggesting a similar mood, also presaging triumph in Bolingbroke's speech:

> That sun that warms you here shall shine on me,
> And those his golden beams to you here lent
> Shall point on me and gild my banishment.
>
> [*Richard II* 1.3.145–47]

5. Cyril Bailey in his commentary on *De rerum natura* notes that in the *Aeneid*, when there
is a line ending in a pentasyllabic word, it is usually a proper noun. And of the five
pentasyllabic endings that are grouped closely together at the close of book 6 of *De rerum
natura*, he notes: "This may be intended to give a special dignity to the conclusion of the
poem."

Drayton in his "Of Poets and Poesie" varies this pattern slightly (as did Tennyson also in the line cited above) when he says of Marlowe himself that he

> Had in him those brave translunary things.

This rings a fascinating change on the basic finite-infinite motif, with the final monosyllabic coda constituting an echo of all that precedes the penultimate polysyllabic term, as in the long, sequacious notes concluding Coleridge's "The Eolian Harp":

> Peace, and this cot, and thee, heart-honored maid!

It is a structure not unlike the ABCA or ring pattern familiar to students of classical literature, and its appearance in the following line from Pope's *Essay on Man* may explain in part Lytton Strachey's enthusiasm for it: "If that is not beautiful, what is?"

> Die of a rose in aromatic pain
>
> [1.200]

This kind of circular development is extended for four lines in "L'Allegro":

> Quips and Cranks, and wanton Wiles,
> Nods, and Becks, and Wreathed Smiles,
> Such as hang on Hebe's cheek,
> And love to live in dimple sleek.
>
> [27–30]

Here the brevity of the line modulates the effect as does also the softening or suppression of the Latin–Anglo-Saxon collision—all quite unlike the following from the later Milton, from Arnold, and from Bishop King respectively:

> Then feed on thoughts that voluntary move.
>
> [*PL* 3.37]

> As with new wine intoxicated both
>
> [*PL* 9.1008]

> Pierce fate's impenetrable ear
>
> ["Resignation," 274]

> Should let so deare an obligation dy
> > ["An Acknowledgement," 10]

With these one might compare Vaughan in "The Retreate":

> But a white celestial thought

Or one might compare also the following—which is a kind of refrain from Crashaw's "To the Queen upon her Numerous Proginie":

> Shine then, sweet supernumerary Starre.
> > [99]

Here the Latin–Anglo-Saxon collision follows the Drayton scheme closely, while the following from Spenser's "An Hymne of Beavtie" thematically anticipates Vaughan:

> But that faire lampe, from whose celestiall ray
> > [99]

And both phosphenic images anticipate the best of Wordsworth on "Lucy," and on Dorothy in "Tintern Abbey,"

> Rolled round in earth's diurnal course
> > ["A Slumber. . . ."]

> > let the moon
> Shine on thee in thy solitary walk.
> > [135–36]

and Robinson in "The Dead Village" and "Discovery" respectively:

> The strange and unrememberable light

> And seen for us the devastating light

My last example of this structural *longueur infinie* is also from Robinson, "The March of the Cameron Men," where the title both echoes Byron's chord in *Childe Harold*—"And wild and high the Cameron's Gathering rose!" (3.226)—and also sets the pattern for the following: "In your smile was a gift of ineffable things."

Before looking at the poet whom I left unidentified earlier, I want to consider a few additional illustrations of *poésie pure* and their

relation to my own patterns. The whole of "Clair de lune" is regarded as a kind of touchstone by French critics, and I have used it
frequently. Its coda is,

>Les grands jets d'eau sveltes parmi les marbres.

Here the monosyllabic initiating terms come to a climax at the
displaced and somewhat exotic "sveltes," which then prepares for
the disyllabic denouement. Here, also, the paradoxic unity-
multiplicity chord reflects the "narrative" theme of the conjoining
of fluidity ("jets d'eau") and solidity ("marbres"). A similar development, though now in the opposite direction, *le mode mineur*, is
evident in my last two examples from French poetry, fittingly,
from Racine's *Phèdre* and from *Andromaque*—the latter dedicated to
the daughter of that other "Andromache," that other *reine dépossédée*,
Henrietta Maria, widow of Charles I:

>Au tumulte pompeux d'Athène et de la cour
>>[*Phèdre* 1.1]

>Le perfide triomphe, et se rit de ma rage.
>>[*Andromaque* 5.1]

Unfortunately, I have no structural explanation for that other
familiar touchstone from *Phèdre*:

>Ariane, ma soeur, de quel amour blessée
>Vous mourûtes aux bords où vous fûtes laissée!
>>[1.3]

Here there is again a subject of great melancholy, and a text heavy
with assonance; and perhaps there is a certain circularity, paralleling that of the statement, in the inner rhyme of the second line,
much like the adjective-noun unit in both halves of the so-called
Vergilian "golden line." John Hollander talks of this kind of interior
balance as suggesting that the line is, as it were, looking in a mirror
and gazing back at itself.[6] This is a happy conception that bespeaks

---

6. There is a similar "mirroring" in Milton's use of the adjective-noun-adjective formula;
here the adjectives do not line up in homage before the sovereign substantive but instead take
dominion over it, and thus assure that their modifying presence will be felt; as traditional
"enemies of the noun," they democratize the relation by surrounding the noun. The form is

the unifying of dualities, the back-forth and up-down fusion, that defines the act of making poetry—for example, the "doubling" that Angus Fletcher says "produces magical relations between the terms," and that is so typical of Wordsworth, as in "Yarrow Unvisited," "The swan on still St. Mary's Lake / Float double"; the mist that accompanies the hare "Wherever she doth run" in "Resolution and Independence"; or "the water mirrors" of Yeats; the "fish for fancies . . . in the watery glass" of Blake; or this passage Blake illustrated in which the very pattern I have been discussing above twice recurs:

> And let some strange mysterious dream
> Wave at his Wings in Airy stream.
>
> ["Il Penseroso," 147–48]

The unidentified line bracketed by du Bellay and Villon above is "Celle qui fût Héaulmiette." In this characteristically audacious title we have an excellent example of the "sophisticated looniness," the "dandyism," of a poet who was described by his critics as an "ecstatic eunuch," a "francophile," a "hedonist." The structure occurs frequently:

> A sunny day's complete Poussiniana
>
> ["Le Monocle de mon Oncle"]

> After that alien, point-blank, green and actual Guatemala
>
> ["Arrival at the Waldorf"]

> I love to sit and read the *Telegraph*,
>
> ["Mandolin and Liqueurs"]

Italian, as in Milton's own "alto valor vago" from the sonnet "Giovane piano," and one would be tempted to think its use, relatively infrequent, is reserved for the most solemn moments in *Paradise Lost*: "human face divine" (3.44)—later echoed in Blake's "human form divine" ("The Divine Image") and in Coleridge's "bright eyes divine" ("Christabel," 597); "mortal Sin original" (9.1003); "written Records pure" (12.512). And so the rightly admired closing, "wand'ring steps and slow" (12.648), is balanced with the equally effective opening triad, "upright heart and pure" (1.18). The temptation to regard this pattern as suggesting a note of solemnity is strengthened by what seems the willful avoidance of it in the beginning of the twelfth book when what must have been for Milton the unforgettable phrase "dolce stil nuovo" was rearranged in the hastily devised and redundant opening: "Then with transition *sweet new speech* renews" (12.5). Unfortunately, while one's Kabbalistic instincts favor succumbing to the temptation, there are some triads that—so at least it appears on the surface—seem to key passages of no great significance: e.g., 3.439; 3.568.

Force is my lot and not pink-clustered
Roma ni Avignon ni Leyden.
   ["Examination of the Hero in a Time of War"]

It is a cat of a sleek transparency.
   ["An Ordinary Evening in New Haven"]

Not as it was: part of the reverberation
         [Ibid.]

One would be moved to cry out "Stevens" if one heard these lines in the deserts of Arabia. So, too, with the movement in the opposite direction, the minor mode:

Tristesses, the fund of life and death, suave bush
   ["Credences of Summer"]

Giovanni Papini, by your faith, know how
   ["Reply to Papini"]

Remembrances, a place of a field of lights
   ["Sombre Figuration"]

These are all linear fragments, abstracted texts, but one may believe that in another century or so they will be as cited and memorized as anything from Racine or Verlaine—and for much the same reasons. Stevens had written in a letter to Henry Church, which is not included in Holly Stevens's collection: "I am, in the long run, interested in pure poetry."[7] Now, it is difficult to believe that Stevens, so close a follower of French artistic and literary activities, and writing to Henry Church, a man of similar disposition who had been living in Paris at the time of the controversy over Henri Bremond's book—a controversy which involved among others Maurras and Valéry—would have used the phrase without intending to give it at least some of the connotations attached to it in its most salient twentieth-century critical context. It would have been redundant of Stevens if he had meant merely that he was not

7. This should be read in the context of an earlier letter (31 October, 1935), which is in Holly Stevens's collection, to Ronald Lane Latimer; in this letter Stevens qualifies his commitment to "pure poetry," all the while making it apparent that his interest in it remains strong.

interested in poetry as a vehicle of political indoctrination; and it is inconceivable, given his practice, that he was embracing the kinds of principles advocated in the name of Imagism or enunciated in George Moore's collection, *Pure Poetry*.

There may, of course, be additional reasons why the various "touchstones" analyzed above are affecting; I am supplying only one kind of reason. But it is at least *a* reason. Thus, if there is "magic" in these kinds of patternings it is the magic of Stevens's "sleight-of-hand man." The magician, says Edward Young in *Conjectures on Original Composition*, "raises his structure by means invisible"—invisible but not inaudible, and therefore *not* inexplicable. Such structures are not mere verbal friskings; they are a response to the ontological possibilities of language as such. And certainly, with regard to poets writing in English, they represent a poetic format that springs from the very hybrid nature of the language, a format that emerged in our literature at the time that the "Perle" poet extended "one hand towards Langland and one towards Chaucer" (Israel Gollancz), and a format that was permanently stamped upon the language in the Henrician period.

Though it went unremarked by Ransom, Shakespeare was less the originator than the inheritor of this linguistic practice. Given the nature of English as a distillate of Latin and Anglo-Saxon, such conjunctions would occur more or less spontaneously. But they seem to have been first employed consciously by the great creators of the English biblical-liturgical tradition: for example, Tyndale ("peace maker," "scape goat," "jolly captains") and Cranmer, who in *The Prayer Book* raised the practice from the level of more or less mechanical devisal to that of intentional artifice. Such well-known doublings as "erred and gone astray," "assault and hurt," "covetous desires and inordinate love" are often as effective as anything in Shakespeare.

Lastly, I repeat that, although I have concentrated mainly on the movement *from* the multiple *to* the unified, one could as easily concentrate on the opposite development as, say, the reflection of the absolute attracting the contingent. There is nothing unsignificant about these patterns. As William James frequently warned his students, there is a danger in introducing too many and too fine distinctions into the realm of the affective; there is no one correct interpretation, no single mode of explicitating the fundamental structures of the human utterance. The final argument cannot be in favor of a specific interpretation of a given development (multiplicity to unity or vice versa) in the pattern, but of its postulation as the point where vexing "contraries meet in one."

F. P. Wilson in his study of seventeenth-century prose has called such patterns "utraquistic," and though he is somewhat hesitant about employing the ascription, it may prove to be a more apt term than he intimates. The original Utraquists were a relatively obscure band of sectaries persecuted by the official church for wanting to take the eucharist under both species, as wine and as bread; persecuted, one may say in our larger framework, for wanting to be faithful to the paradox of spirit-matter, of fluidity-solidity (again, Stevens's "fluent in even the wintriest bronze," Yeats's "brimming water among the stones," and Verlaine's "jets d'eau . . . parmi les marbres"). But it is not merely the literary and religious rebels against the power of monistic orthodoxies who have affirmed the centrality of this paradox. Sandor Ferenczi in his *Final Contribution to Psycho-Analysis* has noted that a world view "as far as possible faultless demands a utraquistic attitude (oscillating between introspection and direct observation) [Wordsworth's "looking steadily" and "recollecting in tranquility"] out of which a reliable reality can be constructed."

As final verification of the fact that there is no all-inclusive, all-exhaustive mode of interpretation for these utraquisms, I offer the following from Thomas Browne: "To be knaved out of our graves, to have our sculs made drinking bowls, and our bones turned into Pipes to delight and sport our Enemies, are Tragical abominations escaped in burning burials." For the most part this moves away from the monosyllabic; and among the many possible interpretations (*many*, I repeat, because we are concerned with something that is impatient of formula and recipe), one might suggest that the structure here is similar to the rhopalic pattern examined briefly in chapter 1: a movement from the isolated singular and concrete to the all-embracing and the universal. Indeed, that is the structure of the entire *Urn Burial*, a movement from finite to infinite, with the attainment of the latter commemorated in the ecstatic coda of the last chapter.

It is precisely this movement that has been defined as typical of

all of Browne's mystical speculations in Morris W. Croll's endur-
ingly valuable study, "The Baroque Style in Prose." Croll analyzed
a characteristic Brownean passage and, in a paragraph that marked
himself as adept at this mode of speculation, went on to observe:

> Browne's sentence, on the contrary, opens constantly out-
> ward; its motions become more animated and vigorous as it
> ends, as his sentences are likely to do, in a vision of vast space
> or time, losing itself in an *altitudo*, a hint of infinity.... After a
> slow expository member, this phrase, so strikingly wrenched
> from its logical position, breaks the established and expected
> rhythm, and is a signal of more agitated movement, of an
> ascending effort of imaginative realization that continues to the
> end. In a different medium, the period closely parallels the
> technique of an El Greco composition, where broken and tor-
> tuous lines in the body of the design prepare the eye for curves
> that leap upward beyond the limits of the canvas.

In the brief passage I have quoted from Browne, the monosyllabic
suggests the "broken and tortured," and the polysyllabic the
"curves that leap upward"—again a journey from the fragmented to
the unified.

In the next chapter I shall examine further implications of these
breaks and curves, these particles and waves. But at this point I am
in via—"staggering in the way," as Vaughan says in "The
Retreate"—and not yet at the moment of synthesis. My present
concern is with the nature of the journey, the voyage on which we
are booked and bound—into one volume, as Dante says at the close
of *Paradiso*, at the end of his own cosmic journey.

Man began in what Freud—who is not without affinities to Stevens's "Caliper"—would call a condition of polymorphousness,
"the aquatic mode," and in what the mystic and poet would call a
condition of porosity and union with the absolute. The "perilous
seas" were for Freud, and even more for Ferenczi in *Thalassa*, the
amniotic fluid; for some poets, "the mind that ocean" (Marvell); and
for the mystic, "the infinite ocean of Being" (Sankara). Since acceptance of any of those views entails a leap of considerable faith, there
is no reason to pause over them right here. With Stevens, one must

affirm that "aesthetics is independent of faith" ("Adagia"). What the poet—beyond psychology and perhaps mysticism—uniquely conveys to us is not just something about the goal (though that is ingredient in every poem) but something about the nature of the journey itself.

Thus, Crispin conceived "his voyage to be / An *up* and *down* between two elements." Crispin, of course, is a comedian and as such sings Thomas Nashe's "A Clownish Song":

> Trip and go, heave and ho'
> Up and down, to and fro.

And in Stevens's "Homunculus et la Belle Etoile" the unifying light causes the salty fishes to go "in many directions / Up and down." A close relative of Stevens's "Caliper," John Dewey, in *Art as Experience* observes, "Up and down, back and front, to and fro, this side and that—or right and left—here and there, feel differently. The reason they do is that they are not static points in something itself static, but are objects in movement, qualitative changes of value." This banal tautology postures as *éclaircissement*—so much for the "electric lamp / On a page of Euclid." One would do better to have Stevens himself chart this voyage.

For Stevens, the poet—and the poet is precisely everyman in his highest condition—is essentially a wandering mediator whose mission is to bridge the chasm in ordinary experience between the imagination and reality; he is therefore, as I have said, the peacemaker between foundational antinomies:

> there is a war between the mind
> And sky, between thought and day and night. It is
> For that the poet is always in the sun,
> Patches the moon together in his room
> To his Virgilian cadences, *up down,*
> *Up down.*
> ["Notes toward a Supreme Fiction"]

If for Stevens *qua* poet the obsessing duality is that of imagination and reality, then all other polarities—spirit-body, interiority-exteriority, unity-multiplicity, and so on—will be seen as ramifications and/or paradigms of this polarization. And hence, for example, the antimony of up and down in the passages quoted above is only a variant of the root antinomy of the *Geist* and the *Welt*, to use Karl Rahner's pregnant phrase.

Thus, there is a great play throughout Stevens's opus on the poet's attempt to fuse such symbolic extensions of this relationship as red-blue, beginning-end, stability-mobility. The poet seeks to live in the domain of the blended opposites: though he is always in the sun, yet he patches the moon in his room in order that the conflict of "mind and sky," or "thought and day" may be adjudicated. Yet the conflict is never utterly resolved. Indeed, if it were, there would be no need for the centos of poetry—for the poet's "purple patches" never quite heal the breach, never quite fuse the blue of "spirit" and the red of "matter." Though one may bring the polarities almost into union, so much so that the triplet "up and down" of Crispin becomes the doublet "up down" (just as "beauty is truth," becomes "truth beauty"), yet the elusive perfect unity is not attained: "I cannot bring a world quite round, / Although I patch it as I can," says the man with the blue guitar.[8] To bring a "world quite *round*" would be to end the opposition between all polarities, for these opposites would meet and close in the perfect harmonious circle of my final chapter, that circle which tra-

---

8. This vision has recently been stigmatized as "Manichaean," which of course it is to the degree that it forecloses *any* resolution of the polarities; but neither in Stevens's total opus nor in what is being affirmed here is that foreclosure definitively established. "No true poet is Manichaean," notes Octavio Paz tersely. Though I shall return to this matter of dualism in the next chapter, the argument at this juncture requires some consideration of the issue. It is customary among contemporary theologians to dissolve all polarizations (e.g., Harvey Cox on the sacred-profane in *The Secular City*) and among contemporary philosophers to decry the "men-things" duality (e.g., Merleau-Ponty on the Cogito in *Phenomenology of Perception*). But, it may be argued as a first line of defense, that is nevertheless how poets see reality: unremittingly dualistic. If the poet is everyman in his purest state, this argument has weight. But, secondly, one may question the theologians and philosophers themselves. Thus, for Cox the profane is the sacred "in a certain sense"—but that "in a certain sense" is precisely what continues to define the duality. Similarly, when Merleau-Ponty in *Adventure of the Dialectic* notes that beyond men and things there "is also the interworld, which we call history, symbolic, truth-to-be-made," he is no doubt right. And there is also, and preeminently, aesthetic, sexual, and mystical experience. But each of these mediating realities is, some memorable prose has it, "in perpetual flight." And of each "it may ever be more truly said that it has ceased to be than it is." There is possibly a naive meliorism behind Merleau-Ponty's declaration following immediately on the quoted passage above: "If one sticks to the [Cartesian] dichotomy, men, as the place where all meaning arises, are condemned to an incredible tension." Indeed—precisely as the poets affirm. But it is this tension, this "exhausting oscillation" (as Merleau-Ponty later defines it) in life and in art that impels man to continue his journey to reach the *nunc stans*.

ditionally symbolized "God," the *coincidentia oppositorum* in which
alpha and omega, beginning and end—and up and down—are
merged. For Stevens, all attempts to "be as gods" are, therefore,
foredoomed. (On this, one may compare the "Eve" of "Sunday
Morning" and the Eve of *Paradise Lost* 9.1010.) The circulating of
man is never "quite round" and remains always eccentric patch-
work.

Nevertheless, man is compelled to journey forth in quest of
union. Pitilessly driven by the impulse (philosophy's eros, poetry's
belle dame) to close the great circle of being, he conceives

> his voyaging to be
> An up and down between two elements,
> A fluctuating between sun and moon.
>   ["The Comedian as the Letter C"]

Seeking the up and down at once, spending the currency of words
"like a drunken sailor"—for "money is a kind of poetry"
("Adagia")—he cannot travel in a straight line, for this will give him
only "one" *or* the "other." Rather, seeking both at once, he fluc-
tuates between them and travels in "cadences."

There is no need here to go into Stevens's varying, but generally
pessimistic, views on the destination of the voyage as such. The
best prose clarification of those views is by another parareligious
atheist, Lucien Goldmann, in his commentary on Pascal's "On the
Conversion of the Sinner." But others, and here I confine myself to
poets, have been more optimistic and glimpsed a different destination: for example, Hopkins who in effect tells us in "Hurrahing in
Harvest," "I lift *up* heart, eyes, *down* all that multiplicity to glean
unity"—or, again, in "The Starlight Night,"

> Look at the stars! look, look *up* at the skies!
>   O look at all the fire-folk sitting in the air!
>   The bright boroughs, the circle citadels there!
> *Down* in dim woods the diamond delves! the elves' eyes!

—or Milton,

> Taught by the heavenly Muse to venture *down*
> The dark descent, and *up* to reascend.
>   [*PL* 3.19–20]

But it is the nature of the voyage itself that is of interest now. And if it be taken as established that the voyage is as described by the poets, then there should be some reflection or indication of its up-down character in the structure of poems—and I here return to my original theme, preferring now text to gloss.[9]

This cantering pattern (Vaughan's "staggering," Stevens's "fluctuating," Ferenczi's and Merleau-Ponty's "oscillating") is imposed on language by the poet's inborn sense of the paradoxic nature of man's pilgrimage to his ultimate shrine. Geoffrey Hartman has discussed a kindred pattern in several passages from Wordsworth under the rubric, "structures of consciousness," and I will consider Wordsworth shortly. First, I want to examine in some detail two remarkably condensed maps of this pilgrimage.

E. A. Robinson has a sonnet called "Credo" which, like a few of Stevens's poems, seeks almost by an act of will to affirm the capability of the finite imagination's attaining the infinite reality—the very large difference between the two poets is that Stevens usually resigns himself to failure, whereas Robinson, as in the disastrous sestet to this sonnet, blindly and like a mechanical optimist affirms fulfillment. This is the octave, "audible, most audible":

> I cannot find my way: there is no star
> In all the shrouded heavens anywhere;
> And there is not a whisper in the air
> Of any living voice but one so far
> That I can hear it only as a bar
> Of lost, imperial music, played when fair
> And angel fingers wove, and unaware,
> Dead leaves to garlands where no roses are.

9. In this chapter, unlike the one that is to follow, I am concerned more with the phenomenology than with the ontology. Ferenczi, on the "Thalassal Regressive Trend," would identify this up-down motion with "the motion of the embryo as it is rocked to and fro in the amniotic fluid." This, I have said, is a "religious" view, and its acceptance entails an act of faith in an insight of no more intrinsic credibility than the Kabbalistic belief that during a woman's pregnancy an angel burning as a small flame on the head of the fetus leads it on a pilgrimage up and down through the entire cosmos. That notion is no more verifiable than Lacan's determinist universal language code which "awaits the newborn even before his birth and seizes him with his first scream so as to appoint his place and his role" (Althusser). Lastly, to have done with these nativity creeds, Lacan's notion is no more believable than the ancient Christian tradition that the "guardian angel," the appointer of one's place and role, comes to the infant in the "trembling of the waters" in the up-down immersion at baptism.

The enjambment should not be overlooked but needs no elaboration now. I am concerned with the "cadenced" quality of these lines, the oscillation they impose on the reader by their movement between plenitude and vastation, between positive and negative images or concepts—all of which may be crudely sketched:

And there is not a whisper in the air	(negative)
of any living voice	(positive)
but one so far	(negative)
that I can hear it	(positive)
only as a bar of lost	(negative)
imperial music, played when fair and angel	
fingers wove	(positive)
and unaware, dead leaves	(negative)
to garlands	(positive)
where no roses are	(negative)

The sestet fails utterly, as I have said, because, as with weak religious poetry, there is no tension between these polar elements; it is, to adapt Eluard, "l'appareil banal de l'espoir."

Robinson's configuration of the up-down journey is more simply extrapolated and therefore may be more pedagogically cogent than the complex orchestration of Keats—again, I follow text with scheme:

> But when the melancholy fit shall fall
>   Sudden from heaven like a weeping cloud,
> That fosters the droop-headed flowers all,
>   And hides the green hill in an April shroud;
> Then glut thy sorrow on a morning rose,
>   Or on the rainbow of the salt sand-wave,
>   Or on the wealth of globed peonies;
> Or if thy mistress some rich anger shows,
>   Emprison her soft hand, and let her rave,
>   And feed deep, deep upon her peerless eyes.

But when the melancholy fit shall fall	(negative)
sudden from heaven	(positive)
like a weeping cloud	(negative)
that fosters	(positive)

the droop-headed	(negative)
flowers all	(positive)
and hides	(negative)
the green hill	(positive)
in an April shroud	(negative)
then glut	(positive)
thy sorrow	(negative)
on a morning rose	(positive)
or on the rainbow	(positive)
of the salt-sand wave	(negative)
or on the wealth of globed peonies	(positive)
or if thy mistress some rich	(positive)
anger shows	(negative)
emprison her soft hand	(positive)
and let her rave	(negative)
and feed deep, deep	(positive)

upon her peerless eyes

At this point ("upon her peerless eyes") the oscillation between poles is resolved in the play on "peerless," meaning "without peer" (positive) and "incapable of peering," that is, "sightless" (negative). The genius of this resolution is that it is founded on the traditional symbol of the beautiful blind woman as paradigmatic of the finite's relation with the infinite: a symbolism that includes the Zohar's description of the Shekhinah as "a beautiful woman without eyes," the blindfolded maiden as "Old Testament" in medieval art, the blinded women in Chagall's paintings, the blind Trophaëa of von le Fort's *Papst aus dem Ghetto,* and the blind Pensée of Claudel's *Père humilié*—all Jewish, and all affirming with the figure of Keats's mistress the paradox of Ben Jonson, "Speak that I may see thee."[10]

I have already referred in my first chapter to the oscillatory structure of "Lycidas" and will not repeat what I have said there.

10. The significance of Jewishness here is in the parallel of that religious tradition and the poetic tradition, both of which rely for inspiration and insight on the oral and the auditory. The poetic tradition speaks in all the passages I have cited; for this religious tradition, one need read only Simone Weil, Buber, or Rosenstock-Huessy. On the latter two philosophers of language, the most important study is Harold Stahmer's *Speak That I May See Thee*—a title that Stahmer derived from Hamann, all in happy illustration of the priority of poetic vision over philosophic, since Jonson anticipated Hamann by a century and a half.

My other examples are from Wordsworth, Yeats, and Ransom, and with the exception of the example from *The Prelude*, they are presented with a minimum of commentary. "Tintern Abbey," "The Wild Swans at Coole," and "Among School Children," oscillate between "then" and "now," between exultation and depression, or as Goldmann would say, describing "tragic tension," "from being to nothingness, and from presence to absence." This "mouvement de va-et-vient" would in English be called a "seesaw" movement and is in fact exemplified in Donne's "The Extasie": "We *see*, we *saw* not what did move." The effect of this structure in the second of the Yeats poems is the more powerful because the entire pattern of oscillation is neutralized by the coda of the last four prosaic stanzas of portentous enunciation and pretentious rambling. The poetry remains in the tension of past and present, of dreaming and thinking, of outside (smiling public man) and inside (my heart is driven wild). The philosophizing, however much range to critical debate it fosters, remains only that, philosophizing. Ransom's modest masterpiece, "The Equilibrists," is in many ways the lyric of oscillation par excellence: in its title, its plot, its imagery, and its rhythm.

In *The Prelude* this oscillation is between a mood of acquisitive arrogance in which the ego of the poet is seen as reshaping Nature and a mood of passive responsiveness in which Nature dominates the poet. Since Wordsworth's recurrent imagery for the second experience is heavily sexual, Coleridge's much-cited judgment about Wordsworth's sensibility lacking a feminine side is true only of the "older" Wordsworth, of the poet after 1804, for whom the great virtues were not candor and openness but strength and security, and who submitted himself to the "new control" of a self-generated concept of duty while rejecting the "old control" of Nature's Being. "The World Is Too Much with Us" is not an attack on materialism but an indictment of Wordsworth himself, who could not fulfill the poet's classic vocation as recipient of the logos spermatikos, and whose mortal being would not "bare her bosom" to Nature's "mighty being." His soul could no longer "put off her veil" (*The Prelude* 4.150) and be penetrated and possessed in the moment of poetic-nuptial union, the moment of what Carew called "holy rapes." Rather, "strong" and "secure" (obsessional key words) in the fortress of the self, the soul was "incased in the unfeeling armor of old time." Wordsworth's growing terror at the prospect of psychic ravishment, his fear of violation by Nature's Being, led with pathological determinism to his vengeful attempt to violate Nature itself. Nuns do fret indeed, and fret with an envy akin to that penile *ressentiment* which motivated the attempted castration of Nature symbolized (and unconsciously betrayed in the title?) by "Nutting."

It would entail too extensive a digression to go even briefly into this inversion of the traditional concept of the poet's relation to Nature's Being: from recipient and conduit of the Word ("Let me express Thee unblam'd," prayed Milton) to transformer of the Word and rival Creator ("I made it," vaunted Wordsworth)—the development is almost the theme of M. H. Abrams's *The Mirror and the Lamp*. It is part of that vast cultural sweep Lord Acton saw beginning with the discovery of the Stoic writings in the late Middle Ages and peaking in the license of the French Revolution. But for Wordsworth phylogeny and ontogeny are not homologous; Wordsworth "grows" *from* orgiastic ecstasy in freedom *to* a state of Stoic self-control. This conflict of rival principles, engendering the oscillatory structure, runs through all of the superb blank-verse poems, particularly *The Prelude* (superior, one sometimes thinks, to *Paradise Lost*, save where it attempts to confront Milton on his own ground—for example, Wordsworth's "Limbo of Fools" in 7.682 ff., and "Eden garden" in 8.70–110), and is briefly compassed in the subjective-objective conflict in the first two stanzas of the *Intimations* Ode, and in the objective-subjective conflict in stanzas 12 and 13 of "A Poet's Epitaph." Wordsworth sought to resolve the conflict by denigrating and then destroying the spousal yoke with Nature's Being—his aeolian harp became a tetrachordon.

This conflict in Wordsworth was laden with freight from the tradition and raised the problem of how to respond to the muse who stood behind the beauty of natural phenomena, the muse whose very raiment was the phenomena of nature. The imagery is sexual: the poet was either submissive, supinely acquiescent, and concomitantly inspired or he was rebellious and assertive, with the result that vision was not allotted. The consequence for Wordsworth was what Francis Thompson called "superb felicity and prosey twaddle." These two views of the poet's relation to his

muse engendered what Herbert Lindenberger has called Wordsworth's "two irreconcilable literary systems" and what Dwight Culler has discerned in a true Wordsworthian, Arnold, as two irreconcilable "selves." The dilemma embodied in both men's works is
the watershed of "modern" poetry. Both Wordsworth and Arnold
were in the end paralyzed into silence—resulting in what might
be called "the soliloquy of the interior paraplegic"—while the
poets of modernity, of whom Stevens is preeminent, reject the
muse of "the really out there now," the muse of "naive realism";
they reject all imagery of sexual submission to Nature in the name
of the subjective paramour, the fictions and figurings of their own
imaginings, which, somehow, mysteriously (it is the inexplicable
dialectic of Stevens's opus) seem truly to simulate reality in the
strange concordism of a preestablished/reestablished harmony.
This dialectic is discovered by Crispin on his return to North
America from Yucatan:

> He gripped more closely the essential prose
> As being, in a world so falsified,
> The one integrity for him, the one
> Discovery still possible to make,
> To which all poems were incident, *unless*
> *That prose should wear a poem's guise at last.*

Wordsworth's dialectic is considerably different, and to trace its
causes would take this discussion too far afield; in any case I am
interested in the oscillatory pattern engendered by the play of these
rival forces within him. The following from book 2 is a very rich
example:

> 'Twere long to tell
> What spring and autumn, what the winter snows,
> And what the summer shade, what day and night,
> Evening and morning, sleep and waking, thought
> From sources inexhaustible, poured forth
> To feed the spirit of religious love
> In which I walked with Nature. But let this
> Be not forgotten, that I still retained
> My first creative sensibility;

> That by the regular action of the world
> My soul was unsubdued. A plastic power
> Abode with me; a forming hand, at times
> Rebellious, acting in a devious mood;
> A local spirit of his own, at war
> With general tendency, but, for the most
> Subservient strictly to external things
> With which it communed. An auxiliar light
> Came from my mind, which on the setting sun
> Bestowed new splendors; the melodious birds,
> The fluttering breezes, fountains that run on
> Murmuring so sweetly in themselves, obeyed
> A like dominion, and the midnight storm
> Grew darker in the presence of my eye.
>
> [352–74]

The movement is from union with Nature to rebellion against it, then back again to general subservience to Nature, and finally to extreme self-exaltation. The whole passage is comparable in poetic and psychological density to lines 121–42 of book 3 with its oscillating sequence from subjective to objective: I gave . . . , I saw . . . , I linked . . . , I beheld . . . : with the whole culminating in the rapacious accents of "Nutting":

> Yet I was most rich—
> I had a world about me—'twas my own;
> I made it, for it only lived to me,
> And to the God who sees into the heart.

That last dutiful addendum ("And to the God . . .") has the same ring of authenticity one hears in the brief advertence, "and for thy sake," to Dorothy at the end of "Tintern Abbey"—an afterthought, like Browning's "One Word More."

As a final illustration, I would like to look briefly at the one poet of the nineteenth century whose language betrays an almost psychotic terror at this oscillation between polarities and whose most frequently reconceptualized imago invariably takes the form of circular motion. Not surprisingly, he is a poet most admired in the dourly earnest mid-nineteenth century and most contemned in the mid-twentieth century—though, as the advocates of "sincerity" man the literary redoubts, there may occur, there is in fact already occurring, a renaissance of interest in Matthew Arnold. (It is not without its lessons that the author of the first critical biography was also the author of a book on the evolution of the idea of sincerity.)[11]

Arnold, I have said, was tormented by the strain of these antipodal foundations of human existence; and his entire work, much more clearly than Wordsworth's, traces the path from an early muted hope that they could be mediated to morbid despair in the face of their unrelenting opposition. The result of this cognitive dissonance was the idealization of a state of total univocity, a state in which he sought to be free of any relationship with the non-self, to be immote and isolate: "Self-schooled, self-scanned, self-honoured, self-secure." (The unwitting parallel can only be with Satan and his followers, "self-begot, self-rais'd" [*PL* 5.8601].)

The trajectory of this growing autism is clearly drawn, from the inconclusiveness of "Mycerinus" and the vague wish in "To a Friend" that Sophocles could mediate Homer and Epictetus up to the conviction in most of the subsequent poems that mediation is utterly impossible. (Interestingly, his best poem, and a relatively early one, "The Forsaken Merman," does not display this schizophrenia.) Goethe and Byron are unmediated by the "dumb voice" of Wordsworth; Callicles and Pausanias are unmediated by the suicidal Empedocles—Arnold's own temptation to self-destruction being perhaps the real reason for deleting the poem from the 1853 collection (but he is in the grave, and oh! . . .); the Iseult of Ireland and the Iseult of Brittany are unmediated by the defeated Tristram; the "two desires" of the first Obermann poem, roughly symbolized by Wordsworth and Goethe, are unmediated by Obermann whose "unstrung will" ministered to a "broken heart"; the "two worlds," commemorated at the Charterhouse outside Grenoble, which should have been mediated by Arnold's own achievement, remain inviolable; the scholar and the gypsy are unmediated by the

---

11. On this in Wordsworth, David Perkins is revealing: "an ideal of sincerity, if pursued too remorselessly, can be devastating. Once it has been invoked, the eye fixes upon the self. . . . In this labyrinth of scrupulosity, one can even become bored and listless." The latter condition should not be confused with the paradoxic "ardent listlessness" of Keats; rather, it is identical with that capital sin the Middle Ages called *acedia*, and which Abrams identifies with Romantic "dejection."

scholar-gypsy who is only an unattainable wraith; and lastly, there is the monstrous egoism of the "From Switzerland" sequence where the polarization of male and female is unmediated by human love.[12] Arnold's immense capacity for self-enamorment in these "love poems" is that of the abandoned Endymion (4.309–10), "her hand he kissed, / And, . . . kissed his own." This was perhaps the moment of the fundamental option, the crucial point in Arnold's decline into univocity: to respond to the allures of eros incarnate or to reject them, and by that rejection become the permanent practitioner of intellectual ipsation. The choice he made is evident in the icy, "I bear that ye remove," of "Absence."

The circular movement that draws one toward a higher unity became for Arnold a dreaded experience. And if one may compare the oscillation discussed above with the oscillation between positive and negative poles with its resultant circular generation of electric power, it is clear that only by maintaining these "contacts," only by mediating this relationship between polar realities, is poetic power realized. Arnold could not mediate the strain of the antagonist poles, and he regarded all circularity with terror. For him there was no resolution in the "whizzing wheel" ("The Forsaken Merman"), no escape from the "iron round" that "hems us all in" ("Resignation"), from the "benumbing round" ("Memorial Verses"), from going "round" in an "eddy" ("Rugby Chapel")—there was no escape except into the disinterestedness and detachment rightly lauded in the essays and disastrously embodied in the poems.

Dwight Culler in his *Imaginative Reason* is not aware of the irony in his faltering parallel of Newman and Arnold, which is founded, and founders, on Newman's statement in the *Apologia* about two

12. Just as one reads Wordsworth's "Lucy" poems as elegies for the poet himself and the murder of his muse (it was a transmogrifying leech-gatherer put the poison), so too one may read Arnold's "Marguerite" poems—though there was no doubt a real Marguerite as there probably was not a real Lucy. From "Perle" to Hopkins's "Spring and Fall," all Margarets, Wordsworth's and Arnold's also, have affinities with the gospel *pretiosa margarita* for which one should *abandon* all. It was this radical failure of self-abandonment, this obsession with *se-curitas*, that Arnold suffered from, as had his master. "I only have relinquished one delight," says Wordsworth in the last stanza of the *Intimations* Ode, but that "only one" is the *una necessaria*, the radiant Lucy, the all-conquering Vincentine of Stevens; truly, the "*pearly spouse*" of great price who is depicted by Stevens in all her poetic and sexual glamour: "Abundantly beautiful, eager, fecund"—nothing here nobly planned "to warn, to comfort, and command."

and two only luminously self-evident beings, God and the self: "Arnold believed in two and two only luminously self-evident beings, his Best Self and his Ordinary Self. Newman's task, then, was to strengthen the links between himself and his Creator, Arnold's to repudiate the Ordinary Self and strengthen the Best Self." The upper-case reifications cannot obscure the fact that unlike Newman's "two and two only" affirmation, anything comparable to this for Arnold could entail no real alterity. Newman chose as motto, "heart speaks to heart"; Arnold's motto could only have been, "heart speaks to self"—hence Arnold's erection of a solipsistic prison of negativity, as in "Self-dependence," to be "unaffrighted," "undistracted," "bounded" by oneself, and "unregardful"; or, as in "A Summer Night," to be "untroubled and unpassionate."

In all of these poems and most explicitly in "Isolation. To Marguerite," with its diseased sense of *honte*, Arnold repudiated the finite-infinite conjunction central to all the great Romantics from Blake to Newman. Thus, where Arnold seeks in poem after poem some kind of starry state or astral condition for himself, it is apparent he is seeking it because such a state or condition is monadic, remote, and unchanging; Keats on the other hand seeks it, as we have noted, for its paradoxic qualities, "steadfast" and restless, "falling and swelling"; that is, Keats seeks it precisely for its cadenced, up-down qualities. Once again, Arnold is faithful to the Wordsworth of the postecstatic cogitations, the Wordsworth who in a justly criticized passage assigned to "duty" the office of maintaining order and stasis in the heavens:

> Thou dost preserve the stars from wrong;
> And the most ancient heavens, through
>   Thee, are fresh and strong.
>
> ["Ode to Duty"]

Coleridge, originally a greater visionary than the balladeering Wordsworth, corrects this univocity in his prose comment on the "protoevangelium" embodied in lines 263–66 of "The Rime of the Ancient Mariner," where the astral condition to which we must aspire is seen as intrinsically paradoxic: "In his loneliness and fixedness he yearneth towards... the stars that *still sojourn*, yet *still move onward*."

PART THREE: ONTOLOGICAL
PHENOMENOLOGY

IX: *Complementarity*

The rather pretentious title to this section, "Ontological Phenomenology," is intended merely to indicate that in these last two chapters, as in the first two, I will be relating the structural patterns more explicitly, and more prosaically, to the heuristic myth.

In the fifth chapter of the second book of *De Docta ignorantia*, Cusanus amends Anaxagoras's "Everything is everything" to read "Everything in everything." The shift is from a relatively undifferentiating pantheism, which really is indistinguishable from chaos, to an ordered totality, all the constituents of which are correlative. So, too, with the various structures I have been describing. Depending on one's vantage in considering them, they may be seen as functioning differently but always in consonance with one another and with the whole.

I have maintained that the unremitting duality of human existence is not truly mediated by such symbolic constructs as history or philosophy, or by language itself. One may refer to them as mediators only if one gives the word its twofold sense as "that which connects" and "that which stands between." They thus do not in any way resolve the conflict of opposites but are merely propaedeutic to that partial resolution that comes in the aesthetic, the sexual, the mystical experience. For that reason aesthetic, sexual, and mystical union is rightly characterized as "ecstatic," and it is under that heading that I want to consider my last formal pattern, waves and particles. In exploring this pattern I will examine in detail the works of a poet I have cited often, a religious poet at that, who, as certainly as one can speculate, experienced the ecstasy of union, and whose imagery, perhaps more consistently than that of any other poet in English, directly reflects the thematization of that experience.

But before taking up several of Hopkins's poems, I want to examine quickly two very familiar passages that are descriptive rhythmically of this phenomenon that Hopkins bodied forth figuratively.

Twice in "Tintern Abbey" Wordsworth described what he called the "decay" of spirit and the "wild ecstasies" of liberation. The first passage conveys a sense of an all-environing pressure, a sense of the terrifying *pondus* of existence; thus, the modifying phrases are less in apposition to each other than they are cumulative upon each other, and so expressive of the greater and greater gravamina heaped upon afflicted humanity:

> In which the burthen / of the mystery /
> In which the heavy / and the weary weight /
> Of all this unintelligible world.

What is being experienced here is the seemingly inexorable downward thrust and pull of what the classical philosophers called simply "matter."

But in the second passage what is described is the multiplicity, the chaotic and fragmented nature of reality—and again the classical philosophers concur with Aristotle in defining this as another aspect of "matter"; discrete part outside of part. Since this is an important element in the larger pattern I am analyzing here, it might be well to look briefly at some examples of this multiplicity, which is underlined by the heavily punctuated verse. In Stevens's "A Rabbit as King of the Ghosts," the oppressive and hateful cat is the very embodiment of the discrete:

> There was the cat slopping its milk all day,
> Fat cat, red tongue, green mind, white milk.

In Stevens's poem, when the cat is negated in the moment of ecstatic transcendence, the descriptive comment is simply, "no *matter*."

The archetypal oppressor and object of hate is Satan, who experiences the cumbering burden of his materiality when he attempts to escape the domain of density:

> So eagerly the fiend
> O'er bog or steep, through strait, rough, dense, or rare,
> With head, hands, wings, or feet pursues his way,
> And swims or sinks, or wades, or creeps, or flies.
>
> [*PL* 2.947–50]

It is in the city, the last creation of Urizen, that is established the kingdom of fragmented matter:

> What a hell
> For eyes and ears! what anarchy and din
> Barbarian and infernal,—a phantasma,
> Monstrous in color, motion, shape, sight, sound!
> . . . .
> ... with buffoons against buffoons
> Grimacing, writhing, screaming, ...
> . . . .
> Equestrians, tumblers, women, girls, and boys,
> Blue-breeched, pink vested, with high towering plumes.—
> All moveables of wonder, from all parts,
> Are here—Albinos, painted Indians, Dwarfs,
> The Horse of knowledge, and the learned Pig,
> The Stone-eater, the man that swallows fire,
> Giants, Ventriloquists, the Invisible Girl,
> The Bust that speaks and moves its goggling eyes,
> The Wax-work, Clock-work, all the marvellous craft
> Of modern Merlins, Wild Beasts, Puppet-shows,
> All out-o'-the-way, far-fetched, perverted things.
>
> [*The Prelude* 7.685 ff.]

> trivial forms
> Of houses, pavement, streets, of men and things,—
> Mean shapes on every side.
>
> [Ibid. 8.545–47]

Similarly, the discrete and fragmented is the realm of utterly material love, that is, of grossly concupiscent and purely physical sexual passion, as Donne sought to convey that putative condition in "The Blossome" and "The Indifferent"—where again the Aristotelian definition of matter as "part outside of part" is conveyed by the heavily punctuated line:

> You goe to friends, whose love and meanes present
>> Various content
> To your eyes, eares, and tongue, and every part.
>
> I can love her, and her, and you, and you,
> I can love any, so she be not true.

—or as in Shakespeare's considerably less self-diffident and ironic Sonnet 129:

> The expense of spirit in a waste of shame
> Is lust in action; and till action, lust
> Is perjur'd, murd'rous, bloody, full of blame,
> Savage, extreme, rude, cruel, not to trust.

Even in the religious man this chaotic multiplicity of matter may transform liberty into license, as in Vaughan's "Rom. Cap. 8. ver. 19":

> Shall I thy mercies still abuse
> With fancies, friends, or newes?

Returning now to "Tintern Abbey," this dislocated, shattered condition of "discrete part outside of part" is also conveyed by fragmentation, here by a sequence of repeated dentals that audibly separates syllables, words, and phrases, in effect separating them from a unifying "spirit" or "form," so that they bespeak merely so much "dead matter"—the result is comparable to Blake's "What dread hand? and what dread feet?" or to Byron's "dead doges are declined to dust." Wordsworth's anatomy of this tomb of spirit requires that the dentals be stressed:

> how of*t*
> In *d*arkness an*d* ami*d* the many shapes
> Of joyless *d*ayligh*t*, when the fre*t*ful s*t*ir
> Unprofi*t*able and the fever of the worl*d*,
> Have hung upon the bea*t*ings of my hear*t*.

"Tintern Abbey," then, presents two types of misery, the first deriving from an omnipressive *Umwelt* of fardel (the "burthen of the mystery" passage), and the second from the sheer disjointedness of things—that is, misery derived from the *weight* of matter, and from the *discreteness* of matter (this latter most commonly embodied in the heavily punctuated lines cited earlier). In both cases there is entrapment in a monadic condition, in a state of "pure matter" (not in Aristotle's notion of prime matter as "potency" but in Berdyaev's sense of complete enslavement), a condition of total bondage and oppression. Release from this bondage would by definition be "ecstasy," Wordsworth's professed theme, and one that he here communicates structurally.

In the first example from "Tintern Abbey," transcendence is achieved by a kind of intense and immediate ex-plosion, an outburst of liberating incandescence which is literally momentary and corpuscular:

> In which the burthen of the mystery
> In which the heavy and the weary weight
> Of all this unintelligible world
> Is *lightened*.

The play on "light" stresses both exultation and illumination, and obviously the overall pattern is congruent, as it will be also in my next example, with what I have described earlier in the context of complexification and coda.

But the second mode of ecstasy is somewhat different.

> how oft
> In darkness and amid the many shapes
> Of joyless daylight: when the fretful stir
> Unprofitable and the fever of the world,
> Have hung upon the beatings of my heart
> How oft in spirit have I turned to thee,
> O sylvan Wye! thou wanderer thro' the woods.

When one scans the last line and then accompanies the reading with gesture, the chironomy must take the form of a wave. This resultant flowing arabesque is the opposite of the single punctum of the first mode of ecstasy. The first, we may say, was corpuscular; this is cymatic. Furthermore, since the paradox redoubles (Cusanus's "Everything in everything"), one may note that in the first passage it is the continuum of pressure that is released by the particulate "is lightened," while in the second, the discrete and fragmented is resolved or subsumed by the extended arabesque.

The language I am employing now is obviously modeled on that of physical theory, where a wave and a particle duality has long been evident, with partisans at different periods of history favoring one or the other antagonist view, or more recently in this century, after Niels Bohr, a paradoxic combination of both. The reason for using this kind of language has been hinted at earlier and will be detailed shortly; for now, it is sufficient to note another common base for the metaphors of poetry and religion, and those of science.

Before looking at some poems of Hopkins, one must emphasize that no prior bias sought confirmation of an abstract theory of poetic structure, reflective and reciprocally causal of pleasure or ecstasy, in the work of this or that likely candidate, in this instance an artist, a metaphysician, a religious "mystic," and so on. Furthermore, as has already been adumbrated, the theory is not merely one of the nature of poetry and its attendant ecstasy but a theory of "reality," of "human nature"—at least as those mysterious entities have been understood in our original heuristic myth. And lastly, though I take as point of departure Hopkins's imagery, it should be apparent that all of the poetic structures discussed earlier are congruent with, indeed in their inscape are identifiable with, what Hopkins's poems figure forth.

In the first lines of "The Sea and the Skylark," with their blatant homophonic repetition, the context of ecstasy is defined: "On ear and ear *two* noises *too* old *to* end / Trench." A creature of duality (two) experiences the transcendentally superabundant (too) which is teleologically oriented (to). The "trench" points to the *sillion* of a more renowned poem on the same theme and stresses by its monosyllabic harshness the arduousness and the unpredictability of the conjunction.

    On ear and ear two noises too old to end
       Trench—right, the tide that ramps against the shore;
       With a flood or a fall, low lull-off or all roar,
    Frequenting there while moon shall wear and wend.

> Left hand, off land, I hear the lark ascend,
> His rash-fresh re-winded new-skeined score
> In crisps of curl off wild winch whirl, and pour
> And pelt music, till none's to spill nor spend.

> How these two shame this shallow and frail town!
> How ring right out our sordid turbid time,
> Being pure!

By definition, "tide" is an undulating mass covering a considerable time span, while the lark's ascending song is brief and particulate. But it is the confluence of both that here defines the human reality: man first as victim and then vector of the sequential and the instantaneous as well as of the ponderous and the lyric. The experience of the one divorced from the other is torment; the experience of the two conjoined is ecstasy. Hence the wordplay on "ringing right out," what Hopkins called the "shallowness" and others have called the "one-dimensionality" of "our time"—for there is no dimension without the experience of point meeting line and concreating volume or depth, much like the juncture of two images in a vectograph. The proclamatory "ring out" is simultaneously the tortuous "wring out" (a pun more commonly recognized in the "wring" and "rung" of "Spring" and "The Windhover" respectively), the verb enunciating magnificence, as in Milton's "ring out ye crystal sphere," and torment, as in Shelley's "wring the truth out of these nerves and sinews." This grandeur-misery theme parallels the polarization in Hopkins's "Pied Beauty" of swift-slow, sweet-sour, adazzle-dim; and again, release from the strain of those particularities is found in their union with the unbroken cymatic: "He fathers forth whose beauty is past change." Hopkins then enriches that paradox ("Everything in everything") by the paradox of the last two lines themselves, which are identical with our experience of coda earlier:

> He fathers forth whose beauty is past change:
> Praise him.

And this last undular *and* corpuscular structure is the same as Wordsworth's "O sylvan Wye! thou wanderer thro' the woods" and "Is lightened."

It is of ecstasy as such that Hopkins writes in what is probably his most opulent elaboration of the wave-particle motif—though perhaps we should employ the neologism of some physicists and speak of the "wavicle" motif. In "The May Magnificat," "this ecstasy all through mothering earth" occurs precisely

> When drop-of-blood-and-foam-dapple
> Bloom lights the orchard apple
>   And thicket and thorp are merry
>   With silver-surfed cherry
>
> And azuring-over greybell makes
> Wood banks and brakes wash wet like lakes
>   And magic cuckoocall
>   Caps, clears, and clinches all—
>
> This ecstasy all through mothering earth

—"this ecstasy" (and one may note again the enjambment) occurs precisely when all of this washed and wet, expansive and rolling landscape is intersected by the brief and clinching "magic cuckoo-call."

I said above I would provide a reason for employing this kind of language from physical theory. I begin with the following from Heisenberg's *Physics and Philosophy*, where he observes that Bohr's theory of the complementarity of waves and particles "starts with a paradox"—and we shall see, terminates in a paradox as well. Heisenberg continues:

> Bohr advocated the use of both [wave and particle] pictures, which he called "complementary" to each other. The two pictures are of course mutually exclusive, because a certain thing cannot at the same time be a particle (i.e., substance confined to a very small volume) and a wave (i.e., a field spread out over a large space), but the two complement each other. By playing with both pictures [the "oscillation" described in chapter 8], by going from the one picture to the other and back again, we finally get the right impression of the strange kind of reality behind our atomic experiments.

Though there has been controversy over what is now called "the Copenhagen interpretation," particularly on the part of Bohm and Margenau, no reputable physicist—unlike, say, Daiches's or Hillyer's easy dismissal of paradox and irony in their attacks on the New Criticism—has failed to wrestle with the basic paradox discerned and articulated by Bohr and his disciples; nor has any reputable physicist suggested that this paradox is merely "a feature" of the basic structure of reality. At present, as Heisenberg persuasively shows, it is the only adequate model (read *myth*) of that structure we have.

But I am not concerned with poetry and the notion of complementarity as such—that has been shown to have a growing relevance to any critical enterprise in the pioneering studies of Kenneth Pike on the nature of language, and in the work of Frank Kermode on fiction and of Norman Rabkin on Shakespeare. Rather, it is the language of Heisenberg that I want to pause over. I note, first, the use of "picture" originally intended to convey merely the provisional nature of the hypothesis but with strong bearing on literary analysis—certainly a much stronger bearing than the more currently voguish (after Thomas Kuhn) "paradigm." Thus Yeats was correct in translating literally from Plato with the phrase "*ghostly paradigm*," because the word does suggest something disincarnate and skeletal—and is certainly quite remote from the poet's preoccupation with an embodied totality. I note, second, the notion of "playing with" as suggesting the chanciness, the unpredictability, of what may ensue in the quasiecstatic unity of scientific discovery. Again, Heisenberg's is a happier rendition than Kuhn's much abused problem- or puzzle-solving with its overtones of the purely quantitative and measurable and its indifference to the poet's intuitive realization that the balances of opposites are not "balances / That we achieve but balances that happen, / As a man and woman meet and love forthwith" ("Notes toward a Supreme Fiction").[1] I

1. Interestingly, it has not been theologians or artists—committed to a world view in which the "miraculous," the "inspirational," the "capricious" are fundamental "givens"—who have attacked the cryptopositivism of the Kuhnian conception; rather, it has been the heirs of the father of positivism, the sociologists, Alvin Gouldner preeminently, who have been most critical of a "logic" of knowledge centered on problem solving.

note, lastly, the easy casualness of "we finally get the right impression of . . ." and its conveyance of a kind of graceful uncertitude, the attitude of openness and willingness to be surprised that I have earlier said is characteristic of the spontaneous outburst of "spirit," of *Vernunft*, as it leaps to conclusions unforseen—as it "gets the joke."

There are other symmetries of the physicist's and the critic's job of work that might be explored, but my main concern is the relevance of Bohr's theory of complementarity (which for my purposes is comparable to de Broglie's theory of "simultaneity") to the larger argument of this book. Man experiences joy, fulfillment, "ecstasy," when the paradox of his own being is, however transitorily, resolved; when, to use the most rudimentary language again, his "inside" and "outside" seem to harmonize; when his being *is* his doing, so that he can say, "What I *do is* me." In this moment he experiences that final circular perfection—that I will take up in my final chapter—where "accident is substance, body is spirit, movement is rest" (Cusanus, again, in *Docta ignorantia*), and where, anticipating this last Hopkins text, Cusanus says in *De Visione Dei*, "to have is to be."

Those poetic utterances which delight us do so precisely because they first point to and then induce this sense of oneness, this transitory but re-creative resolution of duality and dubiety. I think this is neither outmoded physics nor outmoded poetics, and I therefore find significant the following judgment by F. S. C. Northrop in the preface to de Broglie's *Physics and Micro-Physics*: "First, the principle of complementarity and the present validity of the Cartesian and common-sense concepts of body and mind stand and fall together." This is the first part of Northrop's judgment, and I want to gloss it fully before taking up his second.

I have indicated earlier that it is almost an a priori and hence unquestionable assumption in literary, philosophical, and theological circles that a severe dualism is anachronistic, medieval or at least antimodern. If not Dewey, then the "linguistic turn," has utterly evaporated the problem, and the Cartesian gap has been bridged. Gilbert Ryle in *The Concept of Mind* is, of course, correct in observing that to define the issue as one of spirit versus body or self versus other is simply a "mistake," because it is not a question of an utterly irresoluble adversary relation but a disequilibrium which occasionally, by chance, *falls* into balance: when, as Blake's saw has it, "Contraries mutually exist" (pl. 17, 33). One may imagine permanent dissolution of this duality and talk on the level of vulgar psychology and sociology of "interaction" and "transaction," and on the level of philosophy after Blondel of simply "action," or after Whitehead and Hartshorne of "relationism" and "biperspectivism"—unfortunately, the experienced facts remain intractable to these labels, just as the seers of dualism like Wallace Stevens may be pilloried in the name of Merleau-Ponty and Wittgenstein without the dualism being any the less suppressed or evaded, or any of us any the less latently schizophrenic. Says Stevens: "Between the two we live and die." Like Struldbrugs, petulant or wracking, surly or silent, the antinomies are there, and they will not pass away.

As for the antiquarian quality and antimodernism of the notion, it is true the continuum begins with the Sophists' phusis-nomos duality, through Aristotle's hylomorphism and up to Aquinas's "real distinction" between essence and existence. But this continuum stretches well past Descartes. ("Sink deep or touch not the Cartesian spring" is one of Joyce's gnomes. A little unicism *is* a dangerous thing.) It stretches up to Durkheim and his *homo duplex* with its subsidiary dichotomies that read like a refrain from the great Romantics: concepts-sensations, sociology-psychology, moral rules–sensual appetites, social-individual, sacred-profane, and so on. We continue to wrestle with the "paradox" of Freudianism, the bimodality of Rokeach, with Lévi-Strauss's nature-culture, Mannheim's ideology-utopia, Saussure's signifié-signifiant, Tillich's dynamics-form, Jakobson's metaphor-metonymy, Wittgenstein's structures–states of affairs, and so on. This testificatory bricolage could be heaped up endlessly, simply because all seemingly successful hyphenations are momentary, epiphanic, and therefore "function" as stimuli to continue the search for permanent resolution of the tension, of the interplay. It is indeed this search which is the motor of all human endeavor. And one could, as I say, marshal uncountable witnesses. I will cap the pile with the following splendid (though tendentious) coda on Pascal from Lucien Goldmann's *The Hidden God*:

Subsequently Hegel, and especially Marx and Lukàcs, have been able to substitute for the wager on the paradoxical and mediatory God of Christianity the wager on a historical future and on the human community. In doing so, however, they have not given up the main demands of tragic thought, that is to say a doctrine which explains the paradoxical nature of human reality, and a hope in the eventual creation of values which endows this contradiction with meaning and which transforms ambiguity into a necessary element of a significant whole. In my opinion this is one of the best indications which we have of the existence, not only of a continuity in what I would call "classical" thought from Greek times to our own day but also of a more particular continuity in modern classical thought within whose framework the tragic vision of Pascal and Kant constitutes an essential stage in the movement which goes beyond sceptical or dogmatic rationalism towards the birth and elaboration of dialectical philosophy.

This judgment could be corrected by a less doctrinaire Marxist like Bloch, but that is hardly necessary here.

It is necessary though to return to that passage from F. S. C. Northrop I left fragmented above. The complete quotation is:

> *First*, the principle of complementarity and the present validity of the Cartesian and common-sense concepts of body and mind stand and fall together. *Second*, it may be that both these notions are merely convenient stepladders which should now be, or must eventually be, thrown away. Even so, in the case of the theory of mind at least, the stepladder will have to remain until by its use we find the more linguistically exact and empirically satisfactory theory that will permit us to throw the Cartesian language away.

Second, one would maintain that the stepladder of the New Criticism in its substantive contributions—not its occasional social snobbism, political elitism, ahistoricism, linguistic nitpicking, arrant triumphalism—such as the centrality of paradox, ambiguity, and irony as structural forces rather than as verbal techniques, has to remain until there is found an alternative, more linguistically exact and empirically satisfactory theory. As to replacing those central concerns, those notions synonymous with "complementarity," by such vague semantic blankets as "tone" or "authenticity," any one who still finds Wimsatt on critical "fallacies" cogent can only doubt the wisdom of the substitute enterprise, of trading a monkey for Leah's ring.

For the scientist, the complementarity of the quanta of Planck and the waves of de Broglie constitutes the best model of the scientific experience and the physical reality; for the "natural-supernaturalist" tradition, it constitutes, as we have seen, the manifestation of the transcendent, which

> will flame out, like shining from shook foil;
> It gathers to a greatness, like the ooze of oil
> Crushed.
>
> ["God's Grandeur"]

Again, there is no need to labor the significance of the enjambment, but one should note that the flame is Wordsworth's particulate moment of being "lightened," as the ooze of oil is the flowing waters of the "sylvan Wye." Not surprisingly, for Hopkins the "Holy Ghost" lengthily "broods" and then comes to plenitude with momently flaming "bright Wings" (this particular *coincidentia oppositorum*, the commentators have observed, being reminiscent of Loyola's "a sole . . . radii; a fonte aquae"—which Hopkins in his notes on the *Spiritual Exercises* glossed, "give off sparks and take fire, yield drops and flow").

In reading Hopkins on God's grandeur one would almost think he were alluding to the major scientific controversy at the close of the last century between those who believed brain conduction to be essentially chemical and those who believed it to be essentially electrical. The proponents of the first assumption were known as "soup" people, and the proponents of the second, as "spark" people—for "soup" one may read "ooze of oil," and for "spark" one may read "shining from shook foil." In fact, these polemical ascriptions were launched several years after the composition of the poem. But had the scientists followed the lead of the poet, they would have realized that it was in the "trenching," in the "complementarity" of the two notions, that truth lay: the brain is now universally recognized as an extremely complicated matrix of electrochemical circuitry.

One is therefore justified in being somewhat taken aback when Marjorie Hope Nicolson, so at home both in the history of ideas and in the interpretation of poetic texts, gives the scientists priority over the poets. In *Newton Demands the Muse* she notes that "Newton himself had vacillated between a wave theory and a corpuscular theory; while he finally committed himself to the latter in the *Opticks*, he did so with evident hesitation." She then goes on to read both Blake and John Reynolds as absorbing Newton's corpuscular theory into their works, whereas in fact it appears that, in response to the paradoxic tension constituent of man, they may have had a vision of complementarity.[2] (The historical parallel of this "visionary company" might be with those Church Fathers who called baptism in water "photismos"—and in effect said that the "soup" *is* the "spark," the pouring waters *are* the illumination, and the sylvan Wye *is* "lightened.")[3] Like Hopkins a century later, John Reynolds wrote in *A Vision of Death* of the confluence of "atoms too fine" and of "swift streams," thus seeming to embrace both particles and waves, while Blake in *The Book of Los* did the same, only in the opposite order:[4]

> Then Light first began: from the fires,
> *Beams*, conducted by *fluids* so pure,
> Flowed round the Immense.
> . . . .
> [Los] seized, beating incessant, condensing
> the Subtil *particles*.
>
> [4.10–12, 29–30]

2. The subjunctive tone of what follows is necessary because of the ambiguity of all terms used to describe the transmission of atomistic particles, *emissio* and *effluvium* being the most common but both connotative of something fluid. The problem of rightly interpreting such lines as Blake's and Reynold's is further compounded by the fact that such originally simple notions denominated by terms like corpuscle, atom, particle are not compatible with the vastly more complex notions of modern physics denominated by such terms as protons, neutrons, positrons, etc. Neither Newton nor Democritus, much less Blake and Reynolds, would know what to make of such language.

3. It is quite literally the baptism of the Mariner that Coleridge describes—"The lightning fell with never a jag, / A river steep and wide" (325–26)—while Jonson in "Though I Am Young and Cannot Tell" sees both loving and dying, both baptismal moments, coming in "a flash of lightning, or a wave."

4. The coupling of light and fluid imagery in Blake is frequent, e.g., "The Evening Star" both lights a torch and scatters dew, and the "glimmering eyes" "wash the dusk"; or, again, the liberated chimney sweepers' baptism comes when they wash and shine.

Bracketing off the failure of Goethe's color theory, the lesson remains that everyone should pay at least as much attention to the poets as to the scientists—Newton with his prism was for Dean Swift a mere "maker of sun-dials," and for Blake a builder of "water wheels." After all, Orpheus did accompany Jason, and there is even a legend that Pythagoras had been instructed by the ghost of Orpheus.

That Hopkins and the poetic tradition failed to lesson the soup-spark polemicists or Bohr and the Copenhagen group is, thus, not the first exemplification of Hermes' bootless tutelage of Apollo. Again, in this context of spark and soup, one thinks of Keats anticipating Polanyi in *Endymion* (4.77): "There is no *lightning*, no authentic *dew* / But in the eye of love." In fact—though I mention Hermes more or less symbolically—one may read in Poimandres, the hermetic counterpart of Genesis, the following explanation of the coming into being of the elements: "the watery substance... was fashioned into an ordered world... and fire unmixed leaped forth from the watery substance." This tradition extends all the way to Eliphas Lévi, the father of what little—and there is truly precious little—is authentic in contemporary occultism, who commenting in the 1850s on the universal stuff of reality noted that it is at once a "fluid and a perpetual vibration... which in creatures takes the form of magnetic light and fluid." Again, for magnetic light one may read "spark," and for fluid one may read "soup."

Because Hopkins like all true poets was writing unprogrammatically out of his vision and not out of any prescribed convention, this motif of complementarity constantly recurs. In a passage from *The Wreck of the Deutschland*, he again indicates that it is by the wavelike and the corpuscular that the absolute affects the contingent:

> With an anvil-ding
> And with fire in him forge thy will
> Or rather, rather then, stealing as Spring
> Through him, melt him but master him still:
> Whether at once, as once at a crash Paul,
> Or as Austin, a lingering-out sweet skill,
> Make mercy in all of us, out of us all
> Mastery, but be adored, but be adored King.

[10]

We have the "fire" (spark) and the "melting" (soup), along with the corpuscular "crash" and the cymatic "lingering-out." And elsewhere in the poem God is "lightning and love . . ., a winter and warm" (9), whose adorers will "bathe in his fall-gold mercies . . ., breathe in his all-fire glances" (24)—similarly with the "dim woods" and the "diamond delves," the "grey lawns" and the "quickgold" (with the latter playing back to quicksilver, the hermetic medium) of "The Starlight Night"; the "yellow moisture" and "tram-beams" (the latter cognate to "ooze of oil" and "shook foil") of "The Candle Indoors"; the "lift me, lay me" of "Henry Purcell"; and finally the "glide" and "hurl" of "The Windhover."

Since, as I have been emphasizing, ultimately all figures are one figure and all patterns are congruent one with the other, it is hardly surprising that in this context of waves and particles I will draw upon some passages embodying structures examined in earlier chapters. I have already discussed Herbert's "Redemption" with regard to its coda, but there is an equally rich—and, now, very relevant—structural "chord" preceding that dramatic closure:

> I straight return'd and knowing his great birth,
>   Sought him accordingly in great resorts;
>   In cities, theatres, gardens, parks, and courts:
> At length I heard a ragged noise and mirth
>
>   Of theeves and murderers: there I him espied,
>   Who straight, *Your suit is granted*, said, & died.

I will not elaborate on the striking enjambment here which signals the discovery of the transcendent; I want only to point out that the overflowing and unpunctuated line, "At length I heard a ragged noise and mirth of theeves and murderers," is structurally undular while the heavily punctuated line which precedes it is structurally corpuscular. The pattern thus exemplifies my present focus: the ecstasy of conjoining the broken and fragmented with the harmonious and unified. "Dramatically," one might say that the poet is indicating here that Jesus is to be found not in the chaos of the discrete and particulate but in the harmony of the unified; or, better, that Jesus—word become flesh, spirit become matter—is the nexus of both; and it is the experience of this structural nexus that engenders aesthetic delight, or ecstasy—as it does also in Coleridge's

> As if / this earth / in fast / thick pants / were breathing,
> A mighty fountain momently was forced.

It is difficult to read the lines above from Herbert's "Redemption" without thinking of a similarly organized passage in a sonnet of Wordsworth also considered earlier:

> Ships, towers, domes, theatres, and temples lie
> Open unto the fields, and to the sky.

The enjambment needs no emphasis, nor does the fact that one is describing the merger of heaven and earth. In the context of this chapter, I want to stress primarily that the corpuscular fragments find their complement in the cymatic unity of the second line—all not unlike the transcendently beautiful opening to "Vertue":

> Sweet day, so cool, so calm, so bright,
> The bridall of the earth and sky.

Again, one is witnessing the marriage of heaven and earth, and experiencing the "chord" of multiplicity-unity, of matter-spirit. One may hear this chord in the following from *Paradise Regained*, which also evokes the Herbert and Wordsworth lines above:

> As one in city, or court, or Palace bred,
> And with fair speech these words to him address'd.
>
> [2.300–01]

And it is a structure that almost redeems the outrageously self-parodistic beginning of Wordsworth's "To the Small Celandine":

> Pansies, lilies, kingcups, daisies,
> Let them live upon their praises.

One of many ancestors of Herbert's "Vertue" is Edmund Bolton's "A Palinode," in which the first four lines are cymatic and the next four corpuscular; and the entire poem follows the circular pattern I shall examine in the next chapter:

> As withereth the primrose by the river,
>   As fadeth summer's sun from gliding fountains,
> As vanisheth the light-blown bubble ever,
>   As melteth snow upon the mossy mountains:
> So melts, so vanisheth, so fades, so withers
>   The rose, the shine, the bubble, and the snow
> Of praise, pomp, glory, joy (which short life gathers),
>   Fair praise, vain pomp, sweet glory, brittle joy.

The overall paradoxic complementarity is brilliantly intensified (as it will be also in Hopkins's "The Windhover") by the fact that the wavelike lines are all end-stopped, while the corpuscular lines are enjambed.

And certainly one of the immediate heirs of "Vertue" is Keats's "The Day Is Gone" (consistently misprinted in succeeding editions of Bernbaum's *Anthology*), with its many direct verbal echoes of Herbert—as well as of Burton's *Anatomy*, as Robert Gittings showed.

> The day is gone, and all its sweets are gone!
> Sweet voice, sweet lips, soft hand, and softer breast,
> Warm breath, light whisper, tender semi-tone,
> Bright eyes, accomplish'd shape, and lang'rous waist!
> Faded the flower and all its budded charms,
> Faded the sight of beauty from my eyes,
> Faded the shape of beauty from my arms,
> Faded the voice, warmth, whiteness, paradise—
>
> Vanish'd unseasonably at shut of eve,
> When the dusk holiday—or holinight
> Of fragrant-curtain'd love begins to weave
> The woof of darkness thick, for hid delight;
> But, as I've read love's missal through to-day,
> He'll let me sleep, seeing I fast and pray.

The poem is almost the perfect exemplification of the major structural formats we have been considering. The first and last lines of the octave are respectively cymatic and corpuscular, while the six central lines, in chiastic pattern, reverse the preceding order and are respectively corpuscular and cymatic. One might say, further, that the fragmented lines in the first quatrain symbolize the spasmodically attained experiential reality, while the unbroken and flowing lines of the second quatrain evoke the now unattainable, remembered ideal. The entire octave is heavily charged and explosive; the chiasm hints at conflict, and the polarization of waves and particles manifests an unrealized complementarity on the personal and the ontological, the sexual and the metaphysical levels. As in several poems examined earlier, the attainment of that complementarity, of that ecstasy of transcendence, is signaled by the heavily enjambed lines of the third quatrain which stand in marked contrast to the bluntly end-stopped lines of all that goes before:

> When the dusk holiday—or holinight
> Of fragrant-curtain'd love begins to weave
> The woof of darkness thick

The actual resolution of this straining vigil will come, as all true lovers like Madeline and Porphyro know, on the good-morrow of their waking souls. Then they shall no longer kiss by the mass book but in their sexual sacrament shall share in the *individual* kiss of Milton's supreme Copula, which the coda-couplet anticipates.

A much simpler example of this complementarity is in Donne's "A Valediction Forbidding Mourning," where he is explicitly contrasting "spirit" and "matter," soul and body, wave and corpuscle:

> Inter-assurèd of the mind,
> Care lesse, eyes, lips, and hands to misse.

A similar contrast between the transitory physical and the transcendent spiritual is drawn by Shelley in the renowned fifty-second stanza, on unity and multiplicity, of *Adonais*:

> Flowers, ruins, statues, music, words, are weak
> The glory they transfuse with fitting truth to speak.

So, too, it is the unifying and harmonizing spirit of "Lucy" that imposes itself on the chaos of nature in "A Slumber...":

> Rolled round in earth's diurnal course,
> With rocks, and stones, and trees.

My two final examples are both quite telling because they involve a dualism emphatically underlined by the poet himself. In Marvell's "The Gallery," the paradoxic fascination of Clora is described in terms of a twofold portrait. On one side are depicted her purely physical charms, her seductive sensuality, with the concluding line heavily corpuscular:

> Here thou art painted in the Dress
> Of an Inhumane murtheress;
> Examining upon our Hearts
> Thy fertile Shop of cruel Arts:
> Engines more keen than ever yet
> Adorned Tyrants Cabinet;
> Of which the most tormenting are:
> Black Eyes, red Lips, and curled Hair.

This last line recalls in its structure the predatory feline of Stevens. But on the opposite of this portrait from Marvell's gallery is the "spiritual" Clora, displayed in all her cymatic allure, as the concluding line brings out:

> But, on the other side, th'art drawn
> Like to Aurora in the Dawn;
> When in the East she slumb'ring lyes,
> And stretches out her milky Thighs;
> While all the morning Quire does sing,
> And manna falls, and Roses spring;
> And, at thy Feet, the wooing Doves
> Sit perfecting their harmless Loves.

But, of course, it is the particles *and* the waves that trace out what—Marvell would certainly agree with Heisenberg—is the delight of "playing with both pictures."

So, too, with Tennyson's "The Sisters," where Evelyn, who is intended to be the less "spiritual" of the two, sings the following:

> O diviner light,
> Thro' the heat, the drowth, the dust, the glare

while her sister, "the paler and the graver, Edith," sings:

> O diviner light,
> Thro' the cloud that roofs our moon with night.

The narrator, their father, remarks at the end of the songs on the complementarity of both: "Marvellously like, their voices—and

themselves!"; that is, in these moments of union, polarities are
fused, and we marvel at the experience.

Returning now to that poem of Hopkins, "The Windhover,"
which is statedly about ecstasy, I want to show its remarkable
dependence on these structures of complementarity:

> I caught this morning morning's minion, king-
>> dom of daylight's dauphin, dapple-dawn-drawn Falcon, in
>>> his riding
> Of the rolling level underneath him steady air, and striding
> High there, how he rung upon the rein of a wimpling wing
> In his ecstasy! then off, off forth on swing,
>> As a skate's heel sweeps smooth on a bow-bend: the hurl
>> and gliding
> Rebuffed the big wind. My heart in hiding
> Stirred for a bird,—the achieve of, the mastery of the thing!
>
> Brute beauty and valour and act, oh, air, pride, plume, here
>> Buckle! AND the fire that breaks from thee then, a billion
> Times told lovelier, more dangerous, O my chevalier!
>
> No wonder of it: sheer plod makes plough down sillion
> Shine, and blue-bleak embers, ah my dear,
>> Fall, gall themselves, and gash gold-vermilion.

As with the examples above, there is the undular-corpuscular
paradox of the "level underneath him steady air" *and* the "striding
high there"; the gliding *and* the hurling already referred to; the
sheer plod *and* the shine; and finally what might be called the
Sunday Puzzle of Hopkins students: "Brute beauty and valour and
act, oh, air, pride, plume, here / Buckle!" Considering the heap of
critical lumber piled around these lines, it would be rash (though
clearly not fresh) to profess to have gleaned the definitive reading;
but following the hermeneutic being pursued here, "buckle" meaning "to clasp," "to join together," seems to be the preferable
reading—even though Hopkins randomly opined otherwise. "Left
hand" there is brute beauty and valor and act—all lexically
synonomous with the instantaneous and the particulate; "right,"
air, pride, and plume, all synonymous with the tremulously undular and sigmoid. Air and pride are here parallel, since pride is to be

read primarily as *superbia*, loftiness—and plumes, if they do anything at all, "wave."

But what I would want to emphasize now even beyond this
first-level reading is the presence of a further *dédoublement*, which
may be compared to a kind of mathematical "squaring" of the
paradox. It is noteworthy that those terms that literally relate to the
corpuscular, to the fragmented and broken, are structurally cymatic, that is, have no punctuation to interrupt their flow: "brute
beauty *and* valour *and* act"; whereas the terms lexically related to
the wavelike are structurally particulate, that is, broken off from
each other by the four commas: "oh, air, pride, plume, . . ." Again,
we have the paradox within the paradox within the paradox—
Cusanus's "Everything in everything"—which we have looked at
earlier in the context of the figure within the figure, play within the
play, and other such devisals. Lastly, the two separate segments of
the Hopkins line are shown to be complementary by their juncture
at the outburst "oh." This, as I shall detail in my final recapitulative
chapter, is a "realer and rounder reply," an ecstatic outburst that is
circular. In fact, the two first recensions of the poem did not read
"oh" but, simply and more graphically, "O".

That figural utterance is more precisely defined in two earlier
images from the octave of the sonnet: "he rung upon the rein of a
wimpling wing" and "As a skate's heel sweeps smooth on a bow-
bend." These, as we will see in the discussion of circularity, are the
classic sexual, poetic, and mystical images of fulfillment. One need
recall only the love poems of Donne examined earlier, the boy
Wordsworth's self-induced—an ominous foreshadowing—ecstasy
while "skaiting" in *The Prelude* (1.447–63), and the Aristotelian "not
overmuch nor over little" of the mystic Richard Rolle. The flight of
the windhover is thus entirely different from the flight of that
"confessionalizing" falcon of Yeats which circles out beyond all
limitations and into oblivion. Hopkins's image might therefore be
better compared to the spiraling contemplation (the finite medita-
ting the infinite) symbolized by a controlled hawk, lauded by
Pseudo-Dionysius, and studied assiduously by all his commentators, including Hopkins's own Duns Scotus.

Because I will discuss the significance of this ascending circle,
generated by the complementarity of wave and particle, in the next

chapter, I want merely to suggest now that this may be more than an empty symbol of the human and natural reality; it may also constitute the very core of that reality. As is well known, the DNA model is a fusion of the discrete and the continuous; and it has been compared by, among others, Nobel laureate John Kendrew to "a spiral staircase," a figure which for present purposes may be identified further with the coiled-up energy of Kundalini yoga or the zigzag "flash of lightning" of the descent of power through the Kabbalistic sephiroth. Similarly, the structures graphed out of the *I Ching* are more and more being recognized as homologous with those of the genetic code, and they too are founded upon the harmonizing of the two polar principles of the pulsodic and the durational—or, in terms of the *I Ching*, the feminine and the masculine.[5] Peculiarly enough, it is the masculine principle, yang, that is continuous, and the feminine, yin, that is corpuscular; whereas in the West, as I shall note briefly, the converse is true.

Since the male-female complementarity is but another analogue of the primordial duality, I will employ this particular polarization in concluding the present chapter. In our poetry, feminine endings are the equivalent of weak endings; similarly, the feminine is equated with the abstract (and therefore largely unreal) and the masculine with the concrete (and presumably more important): hence, the old mnemonic, "Masculine will always be / Something you can touch and see." Finally, the polysyllabic and latinate is regarded as feminine, while the monosyllabic Anglo-Saxon is masculine. The bias of these designations is not relevant here. What is relevant is that, as "drunkards, poets, widows, and ladies soon to be married" (Stevens, "Homunculus et la Belle Etoile") all know, ecstatic delight only comes when the cymatic feminine is conjoined to the corpuscular masculine.[6] From this perspective that *ancien*

---

5. Since all of this may sound like grist for *Hamlet's Mill*, in addition to that fascinating and provocative work one may look at the more rigorous studies of Philip Ritterbush, *The Art of Organic Form* and, more specifically, "The Study of Form in the Life Sciences." For the genetic code and the *I Ching*, there is the somewhat fantastic and somewhat prophetic *The Invisible Landscape* of Terence and Dennis McKenna and the less daring *The Tao of Physics* by Fritjof Capra.

6. Bachelard in *The Psychoanalysis of Fire* supplies a score of passages from the alchemical tradition in which the masculine principle is identified with fire and the feminine with fluid—with "spark" and "soup" though one would hesitate to press the analogy these days.

querelle over Ciceronian waves and Senecan particles, over Attic and Asiatic styles, or that other quarrel initiated by perennial *stilnovisti* over the superiority of the modes of the present era to the modes of the past (as finely discriminated by Josephine Miles), or over the alleged declension from transient action to static image (as asserted by the Chicago Aristotelians)—all are proved to be moot issues. It is by the fusion of the duality that the artwork is achieved and ecstasy, however briefly, engendered. "I like a composition that is Nervous and Strong; but yet I would have it Sweet, and Gracious withal," declared Sir Roger L'Estrange—echoing both the Jonsonian criterion of "strength" with "ease" and the tough reasonableness with slight lyric grace of Eliot.

Because, I have noted frequently, this sought-for fusion is operative on the sexual plane as on the aesthetic and the mystical, I will close this chapter with three illustrations which, as is to be expected, are really one illustration of a single human reality. On the conjunction of male and female, the culture of the present moment has endowed us with no paucity of treatises; I therefore refer only in passing to what may be characterized as the corpuscular nature of male orgasm and the undular nature of female, and emphasize instead that this harmonizing of the discrete and wavelike represents a flow of "interinanimating" energy, in Donne's sexual sense and I. A. Richard's derivative linguistic sense, which can only be defined as circular: a circle that neither partner can be said to initiate or terminate, precisely because it momentarily approximates perfection. "You in me and I in you," as the mystic à Kempis said, echoing the Qur'an on the soul's relation to God: "Gladness that is thine in him and him in thee." Indeed, as I have noted repeatedly, this perfection is every religion's definition of "God," who is at once alpha and omega, center and circumference.

Thus—for my "poetic" illustration—when Marvell says to his silent mistress, "Let us roll all our *strength* and all our *sweetness* up into one ball," he is recalling the Vulgate definition of God as acting both *suaviter* and *fortiter*, as both "feminine" *and* "masculine."[7]

---

7. The aesthetic counterpart of this perfection is lauded by Pope in book 2 of *An Essay on Criticism*: "And praise the easie vigor of a line, / Where Denham's Strength and Waller's Sweetness join" (360–61). The evolution of the two key terms is traced in masterful fashion, bespeaking both strength and ease, by Donald Davie in his pioneering *Purity of Diction in English Verse* and *Articulate Energy*.

And the implication is that the two lovers *are* "God." They are no longer imprisoned behind the "iron gates of life" and exist not in the deserts of eternity but in the superabundant fullness of time, in the ecstatic *nunc stans*. The poet is not talking about Day Lewis's silly rubber ball, much less Bateson's or McLuhan's cannonball, but about the sexual approximation of the spheres of perfection. Any other reading ignores the underlying religious convention of the poem that only an incarnate, seed-bearing word (and not just "talk") can conquer time; just as, in the religious matrix of Marvell's poem, the prophets ("talk") could not maritally redeem the world—only the "incarnate Word" of the Father. In that in-fleshing, the final eschatological revelation, the ultimate consummation (Ransom's "kinder saeculum"), is proleptically experienced. Thus the persona's goal is transformed from lust that brings "vast"—meaning "desolate"—eternity to love that brings plenary eternity, true timelessness. Here time shall run, not backward but forward to fetch the age of gold. True lovers' seasons run not to the motions of the temporal sun of which Suckling regretfully says in "That none beguil'd be": "his motions / Are quicker / And thicker / Where Love hath his notions." No, rather, true lovers seek sexual and eschatological consummation when they, "dissolving, run [Keats's "solution sweet"] into the Glories of th'Almighty Sun."

Here it may be helpful to introduce the parallel frequently glimpsed but rarely fully elucidated between "The Garden" and "To His Coy Mistress," because that parallel helps confirm the present analysis of the latter poem. In both poems there is a crucial transition. In "The Garden," it entails a shift *from* a consideration of all the natural and sensual delights of the place—embodied partially in the two "sisters," innocence and quiet—*to* a preparation for the supernatural delights of the next world attained through easeful death, the "otia sana" of "Hortus," and the contradictory of what is found in "*busie* companies of men": *neg-otium*. In short, it is a movement *from* (these are classically related states or conditions) contemplation *to* action, the latter being here defined in terms of the ultimate *transactio*, death. In "To His Coy Mistress" there is similarly a shift *from* the consideration of natural, sensual pleasures, embodied here in the "quiet" and virginal mistress, *to* that sacramental, "supernatural" *transactio*, sexual intercourse—which, as noted frequently, is the poetic analogue of death. The quiet sister of

"The Garden" is the "alma quies" of "Hortus" and is thus identifiable with the Mistress, since *quies* is the root of the word *coy*. This identification is further supported by the fact that "alma" and "ubera" make up almost a *topos* (much like "alma mater") so that the personified, nurturing Quiet of the garden poems is clearly linked to the woman of the long-adored breasts in the "Mistress" poem.[8] Lastly, the overall parallel structure of the two poems in English is strengthened by their both being poems of preparation for a consummation *not yet attainable*, though *devoutly* to be wished.

This latter datum illuminates that puzzling phrase, "vegetable love"—itself the object of so many coy misreadings. I suggest, first, it is to be taken in a strict literal sense: the persona says: "I would / Love you ten years *before* the flood," and the next reference to precisely *that* love is that it is "vegetable." The gloss is from Thomas Browne's *The Garden of Cyrus*: "And if it were clear that this was used by Noah after the Floud, I could easily beleeve it as in use *before* it; Not willing to fix such ancient inventions no higher originall than Noah; nor readily conceiving those aged Heroes, whose diet was vegetable." Men "before the flood" were "vegetable men"; love before the flood was "vegetable love." The second use is figurative and, as I indicated, lends cogency to the presence of a contemplation-action pattern in the poems. When Thomas Browne equates the phrase "garden delights" with the phrase "vegetable delights," he is in neither instance writing about the pleasures of actually "tending one's garden" after the manner of the *Georgics* or of Columella's *De Arboribus*. He is writing about *contemplative* delights—as is also a more renowned artist:

> And add to these retired Leisure,
> That in trim *Gardens* takes his pleasure;

8. As a final note, and in the interests of strengthening my Cusanian argument (every garden in every garden), I would like to invoke some other cogent *tradita*. There are two sisters in Marvell's garden, "Quies" and "Simplicitas," and since one is addressed as "alma" (topically companioned with "mater"), we may want to think of that archetypal garden where Dante meets his own "*soror* mystica," Beatrice with Matelda—her name being (after a brilliant reading by Gerald Walsh) a cryptogram for *Mater* Dantis. But indeed she is more than that, as the medieval Latin for "alma" (after Paget Toynbee) brings out; for "alma" is translated "sancta." And so the fuller invocation of all these fictive muses is Stevens's "Sister and mother and diviner love."

> But first, and chiefest, with thee bring
> Him that yon soars on golden wing,
> Guiding the fiery-wheeled throne,
> The Cherub *Contemplation*.
>
> ["Il Penseroso," 49–54]

"Otia sana" is literally "retired leisure," and "vegetable love" is literally "contemplative love." The garden delights, the garden pleasures that are to be hurled through the iron gates of life will by the very fact of entrance through those gates and into the sacred-sexual sanctuary (as in the discussion earlier of "Lift up your gates . . .") be transformed from contemplative to active, and their participants from vegetable (that is, contemplative) lovers to coactive and consummate practitioners—sharing in what Thomas Browne would call "the Kisse of the Spouse," which is Milton's "individual kiss."

Thus, "To His Coy Mistress," as several commentators have demonstrated, does not endorse but attacks the *carpe diem* tradition. The "running" of Marvell's daytime sun is to be understood as the exact opposite of Ovid's "lente currite" of nighttime, just as the early Christian eschatological cry, "Come, Lord Jesus," is the opposite of the classic world view's terror at the onrush of the future. The final section of the poem is thus the dialectic counter to the first section, as biblical teleology is the counter to classical cyclicism.

For that reason, perhaps the best gloss on these lines is the two following passages. The first is a fragment from Hopkins (no. 103) on his own encounter with the deserts of eternity, which begins, "—I am like a slip of comet."

> So I go out: my little sweet is done:
> I have drawn heat from this contagious sun:
> To not ungentle death now forth I run.

These lines should not necessarily be read sexually, or at least only to the degree that sexual ecstasy is the image of dying. In Hopkins's fragment "sweet" and "heat" certainly have a twofold implication, and the "contagious sun" is both Christ and the "Sunne" of Donne's "S. Lucies Day." The second passage is from Herrick's "Love what it is," where the restless circle is Marvell's roughly striving "ball," and lust's vast eternity is transformed into love's sweet eternity.

> Love is a circle that doth restlesse move
> In the same sweet eternity of love.

In my closing chapter we shall meditate on the nature of that circle.

X: *Cycle*

Since the original heuristic myth was derived from the circular development of *ingressus, progressus,* and *regressus,* it is fitting that this final chapter should be devoted to the nature of poetic circularity as such. And, for the last time, I emphasize that the heuristic myth may be in fact nothing more than that: a heuristic device which need not necessarily lead to a goal, and a myth, *stricto sensu,* generated by Western man and neither embodying "reality" nor possessing universal symbolic cogency. The best poetic expression of the view that this myth is an empty fabrication is E. J. Pratt's "The Truant," where man as measure of all things declares:

> Boast not about your harmony,
> Your perfect curves, your rings
> Of pure and endless light—'Twas we
> Who pinned upon your Seraphim their wings.
>
> [126–29]

As to the perhaps exclusively occidental nature of this circularity, Rudolph Arnheim in his analysis of the *T'ai-chi tu* notes: "Oscillatory alteration seems to be the most effective way of perceptually symbolizing the interaction of part and part, or part and whole, by which each sharer of the relationship is affecting the others while being affected by them at the same time."[1] I have discussed at some length this interinanimating oscillation as exemplified in the

---

1. It is an understandable assumption that the circle enclosing a straight line symbolized death because theta, θ, is the first letter of Thanatos; but the deeper reason is certainly that the circle with straight line lacks the element of serpentine alternation, lacks, that is, any sign of the vital interplay of part and whole.

poetic structures considered earlier. And it is obvious from that discussion that the answer would be affirmative to Arnheim's subsequent question as to "whether the *T'ai-chi tu* could be an emblem of Christianity or Marxism just as well" as an emblem of Taoism. There seems some warrant for suggesting that some of these patterns relate to universal "deep" structures, indeed, relate to man's entire existence in time.

Thus Croce in *La Poesia* recognized the congruence of the ontological, the biological, and the historical in the symmetry of *circolarità spirituale*, *circulatio sanguinis*, and the Vichian *corso* and *ricorso*. Following his lead I shall organize this final chapter as a kind of meditation on the circular nature of the divine (since Croce's first term translates *circuitus spiritualis*, which, Abrams has shown, is the "supernatural energy" that begins and ends in "God"), the circular nature of the sexual (already alluded to in the context of Marvell's "Mistress" poem), and the circular nature of the historical, as these three realms have been understood by poets and structured into their works. But first the fascination of the circular itself must be examined more closely.

Future historians of recent years, though not necessarily historians of literature, will no doubt express amazement at the attention, critical and uncritical, Allen Ginsberg attracted on various inconceivable occasions by chanting the great Om, a prayer which needed not to be translated—though the translation brings out the paradox of "jewel in the lotus"—because its effect was derived entirely from its droning repetition of the O sound. It therefore paralleled in many ways the "Great O's" of the ancient Christian liturgy for the days preceding the feast of Christmas: "O oriens," "O clavis," and so on—prayers that were also chanted more or less by rote, that is, in rotary fashion like a prayer wheel spinning.

Holiness, peace, communion, again in both East and West, seem to be signified by this sound and this figure of O, a figure which at least in the West indicated, as we have seen, that man has "come home" to himself; his oscillating voyage is over as he enters the "Paradise" where, according to Herbert's poem of that name, "such beginnings touch their END." The perfection of the circle, which Emerson called "the brightest emblem in the cipher of the world," symbolizes that man is no longer split in himself, split from his beloved "other," and split from his world but rather is, in Yeats's transmission of Plato, joined like the yolk and the white of one shell—a shell, as the "Perle" poet said, which is "like the rim of heaven's sphere."

The oscillating voyage we have seen is serpentine, is fraught with ambiguities, as Keats emphasized in "Lamia," a poem, we have noted, whose ancestral vision is embodied in the relics of the Gnostic sect of the Ophites who worshiped the Jesus who had paradoxically compared himself to Moses' brazen serpent. This ambiguity of the serpent in relation to the circle is universal, for example, the snake of Vishnu, one end pulled by the good powers and the other end by the evil powers; it is the amphisbaena dire of Greek myth; and, to bring the image into our tradition, it is the worm as "mother and sister" of Donne's meditation and the "Glo-worm" of Vaughan's "John 3, 2," where the glowworm is to the serpent-Christ as the man Jesus is to God. The same deadly serpent which in Genesis brought schism and rupture was regarded as destined to bear life, to become the salvific circle of union—again, some examples: the yang-yin hieroglyph where the serpentine both separates and joins; the dual symbolism of the serpent in Shelley's *Prometheus Unbound*; Coleridge's definition of the "perfect" poem as the "snake with its tail in its mouth"; Rossetti's explanation of the "heart of the mystery" as "the serpent of eternity enclosing the Alpha and Omega"; and lastly, the "wormy metaphors" of Stevens, close kin to Kenneth Burke's "Ooey Gooey" and to Lévi-Strauss's koro worm.

This serpentine structure has been charted earlier. I am now concerned only with this power of the overall figure itself, with responding to Keats's apostrophe, "O Moon! . . . O Moon!" or to Stevens's question in "Annual Gaiety," "Wherefore those prayers to the moon?" "Because the world is round it turns me on," declaimed and then again declaimed the Beatles, even as their less potted predecessors a generation before chanted with equally tantric intensity: "O the music goes round and round, O, O, O, . . ."—with a "kind of classical sound," Stevens would have added. All this is the paradoxic marriage of the *esprit géometrique* with the *esprit de finesse*: one is talking about Euclidean figures and understanding them poetically—"my serpentining beauty, round on round," says Browning's Andrea.

This obsessive recurrence of the serpent-circle in East and West, in high culture and in low, compels one to wonder whether these are merely apt but arbitrary images, gratuitous designs which vaguely stand for but don't really have a foundation in "reality," and indeed are therefore only like another circular argument that gets one nowhere. The implied question, like every question, is somewhat tautological, since in a truly circular world the figure and the image would be the reality. But the question merely by being asked does underline the need for attempting to posit some less capricious basis for man's spheric penchant than that it, out of scores of geometric shapes, merely appears most assuaging to his various personal, sexual, and social schizophrenias. Interestingly, for Emerson's cosmic "emblem" the seventeenth century had a much more modest counterpart. The following is from Lovelace's "The Snail," one of those Metaphysical exercises in close analysis that are unrivaled up to the poems of Francis Ponge. The first line apostrophizes, "Wise emblem of our politic world," and continues:

> Compendious snail! thou seem'st to me
> Large Euclid's strict epitome;
> And, in each diagram, dost fling
> Thee from the point unto the ring.
> A figure now triangular,
> An oval now, and now a square;
> And then a serpentine dost crawl,
> Now a straight line, now crook'd, now all.
>
> [6–13]

But however modest a figure, it is still circular. But why, it may be asked, shouldn't one extol triangles, which the tradition saw as feminine and inferior, or even pentagons? The contemporary citizen of our "politic world" would, of course, immediately respond with a negative, forgetting the ancient equation of *panta* and *penta,* of the universe and the fivefold. There is, I think, an answer to such questions, and it will affirm the absorbing orb as more than merely an arbitrary symbol, as in fact something structured into man's very substance; but I will reserve that "answer" to the end of the chapter, to the closing of the present speculative circle.

I will start at the center (Croce's *circolarità spirituale*), with anyone's definition of "perfection"—Jalal Ad-Din Ar-Rumi's, Maimo-
nides', Luther's, or Spinoza's—and then move out on various radii
to the "created" circumference. One could, readily enough, think of
beginning with an analysis of the mystic's prayer to the Buddha:

The marks of the wheel beneath his feet are all elegant—
The hub, the rim, and the thousand spokes are all even.

But since, as M. H. Abrams has demonstrated, the circular pattern
of the Bible inspired if not engendered the circularity of our poetic
tradition, it is probably preferable by way of introduction to take
up first something from our own Scriptures—which are not without their own partial relationship to Buddhism. J. Edgar Bruns of
the University of Toronto has shown that the Gospel of John may
owe almost as much to Mahayana Buddhism as to Alexandrian
Judaism, and it is with the prologue to that gospel that I want to
begin. There is a translation of that prologue by Raymond York,
author of a standard textbook of Greek grammar, in which *logos* is
rendered into English as "O so." Thus, where one would conventionally have read, "In the beginning was the word and the word
was with God and the word was God," one now reads, "In the
beginning was the *O so,* and the *O so* was with God, and the *O so*
was God." There is nothing precious or artificial about this "translation"; it is a sophisticated and precise expression of the spirit of
the original. "So" like *sic* suggests finality and perfection, suggests
the Anselmian "than which nothing greater can be conceived," as
when Hopkins defines beauty as "the O-seal-that-so feature." How
seal it? *So.* "Thou art *so* truth," says Donne to the deified beloved;
and Crashaw in the "Hymn of the Nativity," when the fitting
resting place for Jesus has been found, declares: "no way but *so.*"
Nothing more can be said. For in the tradition of "natural supernaturalism," "God" is the self-answering question. But the phrase
"O so" conveys more than divine finality and absolutehood; it is an
ecstatic utterance like the great Om: *O so!* And visually it harks
back to the earlier image of the serpent sphere. For this perfection is
figured forth as two spheres linked by the snakelike arabesque:
OSO. And, since I too am arguing circularly, the created "image

and likeness" of that divine OSO is the temporal OMO (that differentiating "M" being the tortured figure of creaturely contingency) which Dante saw engraved in the face of everyman. "The light of God's countenance is signed upon us," says the Psalmist; but it is signed not in our *face*, according to the Scholastic commentators, but in our intellect.

Again, one may cite the hermetic definition of God as a circle whose center is everywhere and whose circumference is nowhere. This is the inexhaustibly fecund center from which, according to the tradition, all derives and which man can never quite reach; it is, as I suggested earlier, another aspect of the topos of outopos. Or, in Rilke's words blending the visual with the aural, it is the *unerhörte Mitte*, the center whose music one can never quite hear, or hear enough of. All one can hear *in illo tempore* is Robinson's "bar of lost imperial music," or those preludes to the full diapason commemorated by, among others, Wordsworth, Lamartine, and Liszt.

It is this lure of the center that accounts for the fascination of those spheres within spheres within spheres that little children *and* poets play with, in the innermost of which is the startling and delightful "surprise": a miniature figure, an infant doll—the very symbol of Rilke's *unerhörte* (in-fans = nonspeaking) *Mitte* and the very emblem of Milton's and Crashaw's and Campion's Christmas hymns.[2] This "silence" is identified with one's purest self in the Upanishad Chandogya: "Within the city of Brahman, which is the body, there is the heart, and within the heart there is a little [doll] house. This house has the shape of a lotus, and within it dwells that which is to be sought after, inquired about, and realized." Hence,

---

2. The more common name for this kind of toy is "Chinese boxes," a name that relates it to the Chinese magic square of three, a square in which the lesser squares whether totaled vertically, horizontally, or diagonally add up to fifteen, with the center symbolizing perfection, the fusion of opposites, the marriage of heaven and earth, through the combination of the perfect even number, two, and the perfect odd number, three:

$$4 \quad 9 \quad 2$$
$$3 \quad 5 \quad 7$$
$$8 \quad 1 \quad 6$$

Granet in his classic studies on Chinese dance has shown how movement through each of these boxes in search of the sacred center required a choreography based on astronomical patterns. The center was thus attained only by chance in response to mysterious impulses from the outer world. And for this, the best parallel would be with children's games of chance, hopscotch and, more pertinently, the game known as Sky Blue.

too, the fascination of authors as diverse in subject matter as Gide, Joyce, Borges, and Nabokov with the structure of the play within the play; and lastly, the fascination of those strobochromatic paintings of the Italian futurists, best anticipated by Velázquez's "Las Meninas"—on which Foucault has written so reflectively—which in the Prado is ingeniously hung directly across from an immense mirror, so that one looks into the mirror to see the painting in which there is a mirror into which one looks to see..., and so on: all symbolizations of the endless quest for the "heart of the heart," the "deep heart's core," "el profundo centro." This teaching has been best expressed by the Zohar's commentary on Solomon's penetration into the "depths of the nut garden" (6.11), a sexual setting evocative of Perle's repeated "more..., more," or Molly Bloom's self- and world-affirming "yes..., yes."

> The primal center is the innermost light, of a translucence, subtility, and purity beyond comprehension. That inner point extended becomes a "palace" which acts as an enclosure for the center, and is also of a radiance translucent beyond the power to know it.... From then outward, there is extension upon extension, each constituting a vesture to the one before, as a membrane to the brain.

These kernels within kernels, these spheres within spheres and their unknown interiors represent the mystery of an elusive and somewhat capricious perfection. They are thus, in another form, those colored and iridescent spheres hung on ceremonial trees to symbolize the cosmos as mere bauble, as mere plaything of their central occupant, of Jesus or Parshvanatha, both of whom come as infants in "a globe of circular light."

I have already assayed one reason why the circle stands for perfection: its very endlessness. E. J. Pratt notwithstanding, eternity *should be* like Vaughan's "ring of pure and endless light" or like Yeats's sonically chiastic "phaseless sphere." But these are static images, and few world religions worship a deity that is static. Rather, it is both static *and* ecstatic, the immutable *and* the pure actuality, the being that is anchored in unity *and* reaching out to embrace multiplicity—for which other figures are those trees I mentioned earlier in the context of poetic refrain: Yeats's tree, or the Mayan ceiba tree, Buddha's tree of enlightenment, the Yggdrasil, or Moses' bush burning unconsumed, itself identical with the Kabbalistic tree of life. The circle is perfection, that is, "God," because it is at peace with itself. Though drawn outward, it is held inward; though reaching toward the multiple, it is rooted in the one. There is no schizoid conflict between exteriority and interiority, no *fausse conscience*, a Marxist would say, alienating the inner self from the outer agent, alienating—the poet would say more auspiciously—the falcon from the center.

But *conversely*, "evil" possesses its own kind of circular character. *Demon est deus inversus*, as Yeats well knew; Milton's Satan as mimic of God is the Bible's "sign [sin] of resemblance."[3] This perverse reflection is defined in Blake's *Jerusalem* (1, pl. 15):

Of many Wheels I view, wheel *without* wheel, with cogs tyrannic
Moving by compulsion each other: not as those in Eden: which
Wheel within wheel in freedom revolve in harmony & peace.

[17–19]

If only for reasons of expository completeness, it will be necessary to look briefly at this negative circularity and some poetic structures based upon it. In *Jerusalem* (2, pl. 28, 19–20), Blake defines Satan as "a Center from which branches out / a circle in continual gyrations." This is a theme on which Herbert rings an interesting change in the first stanza of "Confession," and which he elaborates less arcanely in "Sinnes round," where again the circular or envelope pattern is the organizing principle:[4]

3. Milton's sign-sin identification is not a facile wordplay. If "sin" is the experience of duality, that experience comes only when one's inner reality is denominated by one's outward appearance: hence the emphasis on the latter in Eve's oneiric "imprinting" by Satan (5.38-47), and Adam's lament: "And in our Faces evident the signs / Of foul concupiscence" (9.1077-78). In contemporary language, one would say that to "evaluate" a person not for what he *is* but for what he *appears* to be is to "instrumentalize" and "functionalize" that person. It is to affirm that such a person is not an end in himself, has no inner "depth," no subjunctive freedom, but rather is a means to be used to attain some other goal; in short, is merely a pointer, an indicator rooted in the indicative, a *sign*. Coleridge catches these implications when he uses the word "sign" in two contiguous prose comments in "The Rime of the Ancient Mariner," not as a neutral term but in both cases as annexed to the threshold of evil.

4. Medieval biblical commentators had noted this kind of circularity in the Psalms, and it is exemplified in Donne's "La Corona" on which Louis Martz has written the definitive historical explication. This technique of repetition is also employed in another marvel of circularity by Herbert, "The Wreathe."

Sorrie I am, my God, sorrie I am,
That my offences course it in a ring.
My thoughts are working like a busie flame,
Untill their cockatrice they hatch and bring:
And when they once have perfected their draughts,
My words take fire from my inflamed thoughts.

My words take fire from my inflamed thoughts,
Which spit it forth like the Sicilian Hill.
They vent the wares, and pass them with their faults,
And by their breathing ventilate the ill.
But words suffice not, where are lewd intentions:
My hands to joyn to finish the inventions.

My hands to joyn to finish the inventions:
And so my sinnes ascend three stories high,
As Babel grew, before there were dissensions.
Yet ill deeds loyter not: for they supplie
New thoughts of sinning: wherefore, to my shame,
Sorrie I am, my God, sorrie I am.

The threefold cycle of sinning in every Christian catechism was
"thought, word, and deed," which constitutes the "three stories"
and three stanzas of the poem which, though it seems to be circular
inasmuch as it begins where it ends, might better be thought of as
semicircular, each line moving the trajectory ten degrees further
into the inverted world of evil.

But for the perfect structuring forth of the figure of Blake's Satan, who is at once alluring and dreadful—even as his circularity is
the inverse of the *fascinosum* and *tremendum* of the true circularity of
"God"—one must look to the *locus classicus* of enticing corruption,
Spenser's *Bowre of blisse*:

Birdes, voyces, instruments, windes, waters, all agree.

The ioyous birdes shrouded in chearefull shade,
    Their notes vnto the voyce attempred sweet;
    Th'Angelicall soft trembling voyces made
    To th'instruments diuine respondence meet:
    The siluer sounding instruments did meet:
    With the base murmurs of the waters fall:

> The waters fall with difference discreet,
> Now soft, now loud, vnto the wind did call:
> The gentle warbling wind low answered to all.
>
> [*FQ* 2.12.71]

This is dangerously charming glamour, as dour Burleigh realized; its purpose is to cast a spell upon the reader, to render him vertiginous, indeed, to lead him, as it were, to leap into the continual gyrations of the verse. But for Spenser it is all meretricious, it is merely the gross effigy of the circular reality of perfection. Here the dizzying music and the circular movement are simulacra of the "diapase" of Alma's Castle, with that diapason posited by Spenser as the authentic counterpart of the heavenly music of the spheres.

Northrop Frye in *The Well-Tempered Critic*, himself very responsive to such music, notes how the following similarly patterned stanza—where the heavy punctuation again "embodies" the discreteness of matter—was quoted in a contemporary manual appearing before *The Faerie Queene* was published:

> Wrath, gelosie, griefe, loue this Squire haue layd thus low.
>
> Wrath, gealosie, griefe, loue do thus expell:
>   Wrath is a fire, and gealosie a weede,
>   Griefe is a flood, and loue a monster fell;
>   The fire of sparkes, the weede of little seede,
>   The flood of drops, the Monster filth did breede:
>   But sparks, seed, drops, and filth do thus delay;
>   The sparks soone quench, the springing seed outweed,
>   The drops dryp, and filth wipe cleane away:
> So shall wrath, gealosie, griefe, loue dye and decay.

Frye comments that the "purpose of a deliberate rhetorical exercise in such a scene is not simply to cast a spell but to suggest the paradox of something which does cast a spell and yet remains evil." It is difficult to detect the paradox, since we ordinarily think of spell-casting as involving at least an approach to evil. In any case, the comment is true of the passage in canto 12, but not in canto 4 where the quasimadrigal pattern functions quite differently, functions as it did in our larger figure of the circle as the model of *exitus* and *reditus*, of perfect fulfillment. Dramatically, the circular

pattern in canto 4 indicates merely that the innocent world after
having been marred by sin shall return to innocence—the parallel
would be with the pithy circularity of Donne's "Death thou shalt
die."

Another pattern in *The Faerie Queene* which does, however, have
as purpose to convey the allure of evil, of Blake's "circle in continual
gyrations, is the *carmen correlativum* in canto 6 of book 2. The
description is, again, of the fascinating and corrupt—this time, the
false delights of Phaedria's isle, that mazing and amazing labyrinth
of multiplicity:

> No tree, whose braunches did not brauely spring;
>   No braunch, whereon a fine bird did not sit:
>   No bird, but did her shrill notes sweetly sing;
>   No song but did containe a louely dit:
>   Trees, braunches, birds, and songs were framed fit,
>   For to allure fraile mind to carelesse ease.
>   Carelesse the man soone woxe, and his weake wit
>   Was ouercome of thing, that did him please;
> So pleased, did his wrathful purpose faire appease.
>
> [13]

This is also the nature of Milton's evil serpent who appears as a
"circular base of rising folds" (*PL* 9.420). And it was no mere
rhetorical exercise that led Milton to employ a dizzying circular
repetition so frequently in his description of Eve's temptation—as
in the following:

> He sought them both, but wish'd his hap might find
> Eve separate, he wish'd, but not with hope
> Of what so seldom chanc'd, when to his wish,
> Beyond his hope, Eve separate he spies.
>
> [9.421–24]

There is a considerably less cosmic seduction apparently being
plotted in Nicholas Breton's "His Wisdom," also ostensibly a circularly flattering argument to the lady:

> I would thou wert not fair, or I were wise;
> I would thou hadst no face, or I no eyes;

I would thou wert not wise, or I not fond;
Nor thou but free, nor I but still in bond.

But thou art fair, and I can not be wise;
Thy sun-like face hath blinded both mine eyes;
Thou canst not but be wise, nor I but fond;
Nor thou but free, nor I but still in bond.

Yet am I wise to think that thou art fair;
Mine eyes their pureness in thy face repair;
Nor am I fond, that do thy wisdom see;
Nor yet in bond, because that thou art free.

Then in thy beauty only make me wise;
And in thy face the Graces guide mine eyes;
And in thy wisdom only see me fond;
And in thy freedom keep me still in bond.

So shalt thou still be fair, and I be wise;
Thy face shine still upon my cleared eyes;
Thy wisdom only see how I am fond;
Thy freedom only keep me still in bond.

So would I thou wert fair, and I were wise;
So would thou hadst thy face, and I mine eyes;
So would I thou wert wise, and I were fond,
And thou wert free and I were still in bond.

There is in all of these passages a kind of Augustinian suggestion that the delights and pleasures of this *orbis terrarum* represent Satan's proper sphere of influence. And indeed, according to the tradition, to the degree that the cosmos is merely the shadow of the supersubstantial circle of perfection, it is partially under the influence of the "powers of this world." As John Donne wrote in one of his own Augustinian meditations, the text for which is, "Lente et serpenti satagunt occurrere morbo":

This is nature's nest of boxes: the heavens contain the earth; the earth, cities; cities, men. And all these are concentric; the common centre to them all is decay, ruin; only that is eccentric which was never made; only that place or garment rather, which we can imagine but not demonstrate. That light, which is the very emanation of the light of God, in which the saints shall dwell, with which the saints shall be apparelled, only that bends not to this centre, to ruin.

But this is the negative side of circularity, the shadow of the sphere of perfection, not the sphere itself; and it is to that larger theme that I now return.

If this circle is perfection, then, by definition it must communicate itself to the imperfect eccentric or broken circle that defines man. And, of course, such communication will itself be circular. Thus Hopkins says of his "Saviour": "what looks, what lips yet gave you a / Rapturous love's greeting of realer, of *rounder* replies." For Hopkins, presumably this greeting was in some mystical or paramystical experience. For others, like Rilke, it was in the aesthetic encounter: "O Brunnen-Mund, du gebender, du Mund, / der unerschöpflich Eines, Reines, spricht"—which Rilke's English translator, Norton, improving on the original, renders: "O fountain-mouth, you giver, O you *round* / mouth speaking inexhaustibly one pure thing." But as we have seen in the discussion of enjambment, most ordinary mortals meet this rounder reality that may make them reel with delight, not in the mystical or the aesthetic, but where Apollinaire met it: in the sexual beloved—"vous dont la bouche est faite à l'image de celle de Dieu / Bouche qui est l'ordre même." In each instance this round speech of the round mouth is the re-ply that re-binds us together, re-stores us to the world of innocence and joy where we are one with ourselves, with one another, and with the world about us: as in Blake's "Laughing Song":

> When the meadows laugh with lively green,
> And the grasshopper laughs in the merry scene,
> When Mary and Susan and Emily
> With their sweet round mouths sing "Ha, Ha, He!"

As we have seen, for all the great world religions and great poetic visionaries, the sexual is preeminently the sacred; Apollinaire's *jolie rousse* is the mouthpiece of "God." Even some anchorite shredding his flesh on a rock in the desert or on Mount Athos, in the Thebaid or the Gobi, whether worshiping the Theotokos or experiencing prajnaparamita, has no other hermeneutic device for fathoming his experience than the erotic language of a Cummings or a Rexroth; or, for that matter, than the language of the Song of Solomon, which was so long and so perceptively interpreted as an allegory of Jehovah's love for Israel. Thus, that the realm of the sexual is the realm of the sacred—and both, the realm of the circular—is a truism as much for the medieval monk illuminating Solomon's "*Os-culetur me Osculo Oris sui*" as it is, from the other extreme, for Juliet's nurse with her "deep O" and for the modern author of *The Story of O.*

We may now move out of the central poem at the center of things to the epicenter, to what is known among psychagogues, ever intent on squaring the circle, as "interpersonal relations." Here, it should be observed that even the most positivist social scientist cannot escape this orbit of language, for to "relate" is to re-latere, to lie down together in a world in which asymptotically every tangent ultimately touches the circle and in which every parallel line ultimately merges. The sphere of sexuality proper need not now much detain us. As we have noted, it is the corporeal-spiritual binding of head, center, and foot, with primacy understandably attaching to the center: again, Donne's "great Prince"—that liberal critics give a grosser name.

It is necessary, therefore, to look at the human reality itself, at that miniature sphere which conventionally and unconventionally thinks of itself as made to the image and likeness of the great sphere. In a justly famous, or infamous, passage—"dumbhead boast," notes Richard Stern in his own cyclical "Work in Progress"—the first modern man of our tradition wrote in *Religio Medici*:

> The world that I regard is my self; it is the Microcosm of my own frame that I cast mine eye on; for the other, I use it but like my Globe, and turn it round sometimes for my recreation. . . . that mass of Flesh that circumscribes me, limits not my mind; that surface that tells the Heavens it hath an end, cannot persuade me I have any: I take my circle to be above three hundred and sixty.

And the last modern man, M. Teste, an infinitely more repellent orb and by definition a more cerebral and Kantian creature than

Dr. Browne, also observed: "J'acquiers l'impression générale et constante d'une sphere de simultanéité qui est attaché à ma présence. Elle se transporte avec moi, son contenu est indéfiniment variable."

But these spheres are of necessity deformed; to be the perfect sphere would be "to be as God knowing good and evil," knowing, that is, at once the ecstatic and the static, interiority and exteriority, existence and essence—all, what the serpentine tempter proffered Eve in Genesis. Thus the very lure of perfect circularity, the very appeal of it, indicates that man is somewhat elliptic or, in Sartre's terms, is an existence without an essence. Again, we are back with Stevens's letter "C". But the cosmic comedy for which Stevens's comedian endlessly cons another part seems to have no denouement. And the symbol for this would be Bosch's circularly organized painting of "The Wandering Fool" or his other painting, "The Kermess," on which William Carlos Williams has developed his own circular theme. This comedy is not quite a tale told by an idiot, but it is a tale which seems forever incomplete: the "C" never becomes the "O" of perfection, the hemisphere never becomes the sphere. Hence the cumulative poignancy of some lines of Milton I have cited earlier:

> But, *O* sad Virgin, that thy power,
> Might raise Musaeus from his bower,
> Or bid the soul of Orpheus sing
> Such notes as, warbled to the string,
> Drew Iron tears down Pluto's cheek,
> And made Hell grant what love did seek.
> Or call up him that left *half-told*
> The story of Cambuscan bold.

But nothing shall rejoin Orpheus and Eurydice; the circle shall not be closed. As Rilke said in his bidding to Orpheus: "nirgends schliesst sich der Kreis." The "half-told" story is man's own history, always incomplete. It is Wordsworth's "hemisphere of magic fiction" (*The Prelude* 6.88) which is never quite maging enough to really close the parenthesis of existence and become the full sphere. Like Browning's "Abt Vogler" (with whom one may compare Hopkins's "No. 19, Let me be . . ."), who thinks by music to plumb and resolve the mystery, man must say at the end of the improvised comedy of existence: "I have dared and done, for my resting-place is found, / The C Major of this life." And one may attend to "the great C Major" of Schubert, his autumnal ode, which precisely because, as Toscanini acknowledged, it does almost approximate formal perfection—particularly in its intricately wrought first-movement rondeau—is really more tragic and incomplete than the "unfinished" or the "tragic" symphony itself.

It is relatively easy to sketch out the metaphors of existence, as I am doing here; it entails perhaps more than a supreme fiction to fulfill them:

> Thyself shalt afford the example, Giotto!
>   Thy one work, not to decrease or diminish
> Done at a stroke, was just (was it not?) "O!"
>   Thy great Campanile is still to finish.
>   [Browning, "Old Pictures in Florence"]

The "great Campanile" here stands not for the artist's sketch, not for the symbolic approximation of perfection, but for the reality, for the lived power to link the hemisphere of heaven with the hemisphere of earth and so close the circle, not metaphorically but vitally and really. Every true artist must imagine he can create this golden age, blend the dark, satanic mills with the new Jerusalem of utopia, end the half-told tale, and bind together the hemispheres ontologically, personally, and historically—the three themes of the present circular exposition:

> Then one shall propose in a speech (curt Tuscan,
>   Expurgate and sober, with scarcely an "issimo")
> To end now our half-told tale of Cambuscan,
>   And turn the bell-tower's alt to altissimo;
> And fine as the beak of a young beccaccia
>   The Campanile, the Duomo's fit ally,
> Shall soar up in gold full fifty braccia,
>   Completing Florence, as Florence Italy.
>
>   [*Ibid.*]

But as all voyagers know, the campanile is never finished; it remains like the tragic broken lines of Vergil, or like Yeats's "broken tower," only another monumental failure "on the Plain of Sennaar." The circle is not closed; the half-told tale is not finished; Crispin the comedian continues his cruise.

This voyage through perilous seas is the same for every man, whether emperor or clown, Prince Henry or Falstaff, Chaucer's Cambuscan or Stevens's Goober Khan, and whether they perform in the circus maximus of their own skulls or in the circus minimus of politics and power. But again, as with Browning's Giotto, it is in both these circles that most people play, like Rilke's acrobats in the fifth Duino elegy. Unlike Stevens, Rilke sees man here as the letter "D," as a semicircle closed in upon itself and with no visible access to the outer world of being and fulfillment. Man's posture is that of the "great initial of D, of Thereness," in which the open half-circle of Crispin no longer allows access to the transcendent but is closed in upon itself. And for this, one may think of that totally cyclical symphony of Franck, the D Minor, which for all Franck's personal piety seems more to express endless repetitiveness than eschatological fulfillment. For Rilke, as for Heidegger, man is simply hurtled into the cosmos: *Dasein* is simply there, its being is a surd, and man remains "unsponsored."

Rilke, it has been suggested, was thinking of Picasso's tumblers whose curse and salvation is to harmoniously play together, to construct out of their bodies the symbols of order and peace, not unlike Stevens's "ring of men" who "chant in orgy on a summer's morn."[5] Both Picasso's acrobats and Stevens's singers are merely trying to participate in that celestial dance whereby, even today in the very streets of our cities, the glazed technicians of the sacred try vainly to exercise away their karma. In all cases by their fruits they are known: the true dancer is known from his response to the dance which has been choreographed elsewhere.

> ... dance, which yonder starry Sphere
> of Planets and of fixt in all her Wheels

---

5. Acrobats, clowns, comedians, drunken sailors accept the precarious balance, the "chanciness" of existence. They thus symbolize the beautiful danger, the terrible beauty, the *sancta inebrietas* of the traditional holy fool, whether Christian hesychast, Hassidic schlemiel, or Hopi koshare. All these brothers of Crispin, living in praise of folly, are foredoomed mediators of the antipodal orders, the utterly sacred and the utterly profane, between which they scurryingly oscillate with such dizzying speed.

> Resembles nearest, mazes intricate,
> Eccentric, intervolv'd, yet regular
> Then most, when most irregular they seem:
> And in their motions harmony Divine.
>
> [*PL* 5.620–25]

Even the individual human dancer, the microcosm, responds to the circular dance within his own being—hence Cowley, "the first desire which does controul / All the inferiour wheels that move my soul."

Thus, according to the tradition, the dance of the body is a response to the dance of the soul, which in turn is a response to the dance of the heavenly bodies, which are responding to the dance of their "souls," the angelic choirs; and the dance of the angels is a response to the Wisdom who dances before the Father; and this in turn is a response to the perichoretic harmony, the ceaseless interior dance, of the Godhead itself. "One mystery," said Jacob Boehme, "proceeds into another, and each mystery is the mirror and model of the other." But in every instance it is a *response*, a dancing *Antwort* to a dancing *Wort*, and therefore, the tradition is equally vigorous in attesting, the dance cannot be self-initiated. There is no method, no technique for attaining this union between the earthly eccentric and the heavenly centrum. Sadly, the woods of what was once called Consciousness III are full of those who think otherwise—as indeed are the obscure selvages from time immemorial: like that deceptive elf Comus who brazenly claims to be in harmony with the heavenly spheres:

> We that are of purer fire
> Imitate the starry quire,
> Who in their nightly watchful Spheres
> Lead in swift round the Months and years.
>
> [111–14]

But regardless of how one seeks to close the circle, it is still incomplete, still a half-told tale awaiting its finish. What is the augur of this finale, the overture to this climax? Well, it is back to the supreme theme of art and song, the blending of the paradox in the act of human love: "*O*, suprême clairon, plein de strideurs étranges . . ." But of this dancing of the rondell, of this ruddy strife, of this playful pursuit of the treasure at the end of the parenthetic rainbow, of this ceaseless giving and receiving, orbing and absorbing, I have spoken earlier and so will here attend only to the affections and faculties that surround this sacred union.

The perennial mythos has it that before the dividing of the image all speech was circular, was the expression of harmonious mutuality, and had a kind of absolute (meaning "godlike") quality to it. And as absolute music is to program music, as Buddha's "wordless sermon" is to the dry rhetoric of Carew's "unscissored churchmen," this silent speech communicated immediately and fully without, as it were, the broken vocatives of postlapsarian programmatic speech: hence, the circularity of Donne's silent "Extasie" which is expressive of the perfect union of the two lovers:

> All day, the same our postures were,
> And wee said nothing, all the day.

That is a very concise version of Eve's candid and beautiful antiphony:

> With thee conversing I forget all time,
> All seasons and thir change, all please alike.
> Sweet is the breath of morn, her rising sweet,
> With charm of earliest Birds: pleasant the Sun
> When first on this delightful Land he spreads
> His orient Beams, on herb, tree, fruit, and flow'r,
> Glist'ring with dew; fragrant the fertile earth
> After soft showers; and sweet the coming on
> Of grateful Ev'ning mild, then silent Night
> With this her solemn Bird and this fair Moon,
> And these the Gems of Heav'n, her starry train:
> But neither breath of Morn, when she ascends
> With charm of earliest Birds, nor rising Sun
> On this delightful land, nor herb, fruit, flow'r,
> Glist'ring with dew, nor fragrance after showers,
> Nor grateful Ev'ning mild, nor silent Night
> With this her solemn Bird, nor walk by Moon,
> Or glittering Star-light *without thee is sweet*.
>
> [*PL* 4.639–56]

In fact, Eve's speech is not so much circular as helical, moving toward that greater simplicity which is the silence of union—here, that union is signaled by the climactic homage in the coda. While in Homer and the classical epic this kind of formulaic device was merely a mnemonic aid to the narrator, here it is functional, as expressive of mutual concord. So it is not surprising that after the fall, as all commentators have observed, when the circle of union is broken, the speech of Adam and Eve becomes fragmented and incoherent, egocentric rather than concentric. It is only with their repentance, with the foretelling of their future healing, that the circular pattern recurs—much like the despair-spare of Hopkins's echo poem:

> What better can we do, than to the place
> Repairing where he judg'd us, prostrate fall
> Before him reverent, and there confess
> Humbly our faults, and pardon beg, with tears
> Watering the ground, and with our sighs the Air
> Frequenting, sent from the hearts contrite, in sign
> Of sorrow unfeign'd, and humiliation meek.
> Undoubtedly he will relent and turn
> From his displeasure; in whose look serene,
> When angry most he seem'd and most severe,
> What else but favour, grace, and mercy shon?
> So spake our Father penitent, nor Eve
> Felt less remorse: they forthwith to the place
> Repairing where he judg'd them prostrate fell
> Before him reverent, and both confess'd
> Humbly thir faults, and pardon begg'd with tears
> Watering the ground, and with thir sighs the Air
> Frequenting, sent from hearts contrite, in sign
> Of sorrow unfeign'd, and humiliation meek.
>
> [*PL* 10.1086–104]

Similarly Keats, who saw his priestlike task as minister to Psyche, the "newest" of gods, whose reign would inaugurate a new era, a new cycle of harmony:

Fairer than these, though temple thou hast none,
    Nor altar heaped with flowers;
Nor virgin-choir to make delicious moan
    Upon the midnight hours;
No voice, no lute, no pipe, no incense sweet
    From chain-swung censer teeming;
No shrine, no grove, no oracle, no heat
    Of pale-mouthed prophet dreaming.

O brightest! though too late for antique vows,
    Too, too late for the fond believing lyre,
When holy were the haunted forest boughs,
    Holy the air, the water, and the fire;
Yet even in these days so far retired
    From happy pieties, thy lucent fans,
    Fluttering among the faint Olympians,
I see, and sing, by my own eyes inspired.
So let me be thy choir, and make a moan
    Upon the midnight hours;
Thy voice, thy lute, thy pipe, thy incense sweet
    From swinged censer teeming;
Thy shrine, thy grove, thy oracle, thy heat
    Of pale-mouthed prophet dreaming.

Possibly the most elaborate play on the circular harmony is the following by Spenser's "sad Alcyon," Arthur Gorges, who was himself elaborating on several earlier versions. The poem is really not so much circular as spheric, not a "flat map" of feminine perfections but a kind of Mercator projection which, in reading, assumes a truly globular dimension and thus offers a veritable "phenomenology of female roundness," to adapt Bachelard's phrase in *The Poetics of Space*. One "reads" this poem almost *ut pictura* because it involves not so much a sequential linear progression as a kind of simultaneous apprehension:

Her face	Her tongue	Her wytt
So faier	So sweete	So sharpe
first bent	then drewe	then hitt
myne eye	myne eare	my harte

Myn eye	Myne eare	My harte
to lyke	to learne	to love
her face	her tongue	her wytt
doth leade	doth teache	doth move

Her face	Her tongue	Her wytt
with beames	with sounde	with arte
doth blynd	doth charm	doth knitt
myn eye	myne eare	my harte

Myne eye	Myne eare	My harte
with lyfe	with hope	with skill
her face	her tongue	her witt
doth feede	doth feaste	doth fyll

O face	O tongue	O wytt
with frownes	with cheeks	with smarte
wronge not	vex nott	wounde not
myne eye	myne eare	my harte

This eye	This eare	This harte
shall Joye	shall yeald	shall swear
her face	her tongue	her witt

Like Sidney's similarly correlative poem beginning "Vertue, beaw-tie, and speech...," Gorges's poem presents a Leibnizian world, each monad virtually identical with the other and differing only in its individual perspective, that is, in its relation to the totality of monads that constitutes the whole. In more contemporary terms, the poem is a kind of holographic continuum in which all points reflect every other point and all points are cotangent. All the parts are "inter-transpicuous"—to borrow a happy coinage of Shelley's from his own climactic vision of the "multitudinous orb" at the end of *Prometheus Unbound*.

All these kinds of antiphonal movements are a variation on the circular structure of innumerable poems (for example, Swinburne's "The Roundel") which, like the voyage of the bright-eyed mariner, end where they began. It is that return to the tonic signified by rhyme, and well exemplified in Stevens's "Anecdote of the Jar" with its repetition of "round," "ground," "surround." And it is also the structure of the two greatest poems in the literature explicitly concerned with the circular journey, "Perle," and "On a Drop of Dew."

Marvell's poem is about the circular journey of a circular being from its perfection in the heavens to the earth where the circle becomes flawed, restless, bent—a "C" or a "D," not an "O"—until it returns in a more purified condition back to the heavens: *ingressus, progressus, regressus.* The puzzling "*So* the world excluding round" I thus understand, quite differently from Poulet, in terms of the medieval notion that the world and man in it after the fall were a flawed circle, a circle which was not "true," and thus excluded the quality of perfection, "roundness." The initial "so" is thus a kind of glyph of the serpentine voyage destined to become harmonized— just as, for example, the initial "O" in Donne's "*O more* than moone" is a glyph of the perfection of Anne More's tear, as that tear is a symbol of that perfect circular union of man and woman which the poet is here idealizing. Like the endlessly repeated ogives in a Gothic temple, "Perle" seeks in all its elements to express its formal circularity. Several critics—notably Norman Davis and P. M. Kean— have emphasized the unique integration of theme and structure in this poem, but none more luminously than Cary Nelson in *The Incarnate Word.*

Though it would take a Helmut Hatzfeld or a Leo Spitzer to do justice to this theme of circularity—and Spitzer at the time of his death had been devoting himself to this topic—I have for present purposes said enough about the circle of the transcendent and the semicircle of the contingent individual. It remains only to examine the universally historical or, as it has been variously denominated, the "wheel of fortune" or the "cycle of history." One might engage the theme with no preamble by referring to the fateful circularity of Margaret's speech in *Richard III*:

> I had an Edward, till a Richard kill'd him;
> I had a Harry, till a Richard kill'd him;
> Thou hadst an Edward, till a Richard kill'd him;
> Thou hadst a Richard, till a Richard kill'd him.
>
> [4.4.40–43]

But if all circles are one circle, we may more profitably consider the circle of history in its relation to the sexual and the divine circles described above.

For this, I want to look at one of Donne's best theological excursions into the dialectic of seduction, "The Dreame." In the poem, one recalls, he is telling his mistress that because she came to awaken him when he was dreaming of her, she must have been able to read his mind (in Scholastic theology a prerogative of God alone); and that thoughts of her suffice to "make dreames truths" (the Anselmian argument for God's existence); therefore, "it could not chuse but bee / Prophane, to think thee anything but thee" (God, the nameless one, is "he who is"—"thou art thou," in perfect circularity): QED, his mistress *is* "God." But Donne is not interested in speculative quibbles; he will, like Marvell with his mistress, *tradere contemplata*, that is, incarnate his seed-bearing word. The historical world is the extension of the divine, a projection of the divine; it is therefore God's "body" (or, in the terms employed above, it is the circumlocution of God's singular word). Thus, Donne in embracing his mistress is, to adapt a phrase, going to make love *and* make war, that is, history.

> thoughts of thee suffice
> To make dreames truths; and fables histories;
> Enter these armes, for since thou thoughtst it best,
> Not to dreame all my dreame, let's act the rest.

The transition is from dreams to truths, and then from fables to histories; but "Enter these armes" is not merely the proclamation of an embrace, it is a stage direction on the world's stage *and* the bed stage, like "enter Caesar's powers," and signals the act of personal and of historical conquest—much like the equally rich coincidence of the two spheres in *Love's Labour's Lost* (5.2.557–58): "I here am come by chance, / And lay my arms before the legs of this sweet lass of France." Nor should this exegesis of the two texts be surprising, for if everything is circumferentially related, all spirals are not merely isomorphic but ultimately seeking to be identical. The sexual (*circulatio sanguinis*) approximates the sacred (*circolarità spirituale*), and both approximate the historical (*corso-ricorso*).

Thus, that dichotomy is simplistic which asserts that in the classical conception history is cyclical and in the biblical, and Marxist, conception it is linear. A modestly encyclopedic knowledge would suggest that all history is circular but that the circularity is envisioned from two different perspectives: the circle which is enclosed upon itself (Rilke's "D") and the circle which may spiral toward a telos (Stevens's "C"), whether the latter be defined as Jerusalem on high, the classless society, or the world process as defined in Emerson's prophetic essay, "Circles": "The life of man is a self-evolving circle, which, from a ring imperceptibly small, rushes on all sides outward to new and larger circles, and that without end." One may refine this judgment on history by seeing Christian-Emersonian time as engendered out of classical time and the result being what Russell A. Peck has called "A triple time sense":

> A cosmology of concentric circles yields a chronology of concentric time. Combined with a Christian sense of linear time progressing from creation to apocalypse, it evokes a triple time sense. Man lives in the moment [Croce's *circulatio sanguinis*]. He also lives within the span of history, a history that defines itself by repeating its own plots [*corso-ricorso*]. And, ultimately, man lives in eternity [*circolarità spirituale*].

In the classical enclosed circle one lives on the periphery of the ever-whirling wheel of change and is doomed to suffer the endless repetition of everyday events and the tyranny of fate. This vision is essentially pessimistic, both in the private, personal and in the properly *geschichtlichen* dimensions, whether as interpreted by a Buddhist or a Hindu seeking to break away from the circumference and return to the cosmic hub, or as interpreted by the rant of a postmedieval Hamlet on the "strumpet fortune," or by twentieth-century existentialists anguishing over *terribile quotidianità*, *Alltäglichkeit*, and so on. However, in a Marxian, say, like Lefèbvre, the strain of the *vie quotidienne* finds ventilation in responding to the current of history and ascending the spiral toward a newly structured harmonious culture of which present-day urbanism is a sad travesty, toward an ecumenopolis in the sense not just of a universal citification but of a universal world mentality—a vision not much different from that animating the great Christian cyclists concerned with *Civitas Dei, Histoire universelle, Scienza nuova,* and *Phénomène humain.* There are innumerable Christian witnesses to the optimistic view, most stridently and most "world-famously" the later poems of T. S. Eliot; though perhaps the best single expression of the microcircle being taken up into the macrocircle is Emily Dickinsons's poem beginning:

> I should have been too glad, I see—
> Too lifted—for the scant degree
> Of Life's penurious Round—
> My little Circuit would have shamed
> This new Circumference—have blamed—
> The homelier time behind.
>
> [No. 313]

On the Marxist side, one could take early Spender, Auden, or C. Day Lewis, of whom the following is representative enough.

> When they have lost the little that they looked for,
> The poor allotment of ease, custom, fame:
> When the consuming star their fathers worked for
> Has guttered into death, a fatuous flame:
> When love's a cripple, faith a bed-time story,
> Hope eats her heart out and peace walks on knives,
> And suffering men cry an end to this sorry
> World, of whose children want alone still thrives:
> Then shall the mounting stages of oppression
> Like mazed and makeshift scaffolding torn down
> Reveal his unexampled, best creation—
> The shape of man's necessity full grown,
> Built from their bone, I see a power-house stand
> To warm men's hearts again and light the land.

This is a sonnet, and sonnets lend themselves to spiraling apocalyptic revelations (When? When? When?—Then), to, in this case, the resolution of class war in a cosmic peace, or in terms of the religious myth to the renewal of the face of the earth after the incineration of the globe. From Joachim of Flora and Thomas Münzer to Marx and Bloch, this is the substance of sonneteers. And each of those revolutionaries would have been pleased by the proleptic eschatology of Sidney Lanier's *Science of English Verse*: "A good sonnet should always therefore be read with a certain suspension of the reader's thought until the end is reached, and the end should always throw back a new and comprehensive interest upon all that precedes it."

The witness of the pessimists, because more universal, is present both in folk art and in more sophisticated forms, for example, Blake's terrifying "The Mental Traveller" with its despairing coda, or Stevens's ominous but lighthearted "Frogs Eat Butterflies. Snakes Eat Frogs. Hogs Eat Snakes. Men Eat Hogs." The popular changes rung on this Daedalian house-that-Jack-built theme are innumerable, and the following is typical:

> Rags make paper;
> Paper makes money;
> Money makes bankers;
> Bankers make loans;
> Loans make beggars;
> Beggars make rags.

Acceptance of the pessimistic cycle is also more fascinating because seemingly more heroic (like Farinata in the Sixth Circle), as long as it doesn't get trapped in Sisyphean posturing or in interminable puling over the dizzying, eddying whirl, as in Arnold.

Again, one hears the authentic accent in Charlotte Mew:

> Not for that city of the level sun,
>   Its golden streets and glittering gates ablaze—
>   The shadeless, sleepless city of white days,
>
> White nights, or nights and days that are as one—
>
> We weary, when all is said, all thought, all done,
>   We strain our eyes beyond this dusk to see
>   What, from the threshold of eternity,
>
> We shall step into. No, I think we shun

The splendor of that everlasting glare,
   The clamor of that never-ending song.
   And if for anything we greatly long,

It is for some remote and quiet stair.

                    ["Not for that city..."]

The coin rings even truer in the rhetoric of that heroic anti-poet ("I hate my verses"), Robinson Jeffers:

While this America settles in the mold of its vulgarity, heavily
   thickening to empire,
And protest, only a bubble in the molten mass, pops and sighs out,
   and the mass hardens,
I sadly smiling remember that the flower fades to make fruit, the
   fruit rots to make earth.
Out of the mother; and through the spring exultances, ripeness and
   decadence; and home to the mother.
You making haste, haste on decay: not blameworthy; life is good,
   be it stubbornly long or suddenly
A mortal splendor: meteors are not needed less than mountains:
   shine, perishing republic.

                ["Shine, Perishing Republic"]

On hearing this one thinks immediately of Spengler; and one should, for Spengler was indeed Jeffers's angel. And, as for Spengler on a vaster scale there was no escape from the *Untergang*, so too for Jeffers: the circumference was an agony, and in "the thickening center; corruption." Chained to his personal and historical catherine wheel, he compulsively spun out his verse like a saffron-robed cenobite spinning his prayers.

If one may homilize before concluding this meditation on what Murray Krieger, after Keats, calls the "teasing doctrine of circularity," one might opine that the proper human stance, if such a thing exists, is neither splenetic eruption over the closed circle with Jeffers nor sullen resignation at the mystery of the intertwining gyres with Yeats nor plucky, stiff-upper-lip optimumism (no "rounder" replies there) at the "fell cirque" with Browning, but the spare-despair ironic honings of a Stevens who—though he knew the broken cartwheel, unlike Coleridge's old coach wheel, would perdure—always delighted in the pleasures of "merely circulating." After all, his very last poem in the complete works is titled after Aquinas on the vision of faith: "Not ideas about the thing but the thing itself."

This chapter has also come full circle. But I have not supplied the promised "answer" to the original query as to whether this universal prevalence of the circular bespeaks something more, on the one hand, than merely conventional poetic-geometrizing or, on the other hand, than woolly "psychic archetypes"—though it obviously bespeaks both, and for most of us that it does is more cogent than auxiliary evidence from any other realm. But it seems that man is not just psychically oriented to the circular; he is so oriented chemically as well. This I suggested in the last chapter is what may be implicit in the so-called double helix. But the irony in the discovery of this chemical configuration is that it would never have been achieved had not the scientists themselves responded to precisely the poetic-geometrizing spheroid convention and the psychic-archetype circularity. At the conclusion of Nobel laureate Watson's book, phrases like the following keep recurring: "a structure this pretty just had to exist," "The structure was too pretty not to be true." Thus it was the psychic-poetic impulse that led to the stereochemical discovery, and it may be that the complementarity of the two is born of a more basic circular force whose trajectory neither poets nor magi nor mystics can trace, though all can glimpse it according to their separate lights and so aid us on the long journey "home."

INDEX